Loving
Our Own
Bones

Loving Our Own Bones

DISABILITY WISDOM AND THE SPIRITUAL SUBVERSIVENESS OF KNOWING OURSELVES WHOLE

JULIA WATTS BELSER

BEACON PRESS
BOSTON

BEACON PRESS
Boston, Massachusetts
www.beacon.org

Beacon Press books
are published under the auspices of
the Unitarian Universalist Association of Congregations.

26 25 24 23   8 7 6 5 4 3 2 1

This book is printed on acid-free paper that meets the uncoated paper
ANSI/NISO specifications for permanence as revised in 1992.

Text design and composition by Kim Arney

Chapter 5 is adapted from Julia Watts Belser, "Priestly Aesthetics:
Disability and Bodily Difference in Leviticus 21," *Interpretation:
A Journal of Bible and Theology* 73, no. 4 (2019).

Beacon Press is grateful for permission to reprint an excerpt
from Laura Hershey's poem "You Get Proud By Practicing." Go
to www.laurahershey.com to read more of Laura's work.

Library of Congress Cataloguing-in-Publication Data is available for this title.
Hardcover ISBN: 978-0-8070-0675-7
E-book ISBN: 978-0-8070-0676-4
Audiobook: 978-0-8070-1370-0

For Devorah,
with gratitude, for everything.

CONTENTS

CHAPTER ONE   Claiming Disability   1

CHAPTER TWO   Grappling with the Bible: Gender, Disability, and God   10

CHAPTER THREE   Hiddenness and Visibility: Passing and Presenting as Disabled   24

CHAPTER FOUR   Ableism: The Social-Political Dimension of Disability   37

CHAPTER FIVE   Priestly Blemishes: Talking Back to the Bible's Ideal Bodies   54

CHAPTER SIX   Moses: Portrait of a Disabled Prophet   73

CHAPTER SEVEN   The Land You Cannot Enter: Longing, Loss, and Other Inaccessible Terrain   93

CHAPTER EIGHT   The Perils of Healing   113

CHAPTER NINE   Isaac's Blindness: The Complexity of Trust   139

CHAPTER TEN   Jacob and the Angel: Wheels, Wings, and the Brilliance of Disability Difference   162

CHAPTER ELEVEN   The Politics of Beauty: Disability and Desire   180

CHAPTER TWELVE   The Radical Practice of Rest: Shabbat Values and Disability Justice   197

CHAPTER THIRTEEN   God on Wheels: Disability Theology   214

Glossary of Jewish Terms   238

Acknowledgments   242

A Note on Translation   245

Notes   246

Index   265

CHAPTER ONE

Claiming Disability

After synagogue one day, a visitor popped the question. "What's wrong with you?" she asked, as her eyes flicked from my face to my wheels. I've been asked this question in an astounding array of inappropriate venues; I didn't flinch. "I have a disability," I said, though it was plain she'd already noticed. A firm stop follows that statement, though I know full well I didn't answer her question. I'm more than willing to talk about disability, but I'm disinclined to do so while waiting in the buffet line for my salad.

In truth, my answer is something of a lie. What's wrong with me has more to do with exclusion, objectification, pity, and disdain than with honest muscle and bone. Most folks I meet assume my disability is a medical story, that the place to start when we talk about disability is diagnosis. I take a different approach. A medical frame centers on bodies or minds that fail to measure up to certain expectations, focusing on symptoms, treatment, rehabilitation. I want to tell you a different kind of story: a story about social attitudes, architectural barriers, and cultural notions of normalcy that value certain modes of being over others. I want to tell you a story about power, about the thousand ways our cultures mark certain bodies and minds as *normal*, while designating others as deviant and defective. It's a story about the way certain bodies and minds get shut out of public space, about the way we get discarded, shunted into care homes or locked up in prisons. It's a story about the endless hours I've spent hunting wheelchair-accessible apartments, about the times strangers on the street have cut in on private conversations to tell me that they'll pray for me. It's a story about ableism, about the deep, entrenched structures of our society that presume it's good and right and natural to live without a disability. It's a story about violence, about harm that cuts against body, spirit, and bone.

It's also a story about joy. I was in college when I first experienced disability community, when I forged my first disability kinships. Though I'd been disabled all my life, I had just experienced a sudden, significant disability change. I started using an electric mobility scooter, and soon after, I got my first wheelchair. I took my first disability studies class, where I led a collective mapping project that documented and analyzed inaccessibility on campus—an experience that finally gave me language to name and make tangible the structures of exclusion that have shaped my life. I fell into friendships with activists and artists, with political crips, disabled dissidents, and dreamers. I learned to dance, shedding the awkwardness I'd always felt on feet in favor of the whirl of wheels. Somewhere along the way, I claimed an uncanny kind of freedom: a recognition that my life, my body, my wheels were so far beyond the confines of the conventional that there was simply no point trying to press my bones into that facade.

Disability movements have brought together many who live brilliantly unconventional lives for activism, artistry, and passionate community. In these circles, disability isn't a medical diagnosis, but a cultural movement. Approaching disability through the lens of culture allows us to recognize disability as a dimension of human diversity. This perspective has often been overlooked in religious circles. Religious communities have more often tended to treat disability as a problem to be solved than a perspective to be embraced. But I follow the lead of feminist, queer, womanist, and liberationist interpreters who have raised up the value of reading sacred texts through the prism of our own particularity. Reading the Bible through the lens of disability experience can transform the way we think about text and theology. Disability cracks open powerful new perspectives on spirit.

Before we go further, let me say a few words about how I use the term "disability." I claim disability as a vital part of my own identity, as a meaningful way of naming and celebrating the intricate unfolding of my own skin and soul. Such a choice is surely a minority position in this world. Living in a profoundly ableist culture, in a world where disability still serves as a seemingly "natural" marker of inferiority, claiming disability as a significant dimension of self remains profoundly counter cultural. We're often taught to "look past" disability, to not bring it up in polite conversation. But I reject both of those approaches. I want you to see my disability.

Disability is an ordinary fact of life and an essential part of my being. Like most identities, it's a mixed bag: sometimes painful, sometimes frustrating, sometimes flush with exquisite, unexpected joy. If you want to know me, you've got to know my disability. It's a core part of who I am, how I experience the world.

I was born with cerebral palsy, and when I walked as a child, my heel used to strike ground in its own distinctive rhythm. My gait was subject to scrutiny and no small disapproval. Everyone wanted to fix it. I was a very compliant child: I tried to "walk right." I stretched the thick anchor of my heel cord. I practiced over and over the motion of heel before toe. But as I did my exercises, night after night, I also remember this. I remember listening to the off-beat of my limp and loving the sound of my own step. The way my foot struck ground, the distinctive rhythm of my walk? They were my signature, something that was purely my own.

This was the first spiritual insight I trace to disability experience, this decision to cherish something about myself that other people didn't value. Maybe you know this insight too. Maybe you know what it's like to say yes to yourself, even in the face of disapproval or disdain. As a kid who couldn't walk right, now as a woman who rolls through the world, as someone whose heart never learned to conform—I trace my own truest sense of self to the decision to embrace those quirky qualities of soul that some folks wished to eradicate, to do everything I could to make sure they survived.

Growing up disabled, growing up queer, the stakes were stark. It was either kindle tenacious love for my self or swallow the world's projections whole. And, so, I chose. I taught myself to trace the lines on the palms of my own hands, a contour of the sacred. I found and felt and claimed the holiness of my own bones. I said *yes* to my own heart, to my own soul. I had the brilliant audacity to call it good and know it whole.

This book unfolds at the intersection of several worlds. I am scholar of disability in Jewish and Christian traditions, with a specialty in classical Jewish texts. I am a rabbi and spiritual teacher, passionate about bringing queer, feminist, and disability culture into conversation with sacred scriptures. And I am a disability activist, committed to building a world where disabled people thrive. For more than a decade now, I've been speaking and teaching about the intersection of disability, the sacred, and Jewish texts—in synagogues and churches, in college lecture halls and community centers, in theater arts circles and dance studios. In all of those contexts, one of the most common questions I hear is this: *What does the Bible say about disability?*

The Bible is a complex text, one that opens up to infinite interpretations. So do the religions that draw inspiration from its pages. People often ask me about "the Jewish view" on disability, but to get a meaningful response, we have to complicate that question. Like all religious traditions, Judaism is a vast and complex terrain, a shifting landscape, not a static body. How would we begin to answer? Would we look to the Torah, the first five books of the Hebrew Bible that, according to Jewish lore, God gave to Moses at Mount Sinai? You could certainly make a case that those texts are central to the unfolding of Jewish tradition. The Torah is read every week in synagogue, and its teachings are a bedrock of Jewish life. But to hold these texts up as some sort of final word on Jewish meaning runs counter to the heart of Jewish experience. Virtually every verse and every word of Torah has sparked a robust line of discussion and exploration, giving rise to a dizzying amount of sacred text: the Talmud, which invites the reader into intricate debates and arguments among the ancient rabbis over Jewish law and lore; the myriad books of midrash, in which every word becomes a springboard for creative interpretation, for probing the possibilities of sacred story; the medieval and modern commentaries, in which scholars laid out their understandings of Torah, verse by verse, line by line. All of this is part of the living body of revelation that Jewish tradition claims as sacred. To read Torah is to enter into a conversation, to participate in a practice of examining and contesting meaning. Torah is never a fixed, final word.

In some Jewish communities today, certain texts *have* become widely accepted as the authoritative word on proper Jewish practice. Jewish tradition orients itself strongly around right action—around rituals, practices, and embodied ethical commitments that shape and ground Jewish identity. Jewish law, known as halakhah, is a complex body of thought that debates and articulates expectations for Jewish practice in virtually all spheres of life, from prayer to proper business ethics. Is a blind person permitted to recite the blessing a Jew says out of gratitude for the sun, or does that act require being able to physically see and benefit from the sun's light? May a wheelchair user lead the congregation in the Amidah, the standing prayer? What is a Jewish community's responsibility to provide equal access to the mikveh, the pool for ritual immersion? Does Jewish law support the redesign of a sanctuary to make sure that all congregants can come to recite the blessings before the reading of the Torah? In observant communities whose sense of Jewish identity is forged in relation to halakhah, these questions are crucial. They shape the texture of Jewish life and directly affect disabled Jews' experience in community. But these aren't the questions that are central to this book.

My purpose here is different. Rather than examine what Jewish or Christian traditions say about disability, I flip the question on its head. I ask how disability experience can shape our inner lives, how disability can offer insights into the textures and tenor of spiritual life. This book is rooted in the bedrock claim that disability can be a generative force, a goad to creativity, a source of embodied knowledge. For those of us immersed in disability culture, for those of us who take disability as an ethical call to resist and uproot the structures of stigma and violence that constrain so many disabled people's lives? Disability is spiritual dissent. Disability politics are a provocative challenge to prevailing conceptions of human value, a refusal to swallow the lie that some bodies and minds deserve to be discarded or disdained. In this book, I bring disability wisdom into conversation with my own religious tradition, with spiritual practice, with questions of the heart. Diving deep into my own disability experience has led me to unexpected insights as a teacher of Jewish text and tradition. Everything I know about God comes through these disabled bones.

I won't spend my time making a case that disabled people deserve a place within religious communities, or that we have an equal claim to divine love and regard. All too often, minoritized peoples get drawn into this trap. We end up asking for acceptance, pleading for recognition, marshaling the case for our own dignity. But none of us should have to argue in this way for our own inherent worth. It corrodes the heart. It saps the soul. I'm not much for pronouncements about God, or for making claims to divine truth. But if there's one thing I know for sure, it's that disabled lives have value. We are cherished. We are beloved. Full stop, no prooftexts needed.

There are many passages within the Bible that affirm the dignity and vitality of people with disabilities. The biblical command in Leviticus 19:14 to "not insult the deaf, or place a stumbling-block before the blind," lays out an explicit obligation to treat people with disabilities with decency and respect. The biblical call to care for the orphan, widow, and stranger has long been a touchstone for Jews and Christians alike, anchoring a commitment to ensure the well-being of people who are vulnerable and at risk, those who might easily end up on the social margins. Stirring words in Genesis call us to recognize all people as created *b'tselem elohim*, in the image of God. And biblical sources offer a vigorous support for the principles of justice and repair of the world. *Tsedek, tsedek tirdof*, calls Deuteronomy 16. "Justice, justice shall you pursue."[1]

But there are other passages that give me pause. There are traditions I find frustrating, principles I judge misguided, texts that feel like a slap against my tender places. In the pages that follow, I'll invite you to explore some of that terrain, in part because I often end up tangling most deeply with the texts that have gotten under my skin. The choice to turn toward difficult parts of the tradition is a deliberate one, a strategy I learned from feminist interpreters who taught me the value of confronting pain and naming harm. Jewish feminist poet and cultural critic Adrienne Rich speaks powerfully of the urgency, the necessity of grappling with the full complexity of Jewish text and tradition. She writes, "To separate from parts of a legacy in a conscious, loving, and responsible way in order to say 'This is frayed and needs repair; that no longer serves us; this is still viable and usable' is not to spurn tradition, but to take it very seriously."[2] This is a book built of love and critique, a book in which I turn unflinchingly toward texts that have cut like razors against the softness of my life. This is a book that says yes, and also no. This is a book in which critique is itself an act of love.

This is a book that imagines disabled words and worlds where they were not built before. For most of Jewish history, Torah has been told by a nondisabled tongue. In Christian circles, the story is the same. Even when our sacred stories feature disabled characters, the texts themselves and the thinkers who interpret them almost always speak from a nondisabled perspective.

To shift this center, I have made a choice to deliberately disrupt the conventional rules for interpreting biblical text, to disrupt the canon of expected conversation partners. In the pages that follow, I dive deep into the worlds of traditional commentary on the Bible. But I also turn to the texts and teachings of disability activists and artists, to the writings of disabled poets and essayists, to disability studies scholarship and to disability memoir. Many of those voices are unabashedly secular. But I claim them as a crucial part of my own canon. The work of disabled artists, activists, scholars, and movement workers is driven by a commitment I hold sacred: the task of claiming the *belovedness* of

bodies and minds that dominant culture all too often treats as disposable, as nothing more than trash.

Disability communities have honed a critical body of knowledge
about what it means to practice interdependence, mutuality, love, and
care. We know something vital about how to live on the underside of
power, how to fight for lives that are often disregarded and disdained.
Disability has taught me much about the potent spiritual subversiveness
of being radically comfortable in my own skin, of daring to find the
presence of God in this fierce and fragile flesh. Disability is a source
of expertise, of insight. I mean not just the reality of living with an
unconventional body-mind, but also the experience of contending
with ableism, with the violent denial of disability as a source of value
in this world. I teach Torah with that knowledge at the center of my
heart. This is Torah, told slant. This is Torah, with a bold and brilliant
limp. Unabashedly disabled.

Let me give you a glimpse of what I mean. During the holiday
of Shavuot, Jewish communities around the world chant from the
first chapter of the book of Ezekiel, reciting the Israelite prophet's
striking image of God. In those verses, Ezekiel describes how "the
heavens opened" and he "saw visions of God": a radiant fire borne
on a vast chariot, lifted up by four angelic creatures with fused legs,
lustrous wings, and great wheels. The wheels, Ezekiel says, "gleamed
like beryl," they were "wheels within wheels" and "the spirit of the
creatures was in the wheels."[3]

In Jewish tradition, Ezekiel's wild, uncanny vision has been the
site of much mystical speculation. In late antiquity, a group of Jewish
mystics used these verses as a guide to spiritual practice, developing an
intense regimen of fasting and prayer, to lead them closer and closer to
the divine throne. I'll confess: While the scholar in me finds that practice fascinating, I've never been tempted to follow their path. I don't
find Ezekiel particularly compelling as a model for my own spiritual
life. But some years ago, sitting in synagogue on Shavuot morning,
Ezekiel's vision split open my own imagination. As I was reading that

description of God's divine chariot, I felt a jolt of recognition, an intimate familiarity, a whimsical sense of kinship. I thought: *God has wheels.*[4]

When I think of God on Wheels, I think of the delight I take in my own wheelchair, the satisfaction I take from a life lived on wheels. My wheels set me free and open up my spirit. I draw a powerful, sensual joy in tandem with my chair: the way her tires grip into asphalt or concrete, the way I lean into a curve and flow down a gentle grade, the way I feel the twinned vibration of earth and wheel through the soles of my shoes or the balls of my feet. My sense of Spirit is bound up with this bone-deep body knowledge: the way flesh flows into frame, into tire, into air. This is how the Holy moves through me, in the intricate interplay of muscle and spin, the exhilarating physicality of body and wheel.

This is the fierce joy that fuels my activism, the body knowledge that grounds my ethics, the wildness that runs like a live wire through my life. It is an ethics bound up with the concrete work of justice, with an activist sensibility, a sense of obligation, a call to recognize and resist violence and oppression, to put my own flesh, my mind, my heart, my fire in service of a world made generous and loving and whole. This body knowledge fuels my hunger for a different world. A world where there are no disposable lives. A world where disabled bodies, Black bodies, Brown bodies, fat bodies, slow bodies, women's bodies, immigrant bodies, Muslim bodies, Jewish bodies, silent, stuttering, blind, and queer bodies, old bodies, trans bodies, homeless bodies are all safe on the streets of our cities.

I dream a world where this is the cornerstone obligation of our souls, the ground of our commitments: a world, as the Psalmist says, "where justice and peace will kiss."[5]

CHAPTER TWO

Grappling with the Bible

Gender, Disability, and God

When the biblical prophet Isaiah proclaims the promise of a better world, he places disability at the center of his vision:

> Then the eyes of the blind will be opened,
> the ears of the deaf will be unstopped.
>
> The lame will leap like a deer,
> and the mute tongue will sing with joy.[1]

If those words sound familiar, it's likely because they were lifted up in Handel's *Messiah*, a centerpiece of the Christmas season and one of the most famous choral works of all time. Like Isaiah, Handel tells the story of a world made new: a world where nothing is impossible, where miracles are manifest, where hope comes even to the desperate, the destitute, and the despised.

It's a promise built on the backs of disabled folk.

In Isaiah's vision, disability is part and parcel of the world we long to leave behind. Deafness is nothing but impediment, blindness the tragic absence of sight. Until they feel the touch of God, the lame and the mute languish. Joy comes with disability transformed.

At the start of his prophecy, Isaiah proclaims that the land itself will mirror this radical reversal. "The arid desert will be glad," he promises. "The wilderness will rejoice; it will blossom like a rose."[2] After he announces the transformation of human bodies, he returns to the restoration of the land. "Waters shall burst forth in the desert," he concludes, "streams in the wilderness."[3] His words draw earth and flesh alike into a divine drama, a startling before-and-after scene. Wastelands are transformed, becoming lush and verdant. When it comes to bodies, the logic is the same. The undesirable becomes perfected, flush with keen perception and with pleasure.

For Isaiah, disability reversal becomes a sign of God's great power. Like a river that bursts forth in the desert, divine healing is proof that even the most intractable realities of the present can change. Isaiah means these words to be good tidings, a promise that will lift the hearts of a weary, wounded people.

But it feels rather different, from where I sit.

In the prophet's telling, disability becomes a sign and signal of a world still waiting for God's touch. Deaf bodies, blind bodies, and bodies that cannot speak stand like sentinels, a silent backdrop of woe. My own lame and lovely leg gets conscripted, proof positive that the world is not yet as God dreams. Every eye is on me, watching for that perfect, agile leap. The slow sweep of my left foot? It becomes a symbol, a sorrow. A reminder that we're all still here, in this land of stone and dust, limping toward Jerusalem.

I never asked to be a part of that story, one of the unnamed extras in Isaiah's drama of salvation. For Isaiah, liberation happens through the erasure of disability. It requires the transformation of our bodies and minds so they match a nondisabled norm. But Isaiah's dream is not my own.

It reminds me of a story I heard from Rabbi Margaret Moers Wening, about a Deaf child in her religious school. A teacher once promised that child, "One day, in the world to come, you'll be able to hear." And the child looked back and said, "No. In the world to come, God will sign."[4]

That affirmation of Deaf belonging isn't precisely laid plain by the ancient prophets. But there is a hint of it here, a handhold. The

prophet Jeremiah lays out a different promise, a promise that God will
bring marginalized peoples into the center of a restored and renewed
community. He describes how God will bring the people in:

> The blind and the lame, among them;
> pregnant women and women with children, together.
> They will return here as a great assembly . . .
> on a level road, on which they shall not stumble.[5]

Jeremiah's vision transforms architectures of exclusion. His future
makes room for wheelchairs and walkers, for limpers and striders.
The athletes and the slow ones all travel a road laid out in intentional,
accessible design. My own dreams linger on that promise of a "level
road," a road on which no one stumbles. I like to think it's God's gift
of access: a long, smooth ramp that cuts through once-inhospitable
terrain, one that offers all of us a way back home.

I tell you these two prophet stories to give you a glimpse of how I read
the Bible, and to tell you why I think it matters that disabled folks and
those who love us grapple with biblical texts and traditions. Open the
Bible, and disability is everywhere. Moses stutters and regards himself
as unable to answer God's call. Isaac's blindness lets his wife trick him
into bestowing his blessing on his younger son. Jacob wrestles with
an angel and limps forever after. Jesus heals people who are sick or
blind, paralyzed or possessed. For centuries, these stories have been
told and retold by commentators who treat disability as misfortune,
as a metaphor for spiritual incapacity, or a challenge to be overcome.

For Jewish and Christian readers, the stakes are probably clear. But
even for those of us who aren't religious, the Bible is a crucial book. It is
a powerful force in American public policy, both at home and abroad.
Its interpretation shapes the policies that guide medical research and insurance practices, prenatal testing and end-of-life care. Biblical themes
shape the plots of blockbuster movies and Nobel Prize–winning novels.

The Bible has been a mainstay in the art world for centuries, shaping our imaginations even when we barely know its stories.

For some readers, the Bible is a book of answers. But for me, it's always been a book of haunting questions. Its characters are complex and often morally ambiguous. Its stories echo with unresolved emotion, with uncertainty, with uneasy endings. I first read the Bible in a sustained way in a high school English class, under the eye of a brilliant teacher who convinced me that it wasn't just a book for believers. Fast forward a few decades and you can find me teaching these texts to students not unlike my younger self. I'm still a fractious reader, as likely to talk back to the text as I am to keep its counsel.

Over the years, I've found the Bible a compelling companion for wrestling with questions that matter, for coming to grips with the foibles and frailties of the human heart. But it isn't the circumference of my spiritual life. To tell you that story, I have to start elsewhere. I have to tell you a story that's anchored in the wide-open wildness of my childhood eye, a story that's rooted in the thin trembling leaves of the willow I grew up with and the oak who spread her sturdy branches around my gangly limbs. It's a story that's grounded in the wonder of this world, in the dirt and in the daydreams, a story of trees and toads and breath and bone.

When I was maybe three years old, my father built a sandbox in the backyard of our Alabama home. My brother and I used to play together for hours, digging our toes into the sand, scooping out holes and fashioning castles, uncovering buried treasure. There was a lot I loved about that sandbox, but the best was this: I used to run my hands carefully beneath the plywood seats my father had built along the sides, into the shaded sand below. Some days, if I was lucky, I'd find a big, beautiful toad.

I remember cradling just such a toad in my cupped hands. His skin was smooth and cool, his belly soft and languid. I remember the perfect moment when he opened his eye, when I realized he was alive.

My own spiritual life is grounded in that recognition of connection: that sense of an eye, opening up and looking back. When I write about spirituality, this is what I mean. I mean that moment of awareness, that visceral knowledge of another presence that opens a doorway, a path into wonder. I didn't grow up in a religious home; not Jewish, not Christian either. But I had a vibrant, voracious spiritual life. I spent my time talking to trees and listening to the stones, inhabiting what philosopher of religion Charles Taylor calls an utterly "enchanted world."[6] My sense of spirit has always been bound up with the stuff of this world, with bread, and dirt, and dragonflies, with that tangible sense of presence alive against my skin, the toad in my hand its own entire universe.

If you and I were talking about the sacred, if we were sitting together over coffee or by candlelight, I wouldn't start by asking you about the Bible. I wouldn't start by asking about God. I'd invite you to tell me about a time you felt a sense of wonder, a time you felt connected to something larger than yourself. People tell me stories about the birth of a child, or the touch of a friend. They tell me about their connections to this world: the feel of the surf or the sight of the stars, that particular moment when sunlight shafted through a forest and tangled them in awe, the stillness that held them while they ghosted in a kayak at dawn across a lake.

I have a moment like that too, a moment when I felt God like a live wire down my spine. I was fourteen, standing on my grandparents' balcony, letting the gravel stones slip through my fingers while I watched the sun sink into the trees. The sky was slowly turning purple, shot through with darkening gold. The wind was crisp and bright against my face, the rocks were humming in my hands and Presence flooded through me: ancient, alive, feminine, entire.[7]

That meeting is the center of my story, the way a stone drops into the surface of a lake and sends the water rippling out in slow, certain waves. In the years that followed, I came into Jewish community. I found myself caught and claimed and cradled by the luminous depth of Torah and Talmud. In graduate school, I dove deep into the study of Jewish sacred text. In rabbinical school, I committed myself to a life of sacred service. But I struggled with spiritual dissonance, torn between talking about God in ways that felt safe and giving voice to the God my own bones know. Decades later, I still remember how lonely it was, to keep my own heart's truth shut tight inside my chest.

Dear reader, I don't know if you think about God, or if you ever give that feeling language. I don't know how the sacred unfolds in your own life, or the words you use to speak of what you cherish. I don't know what memories you might offer if we had a chance to sit together, to speak with softness of the things we love. I don't know the scars you carry, if someone turned their word of God against you like a knife. I don't know what you've lost, or if you've been betrayed.

What I know is this: We need a way to speak more gently and more generously about the sacred, a way that gets us past the bludgeons and the bullhorns. So many of us have been taught to think of religion as a zero-sum game, where one truth triumphs and all the rest is heresy or foolishness. I want a different kind of conversation, one that holds a space for curiosity, for holy playfulness. I approach theology not as a fixed set of firm propositions and unwavering claims but as a field of possibilities. When I speak of God as She or when I tell you what it means to encounter God on Wheels, I don't mean these are the only ways to name the Holy. I mean them as offerings, as invitations.

Religion is, to me, a grammar of the imagination. I want to build a world in which we learn each other's sacred languages, where we strive to become multilingual. I want us to make room for difference. No, even more than that. I hope we seek it out. I hope we cherish it. Each way we speak of God offers a glimpse, a window to the Infinite. "God is like a mirror," a Jewish midrash teaches. "The mirror never changes, but everyone who looks sees a different face."[8]

It isn't quite right to frame all this as a matter of individual choosing, to suggest that the grammar of divinity unfolds for each of us in some purely private key. We live in a world where power and authority are still bound to a particular kind of masculinity, a world shaped by white supremacy, a world that assumes the superiority of certain kinds of bodies and minds. It's not surprising, then, that many of us grow up thinking of God as a thunderous father, with a beard and a throne and a propensity toward rage. Whiteness holds a kind of default setting when many of us imagine the divine, an aesthetic shaped not only by the way that whiteness is still privileged as the neutral position but also by the centering of a decidedly European artistic tradition. And the idea of God on Wheels? It's a shock to expectations, maybe even an affront. To claim a disabled God overturns assumptions about divine power and prowess, about the desirability of certain kinds of bodies, certain ways of moving through this world.

It may well be that you're thinking: *I don't think about God's body. I don't think about God's gender. I don't think about God's race. Isn't God beyond all that?*

Contemporary Christian and Jewish thinkers largely steer clear of talking about God's body. While Christian theology grapples with divine embodiment through the incarnation of Jesus, that interest in the flesh stops before it gets to God Eternal. Most Jews today likewise imagine God as a presence entirely without physicality or form. But classical Jewish sources embraced the notion of God's body. Biblical texts speak without a blush about God's face and extol the power of God's right arm, a phrase that I'll confess has always left me wondering about the unmentioned left. An ancient tradition of Jewish mysticism centers around the measurement of the divine limbs, giving an accounting of God's vast, impossible lengths. The brilliant medieval philosopher Moses Maimonides argued passionately that all these biblical and rabbinic phrases were but idioms and metaphors, ways of drawing our limited human minds toward the divine presence.

In some respects, I would agree. It seems to me quite extraordinary hubris to imagine that we know anything for sure about God, that we can somehow wrap our words around the sacred and pin it neatly into place. Ultimately, I suspect, in some realm far distant from our own, these qualities of gender, race, and body are insignificant. When I turn my mind toward the fullness of *Ehiyeh Asher Ehiyeh*—the

ultimate divine force that will be whatever it will be—I suspect all
these particulars and more are bound up and enfolded and exploded
in the everything of God.[9]

But here and now? We live in a world in which the body matters.
Name God as Goddess, and suddenly the presence of the pronoun
She throws the implicit gendering of God into sharp relief. We live in
a world that consistently devalues Black and Brown bodies, fat bodies
and femme bodies, queer, trans, and disabled bodies. We live in a world
where those bodies are too often held as incompatible with the sacred.
A world where those bodies are imagined as the antithesis of God.

Theology requires a reckoning with politics. It requires that we
confront the question of who has been afforded the power to name and
claim our bodies as close kin to the divine. It requires that we consider
how violent social systems have been rooted in religious assertions, how
the infrastructure of domination is built and buttressed by religious
language. It requires that we recognize how religious doctrine has been
used to claim the inferiority of Black flesh, to prop up the architectures
of enslavement, to justify the hand that held the lash. It requires that
we recognize how the notion of God the Father has helped to make a
world where (certain) fathers have the power of God.

At some point, when we're talking about God, someone always
asks about the real-deal Truth, about the ultimate big picture, about
the final word. I'll confess, I'm quite agnostic on these matters. Even
though I'm a rabbi, even though I've devoted much of my life to teaching and writing about religion, I tend to leave aside such questions as
way above my pay grade. I'm not much inclined toward declarations
about the way God is, save for what I've sketched out here, which is
more a testament to the ways God feels, the thousand ways that Presence breathes into our lives and lights us up in love.

When it comes to evaluation, when it comes to judging and assessing, I suppose my only measurement is this: Does it make you kinder?
Does it open you to gentleness, to wonder, to pleasure and to joy? Does
it tune you toward the heartbeat of the world? Does it help you tend
the hurt inside your skin? Does it offer salve and balm? Does it draw

you to the long slow work of justice—not only for yourself but for the
ones who aren't yet kin? This is the plumb line I bring to the measure
of theology, the foundation stone I return to again and again: *Tsedek,
tsedek, tirdof.* "Justice, justice you shall pursue."[10] Does it help us build a
world where each one has enough, where everyone knows love, where
we all are free?

Don't get me wrong. I don't mean to reduce God to a theory or
a symbol, or turn Presence into nothing more than a utilitarian idea.
For me, religion has relationship at heart: with God, if that's your
way, and with the world. With human bodies, the ones we sing with
in synagogue and stand beside in mosque, the ones who gather at our
kitchen tables, the ones with whom we share our food. And with other
bodies, with trees and toads and the soft curl of a seed as it seeks its
way above the soil.

But if you ask me how I know it, when it's good and true?

I'm not one for judging by the book.

I came of age in a time and a place where the Bible was a whip
and a lash, where grown men chanted *God hates fags*, where employers
appealed to biblical precedent to fire people living with AIDS, where
queer kids learned from Leviticus the cold press of a razor against
skin. Because of that history, because of that memory, because of the
way it curls like a fist in my soft places, I have never been comfortable
with moral language that appeals to the Bible as its source of authority. It's not because I think those teachings are supported by the text.
The ancient scribes who set words upon the page could hardly have
imagined me and my queer kin. The sex and power plays that they
indicted are nothing like our present-day queer lives and love.[11] And
when it comes to God? I know that we are cherished, in my bones.

But because I know so viscerally the way the Bible can be weaponized, I cannot simply grant it power. It's not enough for me to discount
those hateful verses or to argue that they mean otherwise. There are
two things at stake here, two things I need to lay down plain. The first
is the power of interpretation, the role that readers play in shaping
what religion means. When we approach a sacred text, the question

we must ask is not what does it say, but how has it been understood? Our sacred texts speak to us, through us. What they mean is shaped in part by how we read, by what we underscore and what we empha-size, by what choose to see. We can work to peel back veils of history and culture, to ask what those texts meant when they were first com-posed. We can trace the way that they've been understood through long and winding centuries. We can read them now anew and draw forth offerings shaped by our experience, by our scholarship and by our yearning. Each of these are different enterprises. I'll draw on all of them, at different times, throughout these pages.

But here is what I will not do: I won't claim something I believe is right and true simply because the Bible tells me so. That's the second thing at stake, the claim to authority that religious thinking often rests upon. Religious traditions that recognize and honor sacred texts almost always root their own sense of ethics, truth, or God within those scrip-tures. The practice is ubiquitous in Jewish thought, so common that we have a name for it. The prooftext is the biblical verse that buttresses a rabbinic claim, that links an otherwise unfounded assertion back to a recognized, sacred canon. In much the same way, contemporary Jew-ish thinkers also appeal to Torah and rabbinic texts, marshaling our sources to lend credence to our arguments, to show how the idea or claim we want to make is anchored in our sacred sources.

I, too, of course, will turn to text. In almost every chapter, on almost every page, I'll tease out Torah texts and Talmud and midrash and set them alongside commentaries, modern or medieval. But there's a difference here, a difference I want to lay bare. Torah and Talmud are for me a testimony of my ancestors, a witness to the sacred that I value and honor. There is something that I cherish about diving into these depths, even when we're wrangling, even when we disagree. I've learned to tangle with text, to be changed by it, to be in conversation with it.

But I do not trust it.

My first year in rabbinical school, my classmates and I learned a famous and oft-studied passage from the Babylonian Talmud that begins with the question: "How does one dance with the bride?"[12]

The discussion that follows centers on a debate between the students of Hillel and Shammai, two illustrious early rabbinic teachers whose disputes are famous for shaping Jewish law and practice. Both teachers recognize an obligation to celebrate with a bride during her wedding, but they differ in the question of how one should praise her. While Shammai asserts that one should praise "the bride as she is," Hillel advocates the propriety of a stock phrase. "Praise her," he says, as a "beautiful and graceful bride."

There's already plenty I object to. Hillel's answer rests on the assumption that the most praiseworthy qualities of a woman are her appearance and her ease. It is a paradigmatic example of the way women's virtues are commonly framed in aesthetic terms. But as the passage unfolds, the Talmud adds a disability twist. Shammai asks a question designed to scuttle Hillel's argument, a question he assumes will turn Hillel's praise into a blatant falsehood. "And if she is lame or blind?" Shammai asks. "Do you still say to her, 'a beautiful and graceful bride?' Does not the Torah say: Keep far from a lie?"[13]

I remember the first time I learned this passage. Working slowly and deliberately though the Hebrew, the breath sucked out of my body when the meaning snapped into place. Implicit in Shammai's claim was assumption that a disabled woman was the very opposite of beautiful, that her bearing was the very opposite of grace, that any claim to such was obviously false on its face. That reading becomes all the more apparent when we consider the reception history of this text. Jewish interpreters through the ages have read this text as the classic legal discussion of whether it's permissible, according to Jewish law, to tell a "white lie"—to tell an untruth in order to spare another pain.[14]

When Hillel and Shammai debate their question, Hillel counters Shammai's forceful case for telling the truth by asking another question: "Say someone buys poor goods in the marketplace. When he shows it to you, do you praise it or diminish it in his eyes?" Hillel advocates praise, even false praise. Why? "Because we should always strive," Hillel claims, "to be pleasant to one another other."

Hillel has a long-standing reputation as a rabbinic nice guy. But his argument has not solved my problem with this text. Quite the contrary. Hillel's response has made it worse. His is the saccharine sweet voice that praises everyone for any little thing, that swaddles disabled folks with kindness until we choke on false compliments. I don't want Hillel's niceness any more than I want Shammai's brutal honesty. Neither man perceives the brilliant, shimmering, rock-your-world power, beauty, and difference of disabled women's body-minds. Neither one of them can tell the truth about my life. Neither one knows how to properly praise.

This was one of the passages that made me realize I would never "fall in love" with Talmud in some uncomplicated way. No matter how much I honor the complexity, the brilliance, yes, even the beauty of Talmud, I will never trust it to know the truth of my own experience. I do not trust Jewish tradition to side with me, to speak with competence about my own life. I do not trust it to protect, to value the lives of those I hold most dear.

Feminist readers know this problem well, and those of us who remain committed to religious traditions despite their ethical failures have honed many interpretive tools for grappling with such conflicts. When a religious text runs counter to our cherished principles, when it fails to speak to the values we hold close, we often find ways to reinterpret the text. Sometimes we find other shades of potential within the words; sometimes we uncover historical and contextual factors that prompt a different meaning. Sometimes we challenge one text with another, tempering the apparent conclusions of one passage by appealing to deeper religious principles. These are powerful strategies, and they have brought brilliant Torah into the world. But I also want to name another truth, which I've come to realize over many years of building a spiritual life that speaks to my queer feminist disabled Jewish soul: I cannot always find what I need within the text.

There's a famous piece of counsel that the ancient rabbinic sage Ben Bag-Bag gives to those who study Torah: "Turn it, turn it, for everything is in it."[15] Sometimes I believe it. But sometimes I am haunted by the enormity of absence, by a loneliness within the sea of Talmud, by the palpable weight of all the voices, all the worlds that are not there.

Every time I name that grief, someone tries to tell me how to solve the problem. Someone always jumps in to rescue the text, to explain all the ways that Torah and tradition can be read as kind or just or good. But those efforts to rescue the text leave the authority of text in place. They reinscribe the power of text as the true arbiter of worth and value. That, I will not do.

I refuse to pin my life or the lives of those I love to the finer points of historical analysis or hermeneutics. Of course there are ways to read Jewish tradition as life-giving for disabled people, for women, for communities of color, for trans and queer lives. Of course the work of drawing forward those traditions is vital, urgent, and necessary. But let me also tell you this: If we cannot confront the violence, if we cannot come to the edge, look into the abyss, and feel the loss that is there, the anger, the grief, the rage—then we will end up doing harm, most likely wrapped in pious good intentions.

As a passionate queer Jewish feminist, as a proud disabled Jew, as a white person committed to disrupting white supremacy and all the interlocked structures of inequality that drive our world and ways of being, I will not try to paper over the times that text and tradition have let me down. But I also won't assume that there is nothing here for me. I claim this tradition and am claimed by it. I shape it and am shaped by it. I hold it close, and I am held.

I also root my understanding and conviction in other sacred grounds. Vibrant engagement with Jewish practice and text inspires and undergirds my spiritual life, but it is not the sole circumference of my moral circle. My ethical sensibility owes as much to Adrienne Rich, Audre Lorde, Gloria Anzaldúa, Rachel Carson, and Michel Foucault as it does to the Mishnah. I bring to Jewish tradition a passionate rooted-ness in disability community, an interest in and commitment to disabled people's lives. It's with disabled friends and coconspirators that I have felt some of the most potent spiritual insights of Jewish tradition made flesh. My friend and colleague Rabbi Ruti Regan teaches it this way: "The Torah taught me that we are all created in the image of God. But it was disability communities that taught me how to mean it."[16]

In *Black Queer Ethics, Family, and Philosophical Imagination*, Christian ethicist Thelathia Nikki Young argues that the life stories and lived experiences of Black queer people are sacred sources in their own right. These stories testify to the holy work of making family and fashioning relationships, of disrupting oppressive norms and challenging assumed hierarchies to create new ways of living together—what Young calls "the active infusion of queer possibilities into the material reality of family life."[17] I make a similar claim: that the experience of disability often results in powerful insight and expertise. I don't just mean the raw physical fact of living with an unconventional body-mind. I mean the experience of living in a world not built to fit us. I mean the experience of contending with ableism, with the violent denial of disability as a source of value in this world.

Throughout these pages, I'll bring critical testimony from disability communities into conversation with more conventional sources of Jewish sacred wisdom. I do so holding close the luminous words of Black novelist and Nobel laureate Toni Morrison, who refused to situate Black lives in the cracks and margins of white literary tradition. "It is no longer acceptable," Morrison says, "merely to imagine us and imagine for us. We have always been imagining ourselves."[18]

CHAPTER THREE

Hiddenness and Visibility

Passing and Presenting as Disabled

Before we turn more explicitly to the Bible, let us take the next two chapters to dive deeper into the world of disability. Disability is a broad umbrella category, one that encompasses a wide range of experiences. When I use the term "disability" in this book, I include physical and sensory disabilities, cognitive and intellectual disabilities, mental health disabilities, and long-term health conditions like chronic pain and chronic fatigue. The way I use disability doesn't depend on having a diagnosis or demand that you offer up a doctor's note. For some of us, diagnosis is a familiar part of our own disability stories. Some of us pursue diagnosis, while others flee from it. Some of us go for years without recognition from medical establishments.

Disabilities affect bodies and minds in a thousand different ways. Some are present at birth, while others are acquired over the course of a life. Some disabilities change over time, while others are fairly static. Some disabilities are obvious at first glance, but many more are not immediately apparent. I'm a wheelchair user, so my own disability is hyper-visible. The wheelchair is ubiquitous as a sign and signal of disability, so much so that it often crowds out other experiences of disability. Whether in popular media or in the international symbol of access that graces everything from barrier-free entrances to parking placards, contemporary culture has fashioned wheels into the standard marker of disability. Whenever I roll into a room, I often feel a frisson of awareness pass through the gathered group, a reminder of presence. It's as if, through my wheels alone, disability has suddenly entered the building.

But that's a lie. Statistically, the majority of disability experiences aren't apparent at first glance. Diabetes, depression, hearing loss, arthritis, dyslexia—all these experiences fall within the category of disability, but they often pass without notice in casual encounters. Certain factors make disability more likely to register. A white cane or a hearing aid, a guide dog or an emotional support animal often serve as indicators of disability presence. Autistic experience becomes strikingly apparent when a person is facing sensory overwhelm, but in other situations, it may be recognizable only to friends and family or to other Autistic kin.

In disability circles, folks often distinguish between visible and invisible disabilities. It's a useful shorthand for signaling some key differences in the way others register our disabilities. People with invisible disabilities often face dismissive attitudes toward their disabilities, while those of us with visible disabilities often contend with the consequences of being immediately marked as disabled by strangers and casual acquaintances. When I meet new people in the flesh, my disability is broadcast to all and sundry. It's the first thing (sighted) people know about me, my most distinguishing characteristic. While there's a burden to bearing the weight of other people's disability baggage, there's also a relief that comes from having my own disability be immediately legible.

Now let's be clear: just because most passersby can see my disability, it doesn't mean they make accurate assumptions about it. In fact, my life is full of encounters with folks who were outraged that my disability didn't match their expectations. Like a significant number of wheelchair users, I have some ability to move my legs, and I can stand for a moment or two if I'm willing to pay in pain. I rarely do. It's not just the physical cost that holds me back. Standing up from a wheelchair in a public place is a harrowing experience. People are aghast and often angry. I've been accused of "faking" it. I've had folks threaten to take my wheels away. I've heard them make jokes about miracles. Complete strangers get agitated if I move my legs. They assume that wheelchair users are paralyzed, and they get outraged if I don't fit their parameters.[1]

I'm making light here, but it's a brutal experience in the flesh—especially since nondisabled people are regularly in positions of power and authority over disabled people. Want the keys to the locked service elevator? You've got to first convince the gatekeeper who's watching your every move, probing whether or not you deserve the lift. (I'm not sure why access is so closely guarded; it's not like they pay by the ascent.) About to use a disability parking placard? Be prepared to face a gauntlet of vigilante enforcement officers judging your fitness and assessing your limp.[2]

People with invisible disabilities face this kind of scrutiny full on. When disability isn't immediately obvious, people tend to assume our bodies and minds mirror normative expectations. I have friends who regularly use a cane in public, especially in airports or when taking the bus, not so much for the physical support but because the cane makes their disability apparent at a casual glance. Though courtesy and kindness are never assured, a visible marker of disability presence can often smooth the way. It becomes easier to get a seat, to avoid being jostled, to move at a safe pace.

Thanks to the powerful advocacy of disability movements, many countries now provide certain civil rights protections for disabled people. In the United States, public transportation, schools, restaurants, shops, concert halls, and other public venues are often (but not always) required to provide disability access. The Americans with Disabilities Act, a signature US civil rights law passed in 1990, mandates that employers, educators, and agencies must provide *reasonable accommodations* to disabled people who need alternative formats or other arrangements to do our jobs, earn our degrees, and otherwise move through our days. The ADA was a landmark victory, one that reshaped our public spaces and transformed our expectations. While I was born before its passage, my entire life has been made possible by its existence.

But the increasing availability of disability accommodations has also intensified public anxiety about disability fraud—about the way people might masquerade as disabled in order to secure disability benefits or "special" advantages. The idea of the "disability con" has a long and storied history in popular culture, and politicians have often successfully played on these kinds of public fears in order to cut public benefits and impose austerity measures that have devastating impacts on real people's lives.[3] For people with invisible disabilities, this attitude of hostile suspicion makes it harder to disclose disability and ask for accommodations. Not only do folks face the stigma of disability, they also face disbelief about their disability claims. Invisible disability means always making a calculation about the relative costs of speaking up or staying silent, of making a request or letting it pass.

Need extra time to complete an assignment or exam? Despite all the tests and certifications that formal disability accommodations require, students with disabilities still encounter teachers and professors who consider those arrangements a kind of special treatment, a generous favor, rather than an expression of equity. Unable to read the standard menu? Some restaurants now have large print or Braille available, but it almost always requires an ask. Requesting access puts the burden of disclosure on the disabled person.[4] It forces us to disrupt the prevailing assumption that all bodies can take the stairs, read the fine print, or hear the presenter who's declined to use the microphone. It forces us to bear the brunt of other people's frustration, to feel personally responsible for someone else's hassle. The burden of disclosure also means we carry the weight of other people's doubts. *Are you really disabled? Can't you just get by with what we already have?*

We live in a world that generally assumes everyone is nondisabled unless otherwise marked, a posture that means disabled people have to do the work and invest the energy to disrupt those expectations. Arranging a job interview over email, I mention my wheels and ask about access. It can be an odd icebreaker. Sometimes it's clear before I even arrive that prospective employers no longer feel I'm "a good fit." Every time I travel, I disclose these details to manage the logistics.

Countless hosts and hotel clerks know the measure of my wheels and the particulars of my bathroom needs. These aren't private matters, but public facts. In a world that treats my presence as a perennial surprise, I'm always negotiating the terms of my passage. The story of my body gets told and retold, part of the price I pay for a chance at access and accommodation.

Whenever I talk about disability, someone always comes up to me afterward to say, with some embarrassment and uncertainty, that they're not sure if they *count* as disabled. As they unfold a bit of their own story, I almost always end up reassuring them: *Yes, you, too, know something about disability. Your own experience is part of this complex tapestry.*

If you're new to the topic, a working definition of disability might seem like an obvious place to start, a neutral ground that helps establish the basic terms of our subject. But for disabled folks, these questions are perilous ground. Definitions are a matter of power. The act of defining disability isn't an academic exercise. It's an act that's played out on our bodies, our backs.

Definitions of disability are often bound up with access to public support and aid. Societies that offer some form of public assistance for disabled people have to figure out criteria. Who qualities for financial support? Who is eligible for a disability parking placard or for Medicaid? Built into these kinds of initiatives is a need to designate certain individuals as appropriate recipients of public aid. In some ways, of course, that's entirely understandable. Resources are finite, and funding should go to those with need. But the lived experience of these determinations is brutal in the flesh.

Disabled folks face gatekeepers who decide if we qualify for disability benefits or insurance coverage, for school programs, accommodations, or support services. The answer to that question—*are you disabled enough?*—has the power to shape whether we get by or whether we get left behind. These decisions are almost always made by a person whose job depends on denials, who's been trained to hit a fiscal target by turning folks down. These decisions are almost always made by those who can get up and walk away, who've got no skin in the game, who don't live disability from the inside.

Consider the experience of disabled people in the UK. Recent governments have championed austerity politics, an approach to balancing budgets that has resulted in massive cuts to public services and social programs.[5] People with disabilities have faced devastating losses. Journalist and disability rights campaigner Francis Ryan stacks up story after story: disabled people facing malnutrition and starvation, wheelchair users trapped in attic apartments and inaccessible squats, parents with no way to secure disability services for their children, folks in their twenties and thirties who've lost in-home support and have been forced into nursing homes.[6] The last is a cruel irony: institutional care is a vastly more expensive endeavor—but it's one that enriches more powerful corporate interests.[7] In recent years, the British government has turned over the task of determining disability to private companies, a system that often awards contracts to outfits that profess to save the government money. The decisions that these evaluators and their companies make have the power to shatter a life, to pull the rug out from under a carefully calibrated system of *making things work.* Score fewer points and you lose the bursary that pays for a couple taxi trips a month or that shaves down the payments for an accessible car, savings that can offset the cost of a barrier-free apartment, a screen reader, or adaptive kitchen aids.[8]

In the United States, disability determinations are required to assess a person's eligibility for Medicaid. Medicaid is one of the few routes through which disabled people can secure home health care and personal attendant services that makes it possible for many of us to live at home, rather than in a facility, an institution, or a nursing home. At risk is not just fundamental access to basic health care but also the tools we use to navigate inhospitable environments: wheelchair batteries, anxiety meds, hearing aids. Because the options are so few and the stakes are so high, these kinds of disability determinations are fraught with fear and frustration. Will our disability be recognized?

Will we be able to marshal a sufficiently convincing account of our disabled selves to be able to secure the services and support that we need? Or will we be judged as undeserving? Formal determinations of disability are also required to secure accommodations for school and work, which means that disability access is more often granted to those who have the race and class privilege to be able to navigate these systems. Folks without a recognized diagnosis, folks who can't afford a battery of tests and who can't marshal a fresh doctor's note, folks who falter before legions of forms? They're often left in the cold.

In some circumstances, being recognized as disabled is a boon. In other contexts, it's acutely dangerous. We live in a world that routinely judges disability as a negative fact. Educators, employers, and strangers on the street regularly regard people with disabilities as undesirable, judging us too slow, too different, too expensive, too unlikely to succeed. Many disabled folks internalize these judgments, and so we strive to look or act or be perceived as nondisabled—a stance that's commonly known as *passing*. The dynamics of passing are complex. Even if we aren't successful at passing, disabled people often feel pressure to *cover*, what Kenji Yoshino calls "downplaying disfavored traits so as to blend into the mainstream."[9] When we talk about passing and covering, the language we use tends to highlight active efforts to hide, to minimize, to conceal.[10] The social history of disability is full of examples, from hard-of-hearing folks who skate by on lip reading and context cues to physically disabled people who've learned to hide our limps or our tremors, regardless of the cost.

But we must be careful here. If we treat passing and covering as nothing more than an individual choice, we fail to reckon with the social realities that make them such an urgent prospect. When disabled people make the choice to normalize our bodies and minds, it is often a strategic choice, a choice for getting by as best we can in a world that remains profoundly hostile to disability and difference.[11] I am not judging that choice. I am judging the world that makes it necessary.

Consider the example of President Franklin D. Roosevelt. A polio survivor, Roosevelt spent much of his adult life in a wheelchair and could walk or stand only with considerable difficulty. Yet for Roosevelt, the public confidence required for the presidency was incompatible with disability. Roosevelt's biographer, Hugh Gallagher, himself a polio survivor, has documented the extraordinary lengths to which Roosevelt went in order to veil his disability from the public eye, the strategies that he and his son and his physical therapist devised so that Roosevelt could walk unaided for crucial public moments.[12] On the campaign trail, the presidential hopeful was often carried up the back stairs of otherwise inaccessible halls so that he could stride a few steps to the lectern to make a speech. Over the seventeen years of his presidency, Roosevelt surmounted countless stairs with the aid of his bodyguards, who would lift him up and carry him in a standing position in order to give the impression that he was walking on his own. As president, Roosevelt was never once photographed in a wheelchair. In all his public dealings, in all his press, his disability was mentioned only as something he'd overcome.

Roosevelt's ability to pass as nondisabled was not simply a matter of personal drive. It was made possible by his family's wealth and by the power of his position. Roosevelt had access to therapists and strategists; he had lifters and aides at his beck and call. During his presidency, Secret Service agents took responsibility for making sure the spaces he entered were accessible for him. They worked out accessible routes, constructed ramps to ease his entry, and shielded certain moments from public view—even fashioning a special screen that veiled Roosevelt from sight as he was helped in and out of the presidential car.[13] And while Roosevelt's investment in passing was surely shaped by his own desires, it was inseparable from his political assessment that the nation would not have accepted "a cripple" as leader. It might well have been true. Gallagher argues that in this particular historical moment, when the nation had desperate need of Roosevelt's leadership and political acumen, public officials and the press all conspired to bolster the illusion of Roosevelt's physical fitness. "An agreement was struck," Gallagher writes. "The existence of FDR's handicap would simply be denied by all."[14]

For those who can pull it off, passing is a not-uncommon response to living as a minority in a society that is often hostile to our existence. Some queer folk pass as straight. Some people of color pass as white. Sometimes Jews pass as non-Jewish. In some ways, the reasons are obvious. Why call attention to an undesirable difference? Why not avoid the disadvantages of belonging to a group that faces violence, discrimination, disdain? Passing seems to offer an out from the reality of disability stigma, from the exclusions and refusals that disability brings.

But passing comes at bitter cost.[15] I cannot read Roosevelt's story without flinching. I claim no access to the inner life of this man who lived and died years before my own birth. I'll never know what was in his heart. But I know something of what it means to campaign against yourself. To press body and bone again and again through motions that cause pain. To feel legs turn unsteady and to begin that internal calculus, that infernal bargaining with flesh: just two more minutes, just three more steps. I know the haunting of the thing unspoken. I know what it feels like to be afraid the limp will show.

My own disability largely passed unnoticed when I was a child, mostly invisible to a casual glance. I learned to say *mild cerebral palsy* all in one breath, a way of simultaneously identifying my disability and asserting that it didn't really matter. I was a clumsy kid who couldn't play softball to save my life. But I took refuge in books and steered clear of recess. I spent a lot of time in the company of trees, who I largely found more trustworthy than people and more inclined to harbor my own stillness. Looking back, I can see how disability shaped my experience of self, how deeply it contoured the choices that I made, the things I came to love. But at the time, I rarely thought of it. I never gave it words.

Come one summer in college, my disability changed abruptly. Between one day and the next, I lost the ability to walk or stand without pain. After a good six months of endless doctors' visits and fruitless investigations, I gave up on physicians and decided to figure out the new state of things. A beloved friend scored me a used electric scooter, the first and most formative gift of wheels. The scooter was a shock to friends and classmates who saw me as suddenly catapulted into an entirely different category. For me? It was freedom.

Of course it wasn't all roses. The pain was no picnic, and the emotional terrain was equally complex. I had moments of embarrassment so sharp they still cut like a blade. Browsing through the tight-packed aisles of the campus drugstore with a group of college friends, I clipped the corner of a cardboard pantyhose display and found myself suddenly surrounded by a thousand runaway nylons in their little plastic balls. I wanted the earth to crack open and swallow me up, scooter and all. The earth, alas, did not oblige.

Looking back on that moment now, that moment when my body on wheels was so obviously too big for the place I was allotted, I recall vividly one thing that this transition taught me: *I would have to take up space*. It was a startling shift from the protocols of white femme politeness in which I had been subtly (and not so subtly) tutored my entire life. No more tucked knees and demurely crossed legs. No more minute shifts to give way to others on the street, in the classroom, at the concert hall. I hadn't realized how deeply a certain kind of deference was trained into my body until I suddenly lost the ability to accomplish it. On wheels, I was going to have to claim the room.

Whenever I think about the way becoming a wheelchair user shifted my relationship to my own body and to the gender norms I learned to inhabit, I think about a story from the Babylonian Talmud, the story of a woman who had no hand. It's a brief story, a tiny glimpse into an otherwise unattested life. It goes like this:

> There was a certain man
> who married a woman whose hand was a stump,
> but he was not aware of it until the day that she died.[16]

Our story appears as part of a series of brief accounts of surprising events, a chronicle of wondrous happenings that run counter to the expected order of things. In the Talmud's estimation, the fact that the woman's disability passes unnoticed even in the intimate context of her marriage is a marvel—in both senses of the world. It is a marvel meant to surprise, to startle us with unexpected possibility. And it is, for the writers of the Talmud, a marvelous thing, a story meant to underscore the moral virtue of the woman or her man.

Immediately after they tell the tale, two rabbis discuss the significance of the story, trying to decide which party to praise:

> Rav said: "Come and see how modest a woman this was,
> for her husband was not aware of it."

> Rabbi Hiyya said to him: "Such is a woman's way.
> Instead, come and see how modest a man this was,
> for he was not aware of this in his wife."[17]

Rav suggests that the woman herself is the virtuous one in this scenario. He holds up the wife's capacity to veil her disability even in the most private dimensions of her life as a sign of exemplary piety, a testament to her extraordinary modesty. Rabbi Hiyya disagrees. He thinks it's *natural* for a woman to hide her stump, to conceal these imperfections of body and bone, to shield from view anything that others might regard as a blemish. In Hiyya's telling, it's the husband who becomes the hero of our tale. He does not pore over his wife's body, looking for ways it does not measure up. The rabbis inhabit a world not unlike our own, a world in which men routinely pass their eyes over women's bodies and have the power and privilege to assess and to judge. This woman's husband refuses that calculating gaze. He fails to notice her flaw.

Whenever I tell this story, folks are quick to celebrate this man and this couple. In this story, they tell me, we find a relationship that transcends surface judgments. Like Rabbi Hiyya, modern readers are quick to extol his virtues. He's a man who values and cherishes his wife without regard for her disability. He's a man who overlooks the irrelevant fact of the body, to see his wife as she really is.

But this is a story that pierces my heart. While there are plenty of other stories in rabbinic literature that seem on the surface to judge disability much more harshly, this story brings me up short every time. Why? Because it celebrates a practice of "looking past" disability, a practice that still has a powerful hold on contemporary culture. Conventional codes of public propriety dictate that when we encounter disability, the polite thing to do is to look away. The physical practice of averting the gaze goes hand and hand with a broader posture of denying disability's significance. Most of us have been trained to ignore impairment, to refuse to register difference. When did you first hear the words? *Don't look. Don't stare.*

Now I know in my bones how deep a stare can cut. There's a certain kind of look that pins me down like a butterfly tacked into a specimen book, just one more body to press into a collection of curiosities. That kind of cruelty? That surely has to go.

But while I'm all for rooting out the dehumanizing stare, I don't want people to overlook my own disability. The practice of turning away from disability registers, in my experience, as a tremendous loss. It's a silence that swallows up knowledge, that refuses the intimacy of real relationship. When I think about the rabbinic husband who didn't discover his wife's disability until the day that she died, I think of all the knowledge that they didn't share. I think of all the years they were married, all the years he never knew the texture of her flesh, the contours of her arm, the nuance of her skin.

I want a different world for us. If we understand disability as simply something to overlook, if we treat disability as something that shouldn't be lingered on, then we miss something critical, something essential to the narration of the body, to the understanding of a self. Disability is bound up with the stories of our lives, with memory and personal history and a sense of who we are. Disability studies theorist Rosemarie Garland-Thomson argues that disability is an essential characteristic of what it means to be human. Disability, she says, is an inevitable part of our experience, the "transformation of flesh as it encounters world."[18] Transformation is not without difficulty. Sometimes it is a site of pain. Sometimes it is an index of our loss. Sometimes it is a source of shame, a thing we wish were otherwise, a thing we wish to hide.

But shame is not inevitable. Shame can be released. Shame can be transformed. These transformations of mind and heart are long and slow. But anyone can do it, anywhere, with whatever tools they have at hand. The brilliant disabled poet and activist Laura Hershey invites disabled folk to the slow and ongoing work it takes to alchemize shame and come to claim a deep and rooted recognition of the rightness of our lives. In a poem that has become a kind of anthem in many disability circles, Hershey writes:

> Remember, you weren't the one
> Who made you ashamed,
> But you are the one
> Who can make you proud . . .
> You get proud by practicing.[19]

Though much of the task of releasing shame falls to each of us who has internalized it, part of *how* we do it is with others. Part of how we do it is by cracking the chrysalis of silence, the expectation that disability is a thing to be hidden away or overlooked, a source of private trouble, an embarrassment, a truth to be denied. Part of how we do it is by recognizing disability as an essential thread in the fabric of our lives.

CHAPTER FOUR

Ableism

The Social-Political Dimension of Disability

How shall we define disability? Rather than offer the illusion of a simple, satisfying answer, I'm going to suggest that we need to take the very category of disability apart, to look beyond the surface to see how it works and how deeply intertwined it is with power and judgment. I find it most helpful to understand disability as an interplay between three interrelated strands: impairment, ableism, and self-identity.

Disability studies scholars and disability activists often use the term "impairment" to designate the biophysical dimensions of disability, to name the way that disability often (but not always) limits a person's ability to see, hear, move, know, or feel. Impairment has long held a central place in the way most of us conceptualize disability, whether in casual contexts or as a matter of public policy. The Americans with Disabilities Act (ADA) includes in its purview all people with "a physical or mental impairment that substantially limits one or more major life activities."[1]

But impairment isn't exactly a straightforward matter. A robust body of case law has probed the contours of those categories, working to define what counts as an "impairment," what entails a "substantial limit," and what constitutes a "major life activity." Even more significantly, the ADA also recognizes that we cannot simply define disability in functional terms. ADA protections also cover people who have a *history* of a disability, as well as those who are *perceived* as having a disability. Folks in both of these categories often face disability-related discrimination, even if they don't experience any functional limitations.

Impairment alone can't capture the fullness of disability. Sometimes it's not even part of the picture. Consider a person with a significant facial difference, such as a facial birthmark. Facial differences and other highly visible disabilities can have a profound impact on a person's experience, regardless of whether they affect how a person's body functions or whether they have physical effects. Appearance activist Carly Findlay has the genetic skin condition ichthyosis, which causes red, scaly, painful skin. She writes, "I live with the stares, the sniggers and ridicule from strangers, and the expectation to educate people, every day."[2] Her experience underscores the power of social attitudes in shaping the experience of disability. Centering impairment isn't enough to capture this complex terrain.

We live in a highly medicalized culture, and medical thinking often shapes the way we implicitly approach disability. In most medical settings, impairment is the primary focus. A person with a disability becomes a *patient* with a *condition*, for which they seek treatment or cure. In disability circles, this approach is often called the medical model of disability. This kind of framework can be a useful tool for folks grappling with acute health needs. But as a comprehensive approach to disability? It doesn't serve us well. It frames disability solely as a matter of dysfunction, a failure of some element of body or mind. Perhaps even more significantly? It aims to solve the problem of disability by getting rid of impairment.

The ADA takes a very different approach, one that's rooted in the social model of disability. In the 1970s, as disability activists in the United States and Britain began organizing collectively to press for civil rights and more equitable access to public space, they articulated a social model of disability. The social model argues that people are disabled in large part by specific societal choices: by buildings that lack ramps and elevators; by chairs that are built only for "standard-sized" bodies; by public spaces that assume everyone uses sight to make their way through the world. Rather than trying to press all bodies and minds into a single mold, the social model argues that society needs to provide access and accommodation to those of us who differ from the norm.[3]

For me, that insight wasn't an abstract piece of theory. It was a revolutionary reorientation of the way I experienced the world. I take a political view of disability, one that recognizes disability as intimately intertwined with ableism. By ableism, I mean a complex set of power structures that privilege certain bodies or minds as "normal" while designating others as "abnormal." By ableism, I mean a whole host of systems, practices, and policies that stigmatize disability and deny disabled people access, agency, resources, and self-determination. By ableism, I mean the low expectations for disabled kids' achievement, the warehoused classrooms, the state institutions. I mean the taunting on the playground, the snide comments over lunch, the stares at the bus stop. I mean the fact that disabled people are routinely shut out of jobs and turned away from interviews. I mean the fact that many people with disabilities are employed in positions that pay less than minimum wage, that even letting us labor has long been construed as a kind of public charity. I mean the fact that disabled parents routinely lose custody of their children, that housing discrimination runs rampant. I mean the fact that disabled people's health care access is regularly under assault, that many of us risk losing our health care if we marry, if we move to another state, if we publish a book.[4]

I was in college before I heard the word "ableism," before I understood that disability exclusion wasn't simply a private story but a broader public project. Without a framework for naming and recognizing ableism, disability exclusion seemed natural, inevitable, the only way the world could be. Recognizing ableism gave me a way to articulate the violence and stigma that shapes so much of disability experience. Recognizing ableism allowed me to see disability prejudice as an artifact of culture, as an imposition of power and hierarchy. Once I began to probe its dynamics, I could begin to imagine possibilities. I could begin to taste a different world.

Ableism makes the category of disability tick. As a collective group, people with disabilities are an extraordinarily diverse bunch—and our disability experiences are myriad. When it comes to the raw physicality of our bodies, a blind person and a wheelchair user don't actually have that much in common. We fall into the same category not because we share some essential bodily experience, but because we deviate in a significant respect from the way humans are "supposed" to be. We don't measure up. We don't fit the norm.

Standing behind this norm is a figure that gets to pass as "neutral," a figure whose body and mind seem perfectly normal in every respect. But that norm isn't neutral at all. Disability studies scholar Rosemarie Garland-Thomson coined the term "the normate" to draw attention to the figure that powers this fantasy.[5] It's a figure that sociologist Erving Goffman wryly describes as "a young, married, white, urban, northern, heterosexual Protestant father of college education, fully employed, of good complexion, weight and height, and a recent record in sports."[6] Where can such a man be found? Only in our minds. The normate is a fantasy, a chimera. Even people who approximate these norms in certain ways are always at risk of falling out of favor.

Even though the normate is a fantasy, it has enormous cultural power. It is the unspoken force of the normate that makes disability a meaningful category, that forges all the rest of us into misfits. To think politically about disability is to recognize this move, to recognize the sleight of hand. To think politically about disability is to see how the very category itself depends on cultural judgments about the relative worth of different bodies and minds. But to recognize disability as a human-made category is not to dismiss it as irrelevant or fantastical. Quite the contrary. To think politically about disability is to recognize that ableism invests physical and mental difference with extraordinary consequences. It is to track the visceral impact of disability difference, to see how it contours a life.

Whenever I lay out the role ableism plays in creating the very category of disability, someone is quick to propose a solution. Why not stop using the term "disability," they ask me, if it's laced with negative judgments, if it's part of the system that stigmatizes difference and devalues disabled people's lives? To my mind, that's a misguided tactic. Doing away with the category of disability makes it harder to recognize and resist ableism. It distracts us from the work of dismantling the social and structural violence that's done to disabled people. It also cuts away the third strand in my working definition of disability: the power of self-identification.

I don't want to do away with disability. In my own experience, I find that the choice to *self-identify* with disability is a powerful turning point in the work of shedding shame and beginning to work for social and political change. I'm invested in disability as a powerful way to name and claim my own experience, as a marker of identity, as a way of forging connections between those of us whose bodies and minds are on the far side of the ableist line. I use the term "disability" because I believe that living a vibrant, unabashedly disabled life is a brilliant way of refuting ableism's lie. I don't believe there's anything to hide about disability—and substituting out this name for something gentler, something softer seems to me like there's something to apologize for. Euphemisms like "differently abled" or "special needs" feel too saccharine for my skin. While "special needs" has significant currency among parents whose children have disabilities, many disability activists object to the way that term positions disability access and accommodations as a kind of extra consideration, rather than a foundational requirement for equity.

It's worth acknowledging here that the politics of naming disability are complex. When I was first finding my way into disability movements, the most common preferred language for disability was "people with disabilities," a mode of identification known as "person-first" language. Person-first language marked an important shift from earlier, more objectifying disability terminology. These days, the expression "people with disabilities" still gets considerable use. But many more folks are choosing "identity-first" language, identifying ourselves as "disabled people." I use both forms of speech, often shifting between them depending on my audience and the context of my conversation. It's worth noting that certain communities often lay claim to particular language. In Deaf circles, it's common to capitalize the D in Deaf to signal Deaf people's membership in a distinctive cultural community. Autistic activists likewise tend to use the capital A as a strong affiliation with Autism as identity. Both communities strongly favor identity-first language, rejecting terminology that implies that the person can be separated from the cultural identity. A "person with deafness" just doesn't compute.

In other disability circles, there's more variation. If you're not sure what to say, or if you're worried about striking the wrong note, then "person with a disability" is usually a fairly safe bet. Just make sure that what you say affirms the agency and vitality of disabled people. There's a vast difference between a feature story that recognizes someone as "a disabled woman, active in social justice movements" and a news account that calls attention to the "the plight of the disabled." When it comes to identifiers, follow the lead of the person you're speaking with or ask the person you're speaking about. Whatever you do, don't police the way other people articulate their own identities. If you're a nondisabled person used to having your voice respected and accepted, you'd be shocked to know how often disabled people get told we shouldn't call ourselves disabled.

Self-identifying with disability is a powerful kind of alchemy. For me, identifying as disabled has been a way to build community, to forge connections and kinships with others who share similar experiences, who know ableism intimately. It allows me to link my own experience to a broader social movement, to take up the work of social transformation. While people seek disability community for many different reasons, my own affiliation has always been connected to the work of building a different world. I want to bring down ableism, and all the brutal systems of social violence that are its kin.

Allow me to suggest an unexpected text for grappling with ableism: rabbinic commentary on the biblical story of Sodom. Now I imagine that Sodom might well strike you as a bold choice for framing a justice-seeking ethics. Both in popular culture and in some religious circles, the story of Sodom is all too often used as a condemnation of homosexuality.[7] I grew up hearing Sodom as shorthand for castigating queer love, for imagining our sexuality as an affront to God. That's not at all what I mean.

Genesis 19 portrays the city of Sodom as an extraordinarily wicked place, a place destroyed by God after the townsfolk flout the basic laws of hospitality and human decency. Two angels come to town, appearing as strangers, and the men of Sodom decide to rape them. The travelers take shelter with Lot, the one decent man in Sodom. When the crowd comes to his door demanding that he give up his guests, Lot surrenders his daughters to the mob to keep the strangers safe from violence.

There's a lot I could say here about Lot's choice, about the way this story sacrifices female bodies for the protection of men, about the way the daughters of an ancient father could be surrendered at his whim. There's a lot I could say about the choice to imagine God as the arbiter of such sweeping moral judgment, about the way our story fails to ask about the other souls who also call this city home. But on the subject of sex, the story seems clear. Sodom is a condemnation of brutality, an assault on rape. As Rabbi Jay Michaelson argues, "Reading the story of Sodom as being about homosexuality is like reading the story of an ax murderer as being about an ax."[8]

In the classic Jewish sources, Sodom is not a story that condemns male-male love. The rabbis of the Talmud retell and expand the Sodom story, dramatizing the cruelty and hard-heartedness of the city. They use the story of Sodom to condemn violence and greed, to call

out hatred of the stranger, to imagine God as outraged by brutality.
To illustrate, the rabbis tell this story:

> The people of Sodom had a certain bed on which all travelers slept.
> If the guest was too tall, they shortened him by cutting off his feet.
> If the guest was too short, they stretched him out until he fit.[9]

Though the rabbis never frame it in quite these terms, I take this
story as a vivid account of ableism, of how it brutalizes flesh and bone.
This is a story about the kind of violence that follows when we force
people to fit complex, unruly bodies and minds into a simple, straightforward, one-size-fits-all society; when we demand that everyone walk
up a few flights of stairs, read the fine print, and peer at the PowerPoint;
when we assume that everyone's body and everyone's mind better fit
the same bed—or else, face the hatchet. This is the world in which we
live, a world that would rather chop us up and spit us out than cherish
the real, riotous diversity of all human kinds.

Every disabled person I know has stories about the cost of living
in a one-size-fits-all society, about being shut out by attitudes, assumptions, and physical structures that demand everyone's body and mind
fit within the same basic norm. This isn't only a disability story. Fat
bodies, Black and Brown bodies, Jewish bodies, Muslim bodies, homeless bodies, femme bodies, gender-nonconforming bodies, intersex and
trans bodies—so many of us know the cost that normativity exacts from
those of us who don't fit neatly into "standard" spaces and expectations.
Disability activist Eli Clare chronicles the material impact of ableism,
the way it has contoured his own life. "I write slowly enough," he says,
"that cashiers get impatient as I sign my name to checks, stop talking
to me, turn to my companions, hand them my receipts. I have failed
timed tests, important tests, because teachers wouldn't allow me extra
time to finish the sheer physical act of writing, wouldn't allow me to
use a typewriter."[10]

When we hear a story like Clare's, we face a crucial choice. Do
we assume the problem of disability lies in the fact of shaking hands

or slurred speech? Or do we focus our attention on the way certain bodies and minds are denied access? Most disabled people internalize early on that the problem is us. We ask for access, only to be told, "It's not possible" or "It's too expensive." Rather than recognizing inaccessibility as a communal responsibility, ableism privatizes the problem. Ableism convinces us that the mismatch is a consequence of our individual bodies and minds. It puts the burden of dealing with inaccessibility on people with disabilities and our families.

Want to challenge ableism? Anytime you can, flip that script. Put the problem back where it belongs—on a culture that expects all bodies and minds to unfold neatly into standard sizes. Rather than trying to shoehorn disabled people into the narrow confines of the normative, I want us to change the world in which we live. Rather than expecting everyone's body and mind to work the same way, I want us to challenge the policies and social structures that disenfranchise disabled people and make our lives more difficult. Don't shorten the traveler's body; build her a bed that fits.

To commit ourselves to this task, we need a way to tell disability stories that wrestle with violence, that help us name and recognize disparities of social power, that give us critical tools to challenge structural violence. The way that disability shapes my life isn't just a private story about the particularity of my own muscle and bone. It's a political story, a story about collective, communal choices. The exclusion of disabled people isn't a natural, inevitable fact of the body. It's a product of policy choices, of built environments, of cultural norms that have visceral, real-world impact. Human beings designed our cities and our schools, and we built them for a particular sort of people. Human beings designed standardized tests, the fashion industry, and the beauty myth. Human beings developed the nine-to-five workday and came to value efficiency as a signal mark of excellence. Human beings developed mass incarceration, insane asylums, and the eugenics movement. We built this world, and we built it in ways that destroy people's lives.

People with disabilities face profound social and structural violence. Too many of us are unhoused or living on the edge, unemployed or working for subminimum wage, at disproportionate risk of family and caregiver violence, hemmed in by systems or locked away in institutions. These aren't the inevitable consequences of disability. They are realities that flow out of specific policy choices and political actions. *That's* what I want us to think about when we think about disability.

In the nineteenth and twentieth centuries, schools tied Deaf children's hands to deny them access to sign language and force them toward oralist communication—a stance supported by Alexander Graham Bell and other prominent eugenicists who sought to eradicate, in Bell's infamous words, "the deaf race."[11] In Nazi Germany, disabled people were the first ones to be murdered, a program explicitly framed as "mercy killing."[12] Even today, many people with disabilities are sterilized without their knowledge or consent. And the specter of a merciful death still lives in our midst. Most disability activists I know are terrified about the increasing ease of access to medical euthanasia because public debate often assumes our lives are not worth living. My partner has clear instructions: If I'm ever hospitalized, fight for me. Make sure they know *I want to live.*

Solidarity with disability communities demands moving beyond the personal. Theologian Monica Coleman, an ordained elder in the African Methodist Episcopal Church who lives with chronic depression, calls on religious communities to recognize the urgency of political engagement. "It's a political act," she argues, "to advocate for things that would improve the lives of people with depressive conditions: universal health care, sufficient paid leaves from work, health coverage for preventative and non-pharmaceutical care. . . . These are political acts, and they are also deeply religious ones."[13] With the stroke of a pen, disabled people can lose the support that makes it possible for us to hire personal attendants, to live at home, to steer clear of a nursing home. When politicians debate prescription benefits or preexisting condition coverage? It's not abstract for us. It's visceral. It's the thin line between life and death.

My own thinking about the politics of disability is indebted to the wisdom and leadership of disability justice organizers, a movement led by Black and Brown disabled people, especially queer and trans folks. Disability justice roots itself in the recognition that ableism operates in tandem with capitalism, white supremacy, and heteropatriarchy. Consider these words from Patty Berne, cofounder and artistic director of the Sins Invalid performance collective whose insight and organizing has catalyzed disability justice as a movement. "The histories of white supremacy and ableism are inextricably entwined," Berne argues, "both forged in the crucible of colonial conquest and capitalist domination."[14] While different forms of oppression all have their own distinctive dynamics, they often interlock in mutually reinforcing ways. In contemporary culture, ableism runs hand-in-hand with racialized violence and trans-hatred, with misogyny, gender violence, anti-Semitism, and xenophobia. The cultural logics of normalcy and deviance are arrayed against all of us whose bodies and minds don't seem to measure up.

Disability justice activist Talila "TL" Lewis offers an incisive definition of ableism, one that underscores the interlocking relationship between ableism and other forms of domination. Ableism, Lewis argues, is

> a system that places value on people's bodies and minds based on societally constructed ideas of normalcy, intelligence, excellence, desirability, and productivity. These constructed ideas are deeply rooted in anti-Blackness, eugenics, misogyny, colonialism, imperialism and capitalism. This form of systemic oppression leads to people and society determining who is valuable and worthy based on a person's language, appearance, religion and/or their ability to satisfactorily [re]produce, excel and "behave." You do not have to be disabled to experience ableism.[15]

Let me draw out a few elements of Lewis's definition, to flesh out some of its implications. I've already laid out the way that ableism fashions disability into a form of deviance, a departure from the expected norm. We've traced something of the price people pay for falling outside the accepted bounds of what's normal, or normal enough to pass. But let me name now another dimension of this reality, a particular way that ableism and white supremacy interlock. My white disabled body is a magnet for charitable impulses. Strangers on the street are quick to give me unsolicited aid. People rush to open doors, to get out of the way, to give me a hand. Sometimes those impulses are genuinely helpful. More often than not, they're paternalistic and invasive—especially when would-be helpers don't bother to consult before jumping in.

Disabled people of color often face a very different dynamic. Black and Brown disabled bodies are often perceived as dangerous—as out of bounds and out of line in ways that make them targets for surveillance, scrutiny, and discipline. Black disability activist Leroy Moore has spent years documenting and organizing against police violence targeting disabled people of color.[16] The epidemic isn't limited to the streets. In schools, disabled students of color are increasingly subject to harsh disciplinary procedures. Black and Brown students with disabilities are disproportionately suspended and arrested, often for minor infractions.[17]

Let's take another one of Lewis's categories: intelligence. Ableist logics presume that intelligence manifests in one particular way. If you can't show it on a test or deliver it on a deadline, then you don't have smarts worthy of the name. Excellence is similar. Not only do we measure it too narrowly; we use it as a judgment of who is and is not worthy. In an ableist world, excellence is a zero-sum game. Only those who prove their merit deserve respect, dignity, protection, love, or care. Everyone else gets left out or left behind. The flip side of excellence is a whole lot of people treated as refuse, as discards, as disposable.

The rhetoric of disability has long been used to justify inequality in American and European history. Consider the long history of eugenics, rooted as it is in the notion that some people are of "inferior" stock. Or the way that scientific racism deployed false arguments about the supposed physical and mental deficiencies of Africans, Asians, Indigenous peoples, and Jews to support enslavement, repressive immigration laws, and discriminatory policies. Opponents of women's equality likewise leveraged the notion of disability to argue against women's suffrage—citing hysteria, irrationality, and physical weakness as biophysical proof of women's inferiority.[18] And disabled people ourselves? Our inferiority is often figured as something so obvious that it requires no explanation.

The ableist logics of intelligence and excellence often get deployed within disability communities in ways that end up fracturing alliances, turning disabled people against each other in an attempt to capture a few leftover crumbs from the crust of an ableist pie. Many physically disabled people attempt to defend our status as "deserving" human beings by arguing that we're *not* mentally disabled, that our intelligence is not impaired. It's a ubiquitous move, one I learned almost instinctively as a child. *I might not walk right, but there's nothing wrong with my mind.* I flinch now, when I encounter those words. They position cognitive disability and mental difference as the *real* disability, the true marker of inferiority. They claim physical disability as a matter of skin and surface, ultimately insubstantial. But mental disability? That's the real deal, deserving of the full brunt of ableist harm.

I reject that claim on several counts.[19] First, I reject the idea that people with cognitive disabilities are less worthy. I reject the assumption that they are less deserving of access and agency within their own lives. We have often held very narrow definitions of what "intelligence" can be, and then used those notions as a threshold test for human rights or dignity. I believe that move is misguided at the root. Intelligence is no marker of moral standing. Ableism isn't justified when it's deployed against folks whose minds work differently than mine.

Second, I reject the assumption that body and mind can be so neatly kept distinct. Physical disability has, in fact, deeply shaped my mind. It's shifted the ways I see and the ways I think, the ways I understand and process. Some of those cognitive effects are rooted in neurology. Some are a consequence of decades spent wheeling through the world, judging place and mapping terrain with a wheeler's eyes. While I don't want to collapse the experiences of physical and mental disability into one single category, I think it's crucial to recognize the interrelationship between them. Body and mind are virtually impossible to separate. Pain affects cognition, and so do experiences of inequality and oppression. Disability studies scholar Margaret Price urges us to mark this kinship by using the term "body-mind," which marks the interconnected terrain between our physical and cognitive experiences.[20]

Finally, I reject the strategy. When physically disabled people assert that our intelligence is undiminished by our disabilities, when we use that argument to advocate for our fundamental humanity, we leave the basic architecture of ableism intact. That claim doesn't dismantle ableism; it just deflects its force.

Ableist logics persist in part by convincing disabled folks to imagine ourselves as exceptions to the rule, to prove our individual excellence. Arguments for excellence are a crucial part of the ableist landscape, though they often masquerade as good news for disabled folks. Consider the way that popular culture has begun to recognize and celebrate some forms of Autistic genius, or those ubiquitous disability stories where dogged determination and sheer force of will lets us accomplish some spectacular feat. Disabled people get praised when we "overcome" our disabilities, when we show the world how disability has not limited us, how disability has not held us back.

But overcoming is a trap. Overcoming keeps ableist principles firmly in place. It holds out the promise that one or two of us might crawl our way out of the sinkhole of disability, if only we work hard enough. But to do so, we've got to leave disability behind. The whole enterprise rests on the assumption that disability is a negative state and that all those other disabled folks are *deserving* of our fate. Ableism is *right* to target us. Only the few fight their way free.

It's not that I don't celebrate the actual accomplishments of disabled folks, both the spectacular and the small. It's that I'm thinking about the cultural consequences of these accounts, the way they get weaponized against other bodies and minds. All those stories about disabled folks who've done something brilliant and extraordinary? They're like ableist hate mail, letting me know all the ways I fail to measure up.

I've watched my own life get used this way, as a kind of dangling promise of the possible. To have examples of disabled people's accomplishment can be a powerful thing. They can be an invitation to courage, the best kind of dare: *Look, child! Look what you can do.* But turn that story just a fraction, and it cuts against heart, against bone. *She could make it, so why can't you?*

So far, I've focused on the way that ableism targets disabled people, about the way it denies us power, resources, access, and agency—and justifies those denials by setting up a cultural system in which disabled bodies and minds seem to be obviously and inevitably inferior. It's crucial that we recognize ableism as a system that empowers nondisabled people to pass judgment over disabled folks: to grant or withhold accommodations, to commit us to institutions, to assess our lives as not worth living. Disabled people can also become ableist enforcers, especially those of us who can successfully leverage the hierarchy of disability against those judged less worthy than we are. The basic principle holds, regardless. Ableism turns its most brutal effects on those it determines to be least able: the ones whose bodies and minds it marks as failing to live up to society's idea of "normalcy, intelligence, excellence and productivity."[21]

But let's turn now to the last line of TL Lewis's definition, which makes a powerful and important claim: "You do not have to be disabled to experience ableism."

Most of us are used to thinking about oppression as a system that targets a certain social group and gives advantages to another. That's a key part of how ableist logics work. People marked as disabled face the brunt of ableist violence, especially if their bodies and minds are also targeted by other forms of social violence, if they face the brunt

of racism, misogyny, fat hatred, queer and trans hatred, poverty, xenophobia, or other forms of structural harm. When we talk about
ableism, we must center the realities of those most affected. But I've
also come to believe, with Lewis, that ableism can turn on *any* of us.
Ableism isn't good for *any* body, *any* mind.

Consider the final quality that Lewis names: productivity. What defines the good body, the proper mind? Its capacity to produce. Ableism
operates, in part, by turning our ability to work into an assessment of
our worth. It sets up accomplishment as a litmus test for human value.

This logic hits hardest against disabled folks who cannot press their
body-minds into the narrow confines of the capitalist workday or hus-
tle their way through the gig economy. Let me be clear: Some of us
could work, if we could bust through ableist stigma and get a callback
or land an interview, or secure the right accommodations, or find an
employer who's willing to be flexible. But some of our bodies and minds
aren't built for work, aren't made to labor. Some of us need rest; some
of us contend with pain; some of us know that all the support in the
world isn't going to put a paycheck within reach. Ableist assumptions
turn those realities into a referendum on our worth. What's the first
thing most of us ask each other when we're first introduced? "What
do you do?" The script is a kind of default setting, one that's meant to
keep social interactions smooth. But for those who don't have a good
answer, one that lines up nicely with ableist values? It's a punch in the
gut, a wrench in the game.

Failure to *be productive* has visceral, material effects. It means many
people with disabilities rely on public benefits for our very survival,
a reality that is both stigmatized and subject to intense scrutiny. In a
world that fetishizes productivity, disabled people get scapegoated as
shirkers and scroungers, as lazy and worthless, as people who fail because we can't or won't work. But it isn't just disabled folks who face
judgment if we're *not working hard enough*. Ableism doesn't demand a
diagnosis or ask for a doctor's note. It's ready to sweep up *any* body
that seems to be faltering, *any* mind that might not measure up. Ableist
assumptions run through the very fabric of so many of our lives. I

think of all the folks I know who can't afford to call in sick, all the folks who drive themselves to work regardless of how they feel. Those realities are shaped in large part by social policy and public choices, by the fact that so many workers labor without guaranteed sick time or family leave. But I'm also thinking about the way these values get inside our skins, the way we internalize them, swallow them whole. So many of us have learned to use our work as a salve against the fear that we are not enough.

Dear reader, allow me to confess. After writing these paragraphs, I turned away from my computer screen and spent an hour sitting on my balcony, watching the sun slant against the luminous magenta petals of the cosmos I had planted some months before. I read a few pages in a book about delight, a book I'm reading just for the joy of it, not for work and not as part of some enrichment or improvement scheme, but because I savor the particular quality of the author's voice as he works his way with words. This is one of the pleasures that ableism would deny me. It judges that hour on my balcony as nothing more than *slacking off*; it turns our daydreams and delights into *a waste of time*. Slow bodies, soft bodies must always be bettering themselves. Meandering minds must learn to think straight, to press themselves into the solid track of "serious" thinking. A morning spent in bed becomes an unimaginable luxury or else a sign of weakness; either way, it's a moral failure.

Ableism is a lie, my friends. It hits hardest and with greatest cost against those of us whose body-minds fall furthest from its portrait galleries of ideal types, but it is coming for us all. All of us have bodies that creak and crumble. All of us have minds that will not always skip through calculations like nimble little dancers. All of us deserve a world that welcomes us. A world that wants the very quirkiness that ableism would outlaw. A world that savors neurodiversity, that sees our strangeness and our singularity as a witness to infinity. A world that prizes us, that praises our particularity. A world that can embrace our frailties and foibles. A world that celebrates and cradles us. A world that desires us.

CHAPTER FIVE

Priestly Blemishes

Talking Back to the Bible's Ideal Bodies

Years ago, when I was giving a talk to a group of university students, a young woman asked about a biblical passage that troubled her, a passage from the book of Leviticus. Leviticus is devoted to the laws of the priesthood, and it lays out a whole host of instructions that govern how priests perform their sacred duties. In Leviticus 21, God tells Moses that any priest whose body has a "defect" shall not be allowed to come before the altar to offer sacrifice. The student laid out a concise analysis of the ethical problems of the text: the way it portrays God as preferring a certain kind of normative body, the way it seems to sanction discrimination against disabled priests, to bar them from the most sacred duties of their position. "How do you reconcile that?" she wanted to know.

My answer was blunt. "I don't."

Over the years, I've heard many religious leaders grapple with this text. Every now and again, I'll come across someone who uses this text to argue against disability inclusion. But almost always, I hear folks struggle with this passage because it runs counter to their own ethical sense: that disabled people *belong* in religious communities, that we are worthy of love and welcome. I hear pastors and rabbis doing their utmost to read this text against the grain, to wring from these words a more generous message. I hear them searching for a way to avoid the implication that disability makes a person less desirable in God's eyes.

Let me confess: My strategy is different. My goal isn't to gentle these ancient words or to soften their sting. I'm not interested in apologizing for this text or reconciling it with my values. Instead, I prefer to face Leviticus 21 as a powerful and disturbing text: one that makes visible the dynamics by which certain bodies are marked as inferior. I take these biblical words as a visceral reminder of the brutal power of ableism. I hold them as a witness to the deep disdain for disabled people that runs through so much of our histories, our cultures, our sacred narratives.

I flat out don't believe these verses tell the truth of God's desire. But I do believe this passage is a powerful testament to the way that humans have imagined God in our own image, the way we have endowed God with our own prejudices. For me, these words are a cautionary tale, a warning about how easy it is for humans to press our assumptions on the divine. Every time I encounter this text, I hear it as a sacred call: to reconsider the kinds of judgments we make about bodies, to probe why those we judge imperfect are also judged unworthy. This is Torah that calls us to ask ourselves hard questions, questions that are crucial for the long and difficult work of confronting and dismantling ableism. What are the cultural rules that *we* use to disqualify certain bodies? Why do we so often prize "normalcy" above all else? And who pays the cost when we project those judgments onto God?[1]

In the world of the Bible, sacrifice is one of the most important ways that the ancients draw near to their God. The book of Leviticus describes sacrifices of gratitude, as well as sacrifices of atonement and apology. During holidays and festivals, communities come together to offer sacrifice as celebration. Now, the rituals laid out in Leviticus haven't been practiced in Jewish communities since the Roman Empire destroyed the Jerusalem Temple, nearly two thousand years ago. Jewish communities no longer invest priestly bodies with the sacred task of coming before an altar to offer an animal as sacrifice. But it's a mistake to think these laws have somehow been leached of their force.

Leviticus 21 still hits hard against disabled people, a visceral reminder that our bodies are often judged as undesirable.

Let's look more closely at this passage. To sacrifice according to Leviticus's law, you need a priest. But not any priest will do. Leviticus 21:16–23 lays out the biblical criteria for determining those priests who are forbidden to come before the altar:

> The Lord spoke further to Moses:
> Speak to Aaron and say,
> "No man of your offspring throughout the ages
> who has a *mum* [a "defect" or "blemish"]
> shall be qualified to offer the food of his God.
> No one at all who has a *mum* shall be qualified:
> no man who is blind, or lame, or has a limb too short or too long;
> no man who has a broken leg or a broken arm;
> or who is a hunchback, or a dwarf,
> or who has a growth in his eye,
> or who has a boil-scar, or scurvy, or crushed testes.
> No man among the offspring of Aaron the priest who has a *mum*
> shall be qualified to offer the Lord's gift;
> having a *mum*, he shall not be qualified to offer the food of his God.
> He may eat of the food of his God,
> of the most holy as well as of the holy;
> but he shall not enter behind the curtain or come near the altar,
> for he has a *mum*.
> He shall not profane these places sacred to Me,
> for I the Lord have sanctified them.

The biblical priesthood is a hereditary privilege, a responsibility passed down through the lineage of Aaron, from father to son. No one decides to join the priesthood, and no one born to this lineage is free to desist from it. While biblical priests had many responsibilities, the most important of their tasks was the service at the altar, the act of offering sacrifice.

Priests who are blind or lame, priests who have a limb that is too short or too long, priests with a broken limb, priests who have a hunchback, priests of short stature, priests with a growth in their eye, priests with a distinctive scar, priests with scurvy, and priests with a crushed testicle—all of these priests cannot come before the altar. Just a few verses later, in Leviticus 22, the Bible asserts that any animal that is sacrificed must also be "without blemish."[2] Priestly ritual brings together perfect human and animal bodies, who either offer divine service or are offered up for divine consumption.

Let's consider how Leviticus 21 fashions the borders of the acceptable priestly body. The crucial word that drives the logic of this text is *mum*, a Hebrew word that refers to a spot or mark or flaw. The Jewish Publication Society translates it as "defect," a term that captures well the stigma that these physical differences often carry. When I translate for my own purposes, I'm more likely to render *mum* as "blemish," a term that strikes a bit less hard against my heart. But I want to linger for a moment with the word "defect." I want to acknowledge the force of this language, to recognize the kinship between these biblical verses and the invective hurled at certain bodies like stones.

Disability activist Eli Clare writes about the powerful hold *defectiveness* has in our cultural consciousness, the way the language of *defect* has been used to disenfranchise a wide range of marginalized communities. He writes, "Think of the things called defective—the MP3 player that won't turn on, the car that never ran reliably. They end up in the bottom drawer, dumpster, scrapyard. Defects are disposable and abnormal, body-minds or objects to eradicate."[3] I cannot read Leviticus 21 without recalling the history that Clare names: the way the rhetoric of defectiveness has been used time and again as part of the architecture of disenfranchisement to justify slavery and racism, to deny entry to immigrants at Ellis Island, to buttress violence against gay and trans people, to rail against disabled people. The term "defect" has followed me for much of my life: in the medical designation used

LOVING OUR OWN BONES

to describe my birth, in the playground taunts of children at recess. I've felt the force of that word against my own skin.

One thing I never do? I never translate *mum* as disabled. There is no single term in the Hebrew Bible that covers quite the same terrain as our modern category of disability. Rather than collapsing this ancient category into the contemporary one, rather than eliding their differences and smoothing out the disconnects, I want to look more closely at how both the ancient and the modern notions get made. We make a mistake when we think of disability as a fixed, essential category with distinct and certain boundaries. The question of which bodies and minds get marked as disabled is always up for debate, and it has shifted substantially over the course of human history. While the designation of disability is usually rooted in the recognition of some physical or mental difference, the category is produced as much by culture as biology. Certain traits and characteristics, along with certain ways of being in the world, become associated with stigma. They're marked not simply as unusual but as inferior.

Culture doesn't just play a role in determining who is included in the category of disability; it also gives the category its force. What does it mean to be marked as disabled? The answer depends on the specifics of time and place. To understand the implications of Leviticus 21, we have to consider more deeply the way the ancient priesthood operated. The priesthood is not a realm of equal access. Jewish tradition places strict limits on the way that humans interact with the sacred. Only the *kohanim* (priests of an elite lineage) have access to the holiest spaces within the sanctuary; the levites (assisting priests) must stay at a certain distance, while ordinary Israelites are even farther removed. Within this highly structured system, even "blemished" *kohanim* have more access to the sacred than ordinary Israelites.[4] They keep their priestly portion and they are still regarded as holy, a designation confirmed by the fact that they are allowed to eat the holy portions of the sacrifices that are set aside for the priests.

Sometimes I hear contemporary readers of Leviticus 21 lift up the ongoing presence of disabled priests *as priests*, using it as a reminder of the importance of inclusion. In some respects, this is true. Priests with a blemish are not disbarred from the priesthood, and they retain many of the privileges of the priesthood. But it's worth noting how meager this "inclusion" is. Blemished priests are disqualified from the most central priestly duties, the defining ritual practices associated with their position. Rather than serving at the altar within the most sanctified spaces of tabernacle or the temple, they are, in Rabbi Elliot Dorff's words, "put to menial work such as cleaning the kindling wood from worms."[5] Tamara Green, one of the founding members of the Jewish Healing Center, draws on her own lived experience with chronic illness to critique the limits of this model. Green argues that "it is not enough to say that these less than physically perfect *kohanim* were allowed their portion of the offerings, since they were barred from making them on behalf of the people."[6] For Green, the fact that blemished priests still receive a priestly portion doesn't address the problem. It feels like charity, rather than a recognition of their priestly due.

What makes a priest unfit to serve? The priestly blemishes make for a curious list, and scholars struggle to articulate the cohesive organizing principle that drives the specifics of exclusion. Leviticus 21 includes congenital differences alongside characteristics acquired through illness, accident, and the ordinary course of life. The physical changes wrought by scurvy or the injury of a crushed testicle are listed alongside congenital conditions of short stature or a differently formed limb. Some absences are striking. Leviticus 21 does not include certain conditions that ancient writers clearly considered disabling. While deafness was clearly stigmatized in the biblical imagination, it doesn't show up on this list. A Deaf priest would have been allowed to offer sacrifice, as would a priest with an intellectual disability. By contrast, Leviticus 21 singles out a broken arm as a permanent source of disqualification—a fact that often startles modern readers. In a world with good access to medical care, a broken limb is often nothing more than a temporary inconvenience. But the biblical writer assumes that injury leaves a lasting mark, regardless of how well it heals.

Scholars have largely concluded that appearance is a significant factor in driving the priestly logics of exclusion.[7] Priests are held to a stringent standard of physical appearance. Perhaps that shouldn't be surprising, given the biblical writer's investment in forging the priests as a class apart. Biblical priests are drawn from a special lineage and are subject to intense ritual requirements and limits on their behavior. Through the institution of the priesthood, the Hebrew Bible designates a few ideal servants to mediate between God and the rest of the Israelites. The priests act as physical exemplars of holiness within the context of divine service. Any detraction from the priests' physical form represents a danger for both priest and community.[8] When the priest performs the divine service, he takes up a priestly responsibility to represent, in some fashion, the divine presence and to "stand in" for the unseen, perfect body of God. Because Israelite religious practice forbade any visual representations of God, Rebecca Raphael suggests that the priestly body might itself have served as a "visual signifier to mark the unseen body of God."[9] The contours of the acceptable priest's body mirror not only the qualities the community idealizes among humans but also those it projects upon God: a body characterized by symmetry and order, without rupture, distinguished by clear, unbroken boundaries.

This concern for aesthetics might help explain why our biblical writer focuses exclusively on physical impairments. Leviticus 21 is entirely unconcerned by speech disabilities, and intellectual disabilities are also no cause for disqualification. Most of the conditions mentioned are, in Saul Olyan's words, "visible to the eye, long lasting or permanent in nature . . . and more than a few share asymmetry as a quality."[10] While this investment in the visual seems to offer the most compelling explanation, it is not entirely straightforward. Visual concerns do not account for the exclusion of a blind priest, since blindness need not be accompanied by a demonstrable sign or marker. And when it comes to the priest with a crushed testicle? Since priests were required to perform the divine service in vestments and forbidden from exposing themselves when approaching the altar, genital damage would hardly be visible to the humans gathered in the sanctuary. If there is visual offense generated by this body, the only one who might be offended is God.

That's precisely the conclusion that Jeremy Schipper and Jeffrey Stackert reach in a recent article that argues that Leviticus 21 understands Israel's God to have the same visual preferences as a human sovereign—perhaps on the model of King Nebuchadnezzar of Babylon, who, according to Daniel 1:4, instructs his chief officer to bring Israelites who could be trained for royal service: "Youths without blemish, handsome, proficient in all wisdom, knowledgeable and intelligent, and capable of serving in the royal palace." Schipper and Stackert argue that blemished priests—like blemished animals, which were also unacceptable as sacrifices—are disqualified because they fail to satisfy the sovereign's aesthetic preferences. These blemished bodies are "deviations from the design that pleases the priestly god."[11] The God of Leviticus 21 is intensely engaged by the visual. While most priestly bodies are protected by their priestly vestments from God's exacting eye, Leviticus 21 imagines the defects as physical differences that cannot be covered over, that will not allow the priest to pass as a neutral body. Schipper and Stackert perceive the blemishes as "divine irritants," aesthetic characteristics that cause God to feel dissatisfaction. Unlike the inconspicuous bodies of the unblemished priests, each of them garbed in their identical vestments, the defective body disrupts. It snags the divine eye, draws the divine gaze.

Jewish biblical commentary has made much of this notion that God is dissatisfied by blemished bodies. While Leviticus 21:16–23 disbars blemished priests from performing service at the altar, Leviticus 22:17–25 uses almost identical language to forbid the sacrifice of defective animals. Consider Rashi, the medieval commentator whose influence upon Jewish traditions of biblical interpretation can hardly be overstated. Rashi explains the prohibition on blemished priests by way of a verse from Malachi in which the prophet castigates the people for scorning the table of the Lord. "A son should honor his father," the prophet proclaims, "and a slave his master."[12] God is both father and master, Malachi contends, but receives no honor from the people. Exhibit A for the people's failure? They bring a blind, a lame, or a sick animal as a sacrifice and say it does not matter. Likening God to a mortal governor, Malachi asks: Would you offer such to a human official? Would not he consider such "gifts" an insult?

Malachi's questions, taken up by Rashi and echoed by a number of other traditional commentators, assume that God acts according to the principles of honor and dignity that drive humans. It is "not fitting," Rashi asserts, that a blemished priest approach the altar. It is an insult, a slight to the divine honor. The logic assumes that humans should treat God as a magnified reflection of human elites, that you satisfy God in the same way you please a status-seeking governor. The heavens become a mirror image of earth. Divine honor is subject to the same drive for dominance, the same obsessions of honor. Malachi's God demands the same deference, receives the same due. A son must honor his father, a slave his master—and father and master alike must be offered only the best.

I cannot read the prophet's words without flinching. The theological claim that God is father and master has long been used to sanction social inequality: to prop up patriarchy, to undergird centuries of slaveholding. There is violence here, violence that must not pass unspoken. As a scholar, I recognize an ethical imperative to uncover these connections, to invite our critical reflection on the way religious texts have structured our human practices of power. Note how the hierarchies of the present are projected onto the heavens. Observe how neatly the biblical obsession with perfect bodies reinforces the notion of perfect service, how honor demands deference and obedience to authority.

W hat shall we make of this portrait of God? When I read this text as a scholar, I read it with a commitment to understanding Leviticus 21 in its own historical moment, to parsing and illuminating the distinctive cultural and ideological commitments of its author. As a historian of ancient religion and culture, I work to better understand how early Jewish readers imagined the interplay between God and the body. Such questions shed light on the way they conceptualized beauty and difference, how they grappled with disability and its significance within sacred space. When I wear my historian's hat, I try to uncover these critical histories of interpretation, to illuminate the way religious ideas shape and reflect cultural norms, the way religion gets intertwined with the practice of power.

But when I approach Leviticus 21 as a religious reader? I am always winnowing, winnowing and gleaning. What is here for me? What illuminates the presence of the God I know, the God I love, the God whose signature is written into my bones?

Take Schipper and Stackert's recognition that bodies that stand out as different displease the divine eye, or Olyan's insight that the Hebrew Bible often judges beauty on the basis of symmetry and wholeness. These are smart historical insights, and I believe they name well the ancient cultural concerns that shape these texts. But when I engage Leviticus religiously, I find myself deeply skeptical: Is symmetry really something that God likes above all else? Is the priestly blemish really repugnant to God, an irritant that gets under God's proverbial skin? Or are these judgments that certain humans have made, at a particular time and place, and then projected onto God?

Now, I have no way to know what God likes or whether (and how) God sees beauty. I'm suspicious of anyone who considers this is an answerable question, who claims to have this dilemma neatly solved and tied up with a bow. But as I consider the options for approaching the question of what God finds beautiful, here is one thing I know: One interpretive choice imagines the divine as a brilliant artist and capacious creator, in love with the generative possibilities of difference. The other envisions God as the status-obsessed editor of a not especially inspired fashion magazine. Given a choice, I prefer a God who regards with pleasure and satisfaction the vast, riotous diversity of human- and creature-kind. Such a portrait seems much more in keeping with the God who created starfish and katydids, hedgehogs and humans of all different sorts, who seems to manifestly reject the idea of producing one single type and repeating it unchangingly, locking the species in to some static ideal of perfection. Given what I know of the world, I can't really figure God as a paragon of aesthetic rigidity, as founder-in-chief of the fashion police.

So what do I make of these words, this imperative that takes the force of divine fiat? I approach the Bible as a complex record of a human community's striving after God, a text that offers glimpses of revelation, wrapped in human language and filtered through human perceptions. For me, the Bible is a text that offers windows onto the sacred, that reveals the imprint and echo of divine presence. But it is never a straightforward communication, an unmediated chronicle of encounter between the human and the holy.

When I read Leviticus 21, I read a text that has been shaped by human prejudice, a text marked by human assumptions about the beautiful and the good. Consider the words of the twelfth-century Jewish philosopher Moses Maimonides, who explained the prohibition on priests with a blemish as a deference to human limitations. "The multitude does not assess a person on the basis of his true form," Maimonides observes, "but on the wholeness of his limbs and the beauty of his garments." The command for priestly perfection came about, Maimonides contends, not because of God's own aesthetic desires but "because the Temple was to be held in great esteem and reverence by all."[13]

The God I know does not require the semblance of symmetry. The God I know does not share this human fascination with standard-sized bodies, all lined up in tidy little rows. The God I know has made a world brimming over with difference, has fashioned minds and limbs that unfold in their own particular ways. The God I know has chosen variation: sometimes minute and almost imperceptible, sometimes bold and brash and beautiful in its rarity and uniqueness. But the world in which I live has almost always judged with a less discerning eye. When I read Leviticus 21, I take it as a reminder of those false judgments, the way they have been scripted even onto God. I hear this Torah as a different sort of call: a call to witness the long shadow of stigma and exclusion that has shaped the lives of so many disabled people, a call to confront and to challenge entrenched patterns of social and religious violence that have contoured our lives.

Jewish traditions of reading Leviticus 21 offer some models for grappling with this call. As a Jewish reader steeped in the principles of rabbinic culture, I approach the Bible through a tradition that values interpretation, that claims active engagement with texts as a central religious obligation. A famous early rabbinic parable imagines God as a king who gives each of his two servants a gift of flax and wheat. When the king returns after a journey and asks about the gifts, one servant presents the flax and wheat, untouched and pristine. The other servant presents the king with a set table that includes a cloth woven from the flax and bread made from the wheat. The rabbis' telling imagines a God who champions the servant who fashioned something new from the king's gift, a God who delights in the way humans transform God's material and create something innovative and new. The parable is a bold claim to spiritual authority. The rabbis grant their own teachings the status of Torah. They imagine the teachings of the sages and their students to be part of the oral Torah that was given at Sinai, an expression of divine revelation that has been unfolding ever since. For the rabbis, this oral Torah is the interpretive key that gives meaning to the written Torah, the tradition that unlocks the meaning printed on the page.

One of the chief aims of the rabbis was to articulate a system of religious practice that would govern all aspects of Jewish life, a way of living out the commandments and principles expressed in the Hebrew Bible. The Mishnah, a foundational rabbinic text that was canonized circa 200 CE, laid out a vast, interconnected set of obligations that its rabbinic authors regarded as incumbent upon all (male) Jews, a set of practices that would remain formative (if not uncontested) for the practice of Judaism as we know it today. The Mishnah takes up the subject of Leviticus 21, when it discusses which priests are allowed to perform the priestly blessing in the synagogue. This text gives a strikingly different take on the subject of priestly imperfections, an interpretation that will influence virtually all later Jewish discussion of the subject.

But before we consider the Mishnah's treatment of the priests themselves, let's consider how the text is part and parcel of sweeping changes in Jewish culture and practice. In its original biblical context, Leviticus 21 was a passage written to describe proper ritual conduct within the tabernacle, the portable sanctuary that the Israelites used to approach God during their forty years of wandering in the wilderness. Once the Jerusalem Temple became the primary site for ritual practice, the earlier biblical traditions were understood to apply there. But the Temple in Jerusalem was destroyed, and Jewish sovereignty was swallowed up by the imperial ambitions of the great powers of the ancient world, first by Babylon and later by Rome. With the Temple in ruins, there was no site available for the performance of sacrifice. Jewish religiosity underwent a tremendous change.

In the wake of catastrophic political and spiritual loss, the rabbis fashioned themselves as the architects of a new Jewish tradition. They faced a substantial interpretive challenge. How to rethink all the Temple rituals that once anchored Jewish practice? How to preserve both a sense of continuity and connection to the sacred past and yet also adapt Jewish life to radically different circumstances? The rabbis eventually claimed the synagogue as a key site for honoring the obligations that had once been fulfilled through Temple ritual, establishing communal prayer services as a substitution for the sacrifices. Before the destruction, the priests had officiated at the altar, performing sacrifice as a ritual offering to God. After the destruction, this practice became impossible. So the rabbis reconfigured the priestly role, investing the priests with the power of benediction. When Jewish congregations gather to pray in synagogues, the priests take up a new ritual responsibility. They recite ancient biblical words of blessing, while lifting up their hands to bless the congregation.[14]

The Mishnah applies Leviticus 21 to this practice of communal blessing. Rather than decree the biblical discussion of blemished priests irrelevant now that sacrifice is no more, the rabbis assert that the biblical protocol about acceptable priestly bodies should now guide the priests' recitation of the priestly blessing. Let's look more closely at the relevant text. Mishnah Megillah 4:7 reads:

A priest whose hands are blemished may not lift up his hands.
Rabbi Yehudah says:
Also one whose hands are stained by woad dye or madder dye
may not lift up his hands
because the people might gaze at him.

Unlike the lengthy list of blemishes that appear in the Bible, the Mishnah claims that the only significant disqualification for a priest is a blemish on the hands. Why focus on the hands? It's probably because the rabbis regarded the hands as the physical conduit for blessing. In one rabbinic midrash, God sends blessing through the openings formed by the priests' fingers.[15] Ancient sources also caution the congregation not to look closely at the priests' hands. According to traditional custom, the priests draw their prayer shawls over their heads and hands while blessing in order to turn away the congregation's gaze. The Talmud states that gazing at the hands of the priest will cause a person's eyes to dim, and Rashi's influential commentary asserts that this is because the divine presence itself rests upon the priests' hands.[16] The Tosafot, a later group of medieval commentators, offer a different reason for the prohibition. Why is it forbidden to look at the priests? Because it risks distracting a person's attention from the blessing itself.[17]

As we've seen, the Mishnah significantly limits the physical qualities that disqualify a priest from blessing the congregation. But let's consider two other elements of the Mishnah that I consider even more important. First, the Mishnah recognizes that "blemishes" aren't necessarily a medical matter. This becomes most apparent in the statement attributed to Rabbi Yehudah, who argues that the Mishnah's prohibition includes priests whose hands are stained with blue or red dye, presumably because of their work. With this clause, the Mishnah drives a wedge in the conventional ableist assumption that the "problem" of disability is the obvious undesirability of a misshapen or malformed body. In the case of the priest with stained hands, there is no disability—at least not in the way we usually think of it. The priest is forbidden to bless not because of an injury or a congenital difference but because his hands have an unusual appearance. The dye hasn't changed his physical ability. His hands are working hands, gainfully employed and fully able. Yet they still exclude him from offering the blessing.

Why? The Mishnah makes Rabbi Yehudah's reasoning explicit. Priests with discolored hands are prohibited from blessing—because the people will stare at them. With this explanation, the Mishnah introduces a second important innovation. It draws our attention to what disability studies scholar Rosemarie Garland-Thomson calls "the politics of staring," the way in which the act of staring creates disability as a distinct social identity and produces disability stigma.[18] Staring is part of the architecture of social exclusion and marginality. The stare is a crucial part of what makes disability a meaningful social category. It's the stare that turns disability difference into deviance.

Now, let us be clear. This isn't precisely the Mishnah's primary concern. The Mishnah is troubled by the congregation's stares not because of their potential effect on the disabled priest, but because the stare is suggestive of distraction. The ideal priestly body is a kind of negative space, one that avoids engaging the viewer. Priestly hands that snag the viewer's gaze threaten to draw attention away from the unseen God, to disrupt the intangible transmission of blessing.

Years ago, when I first wrote about these passages, I argued that the Mishnah makes a crucial shift in the way it approaches the blemished priest. "By explicitly stating the prohibition in terms of the gaze that unusual hands might provoke," I wrote, "the Mishnah implies that the 'problem' has shifted from the priests' hands to the lingering eye of the congregation."[19] Now I still maintain that the Mishnah has made an important change in the way it conceptualizes the blemished priestly body. I believe it matters profoundly that the Mishnah names the problem of the stare. But I'm no longer convinced that *the Mishnah itself* makes the transformation I desire.

Let me explain what I mean. Faced with the fear that the congregation might gaze at a priest's distinctive hands, the Mishnah forbids that priest from performing the blessing. It solves the problem of the stare by disbarring the person who provokes the stare. It's a common cultural move. Consider, for example, how rabbinic culture often responds to the "disruption" posed by women. Like many other ancient and modern writers, the rabbis were concerned about the way that sexual desire could be a disruptive force, particularly when it comes to male self-control. In order to address the social disruption that sexual attraction might cause, rabbinic culture imposes limits on women's presence—constraining women's movement, women's ritual participation, even women's voice. Rather than expecting men to manage their desires, the rabbis often chose to neutralize the threat by removing women from the scene. So too with disability. While the Mishnah lays the groundwork for a different approach to the priestly body, it doesn't make the shift I long for. The Mishnah reinscribes normativity, preserving the power dynamics that position the disabled body as a disruptive risk, as a sight that disturbs the nondisabled gaze.

A few centuries later, the Babylonian Talmud introduces a key point that reorients Jewish legal thinking about priestly blessing. A seventh-century commentary on the Mishnah, known colloquially as the Bavli, the Babylonian Talmud has had a towering influence on later Jewish thought and practice. On the topic of priestly prohibitions, the Bavli offers a set of three statements by rabbis who prohibited a priest with a blemish from reciting the blessing, and then counters with

an anonymous report that the blemished man did indeed recite the
blessing. Bavli Megillah 24b reads:

> Rav Ḥuna said:
> A man with bleary eyes shall not lift up his hands.
> But there was a man like this in Rav Ḥuna's neighborhood—
> and he spread his hands!
> He was familiar in his town.
> Likewise it was taught:
> A man with bleary eyes shall not lift up his hands,
> but if he is familiar in his town
> it is permitted.
>
> Rabbi Yoḥanan said:
> A man who is blind in one eye may not lift up his hands.
> But there was a man like this in Rabbi Yoḥanan's neighborhood—
> and he spread his hands!
> He was familiar in his town.
>
> Likewise it was taught:
> A man who is blind in one eye may not lift up his hands,
> but if he is familiar in his town it is permitted.
> Rabbi Yehudah said:
> He whose hands have stains shall not lift up his hands.
> It was taught:
> If most of the people of the town work in that way,
> it is permitted.

In these examples, the Bavli maintains that certain social factors
might allow a specific priest to recite the blessing, even though his blemish would otherwise render him ineligible. In each case, the anonymous
voice of the Talmud resolves the contradiction by affirming the general
principle but allowing for an exception if the priest was well known in
a particular town or if the condition of his hands was commonplace.

In this passage, the Talmud rules on the basis of the Mishnah's insight that the true problem is not the disabled body but the community's own gaze. But where the Mishnah used that insight to justify exclusion, the Bavli offers a more inclusive gesture: Familiarity defuses the stare. The people will not look at one they already know. A disabled priest who is known to the congregation need not be excluded from the ritual of blessing because the community's gaze will not stumble over his familiar form.

This talmudic principle becomes codified in the Shulḥan Arukh, an influential sixteenth-century legal text that remains one of the primary sources for contemporary Jewish practice.[20] The legal concept of "familiarity" remains influential in most observant communities today, leeching the priestly prohibitions of much of their practical force. What is the threshold for familiarity? According to the Shulḥan Arukh, thirty days in a place, with the intent to stay a while, is enough to make a person familiar. When a person is familiar? Even the Mishnah's modified prohibitions no longer apply.

Familiarity is a powerful principle, one whose practice largely overturns the priestly prohibitions laid out in Leviticus 21. But I am still uneasy about the expectations it encodes. Consider this: When we follow the principle of familiarity, we decide that an unconventional body becomes acceptable when it no longer startles us. The community accepts a disabled body only on the condition that it no longer stands out as extraordinary.

Once again, the sources fail to clarify which body bears the burden of accommodation. In the process of making the strange familiar, who changes? All too often, it's the disabled body that shoulders the obligation. There are a thousand ways we try to make ourselves familiar, to make ourselves more palatable to the nondisabled gaze. We learn to pass, to press the realities of an unruly body or mind into the narrow strictures of "familiarity," to shear away distinctiveness, to disavow difference. In the folds of familiarity, I hear the stories of countless people who have learned to hide their limp, even though it costs them pain. I hear the choice to cover your Autistic sensibilities, to forgo the pleasure of a stim because nondisabled people treat it with disdain.[21] I hear the pressure to train your tongue away from a stutter, the expectation to veil the realities of your depression, your chronic pain, your illness without end. I hear the expectation that we disabled people tame our differences, that we present only the most palatable version of ourselves for public view.

It doesn't have to be like this.

We could, if we chose, read the ethical imperative of familiarity differently. We could insist that the onus to change lies upon the community, rather than the individual. What if religious communities took this principle as an obligation for themselves? What if we recognized a collective responsibility *to become familiar* with people whose differences strike us as strange, whose bodies and minds strike us as undesirable? That might begin to shift the burden back where it belongs.

But even here, we must be careful. It's not enough to "welcome" difference while expecting communal spaces to remain unchanged. Embracing this ethical call will require deep work within our communities. It will ask us to transform the narrow notions of propriety and decorum we impose upon our sacred spaces. It will require a shift in the way that our communities have long constituted power, a release of the presumption that those with conventional bodies and minds are most suited to serve—whether on the bimah or from the pulpit, at the altar or as the conduits of blessing. And for those of us who have lived long at the margins? It might invite us to ask ourselves whether the very qualities that we've learned to hide, that we've been taught to diminish or despise, might be a distinctive aspect of our spiritual service, a kind of offering that our being brings into this world.

CHAPTER SIX

Moses

Portrait of a Disabled Prophet

W hat might it mean to recognize disability as a distinctive aspect of our spiritual service, a kind of offering that our being brings into this world? To consider that question, to imagine the ways that disability might shape a call to spiritual life and leadership, let's turn to the story of Moses. Jewish tradition honors Moses as the preeminent prophet, the man who speaks to God face-to-face. Yet Moses describes himself as "not a man of words."[1] His own mouth is heavy, his tongue unskilled. The description is not simply a rhetorical flourish, a literary contrast between the mortal and the divine. While Moses' difficulty with speech has been understood in a variety of ways, many traditional sources describe Moses as having a stutter or similar speech difference. Moses carries a deep anxiety about his disability that runs through his own narrative of spiritual call, one that leads him to decline when God first summons him to service.[2]

The most explicit discussion of Moses's disability appears early in the book of Exodus, when Moses is in conversation with God. The Israelite people are enslaved in Egypt, oppressed by a cruel Pharaoh and suffering deeply. God has heard their cries and resolves to send Moses to Pharaoh in order to free the people from their bondage. But Moses has deep doubts about his capacity to carry out the mission. In Exodus 3:11, he asks, "Who am I that I should go to Pharaoh and free the Israelites from Egypt?" God tells Moses that God will be with him, but that promise does not assuage his concern. In Exodus 4:1, when he learns he must rally the Israelite people to the cause of freedom, Moses asks, "What if they do not believe me and do not listen to me?" In response, God gives him a visible set of signs so that he can convince the people that he speaks at God's command. But this promise also does not ease his doubts. In Exodus 4:10, he lays out the reason for his hesitation:

> But Moses said to the Lord,
> "Please, O Lord, I have never been a man of words,
> either in times past or now that You have spoken to Your servant;
> I am slow of speech and slow of tongue."

In this verse, Moses describes himself as "heavy of mouth and heavy of tongue", using a Hebrew phrase that conveys weightiness and effort. Moses has a clumsy tongue, a mouth that takes deliberation to use. He identifies himself as someone who has *never* been at ease with words, not in the past and also not now that he has become a man who speaks with God. When I read this verse, I hear a hint that Moses might have imagined a different possibility. Did he perhaps expect that his encounter with God would transform his speech?[3] Or does our text recognize that readers might make this assumption, that being in direct communication with God might eliminate his stutter? Our verse denies this sort of intervention. Moses's mouth remains unchanged.

In the next verse, God affirms that Moses's mouth is, in fact, part of the divine design. It is neither an accident nor an oversight. Exodus 4:11–12 reads:

> And the Lord said to him,
> "Who makes a man's mouth?
> Who makes him mute or deaf, sighted or blind?
> Is it not I, the Lord?

Now go,
and I will be with you as you speak
and will instruct you what to say."[4]

God's questions are meant to overrule Moses's objections, to claim his mouth and tongue as a matter of deliberate divine design. When the Jewish Publication Society translates the first portion of this verse, it renders the question more loosely, as "Who gives man speech?" But the Hebrew phrase *sam l'adam peh* evokes the "making" or "setting" of Moses's mouth. It is a verb used to describe a thousand ordinary actions, like putting a ring on a finger or bread on a table. But it can also be used to indicate something that has been set or fixed, appointed or fashioned. Our verse uses that very verb to underscore God's intention to endow each person with a particular set of sensory qualities: to make them speaking or silent, hearing or Deaf, sighted or blind. Rabbi Darby Leigh lifts up the importance of this verse in his earliest religious understandings, as one that affirmed his worth as a Deaf child. The verse, he explains, "allowed me to feel that I had been created Deaf, as opposed to my deafness being an error, defect, or aberration."[5]

By phrasing this claim as a rhetorical question, Exodus 4:11 calls Moses to affirm that God has fashioned his body and determined his sensory capacities—to affirm that God's hand lies in the making of every human mouth, even his own. In Exodus 4:12, God renews the command to our reluctant prophet, sending him forth with the promise that God will be with him, as presence and as a guide. The Hebrew once again is visceral and corporeal. God says to Moses, "I will be with your mouth." The next phrase might also be translated, "I will direct what you say." While we could imagine this direction as a kind of divine brace, an intervention God uses to smooth or shape Moses's speech, I prefer to read this verse differently. I hear it as a claim that God's presence is in the very particulars of Moses's mouth, in the twist of his tongue, in the physical realities of the body God has formed for him. God has not undone Moses's disability or erased it. God has promised presence, in and through the very tongue that Moses offers to the world.

Moses is manifestly unmoved. He does not want divine companionship during a difficult and urgent task; he wants someone else to go instead. In Exodus 4:13, Moses speaks again:

> But he said, "Please, O Lord, make someone else Your agent."

God has asked him to take up a task, to shoulder a spiritual responsibility. But Moses does not want the job. Because this is a story about Moses face-to-face with the Eternal, because this story looms so large in the mythic history of the Jewish people, it can be hard to recognize how this same scene recurs in our own lives. I think of friends and loved ones who have taken up a call to service, who have shaped their lives in ways that respond to a people's cry, to a human need. Left to my own devices, I tend to imagine this kind of leadership as a foregone conclusion. I admire their conviction; I celebrate their resolve. But these verses? These words draw me to the doubt. These words remind me of the desire to turn aside.

I know this moment, and maybe you do too. I know this moment of recognizing an important piece of work, a task to which I have been called. I know the flinch, the protest, the sense of deep inadequacy. I know the feeling that *someone else* should go, that *someone else* is more equipped to see it through.

And in response? God has a flash of anger, a burst of frustration. I'll come back to that in a moment, because I think that feeling hints at a dimension of this story that we often overlook—God's need for Moses, God's reliance on this very human man. But first, let's consider how the full scene unfolds, how God responds to Moses's request. Exodus 4:14–17 concludes:

> The Lord became angry with Moses, and He said,
> "There is your brother Aaron the Levite.
> He, I know, speaks readily.

Even now he is setting out to meet you,
and he will be happy to see you.

You shall speak to him and put the words in his mouth—
I will be with you and with him as you speak,
and tell both of you what to do—and he shall speak for you to the people.

Thus he shall serve as your spokesman,
with you playing the role of God to him . . .

For many years, God's anger in Exodus 4:14 made me deeply uncomfortable. I wanted God to empathize with Moses, to offer him compassion, and to soothe his disability fears. I wanted God to say, "I know the world is harsh. I know that some of the people will mock you and others will disdain you. I know that many of them will not heed your words. But I need you. I choose you. You're the one I'm going to send."

I still ache, some days, for the comfort of those words. But other days, I'm bolstered by the honesty of divine frustration, by the fact that Moses's disability isn't fashioned into an opt-out clause on spiritual responsibility.

When it comes to spiritual life? I don't want platitudes. I want equity and access. That's what the second half of Exodus 4:14 offers. God heeds Moses's concern and responds to a specific disability need. Moses lays plain his limitations, and God redesigns the plan to match. Aaron becomes a part of Moses's access team, an arrangement Bonnie Gracer describes as "the first reasonable accommodation in the Torah."[6] The biblical scene mirrors a practice adopted by many people with speech disabilities, who sometimes use a "revoicer" when addressing audiences who aren't familiar with their speech. The person speaks; the revoicer repeats. Aaron is likewise tasked with repeating Moses's words, making it easier for the public to understand what Moses said.

Notice, friends, how our verse affirms the relationship between them. When God first mentions Aaron, God lauds not only the excellence of his speech and the fact of his priestly vocation but the emotional connection that binds him to Moses. While the Jewish Publication Society's translation of Exodus 4:14 describes Aaron as "happy to see you," the Hebrew is even more resonant: "He will see you, and he will have joy in his heart." I'm struck by the way our verse lingers on the heart, the way it recognizes the bond between the brothers as a crucial part of the access Aaron offers Moses. To revoice another person's words requires deep familiarity with the patterns of their speech; it is a responsibility that rests on relationship. Aaron and Moses have that kind of intimacy, that kind of close connection. Aaron knows the tenor of his brother's tongue.

And Moses? Moses will put the words in Aaron's mouth. The Hebrew words echo the very phrase that the Torah uses to describe how God makes a human mouth, evoking a kinship that Exodus 4:16 makes explicit. If we were to translate this verse plainly, without appealing to idiom, we might end up with a translation like this: "He will speak to the people for you; and he will be your mouth, and you will be like God to him." If Aaron is Moses's mouth, if Aaron is Moses's voice before the people, then Moses is placed in the position of God: the one who directs the words, who orchestrates the message. The medieval Bible commentator Rashi blunts the force of this claim. The word for "God" here, he explains, means nothing more than "a superior."

But what happens if we linger with this verse, with the recognition that the very way Moses both directs and depends on Aaron mirrors in some way the experience of God? God has power, yes. But God's position is also precarious. Unlike Rashi, I'm not convinced that God is fully in control of this scene. Exodus 4 is not simply a record of God's confident command. It is also a negotiation that lays bare the urgency of God's call. God *needs* Moses in order to accomplish the things that God wants done.

But here's the thing: God has a staffing problem. God faces the perennial frustration of having to arrange and marshal a fractious bunch of humans to undertake the work that God wants to accomplish in this world. Good help is hard to find, and the people God selects aren't always reliable. They don't always execute the job in the precise ways that God desires. Sometimes they don't show up. Sometimes they turn God down.

This is a problem that disabled folks know well. Many of us rely on other people to accomplish physical tasks, whether that's getting out of bed and getting dressed or lifting the books and moving the furniture. An activist friend with little physical strength describes the way disability has sharpened her skills in the art of delegating and directing a staff of personal attendants, friends, and occasional passersby to facilitate her way in world. This, I think, is the nature of God's power.

Reading Torah through the lens of disability experience invites us to rethink the nature of divine power, to jettison the classical image of God as the one who can upend mountains at a whim. I feel divine presence like a live wild current running through this world, intimately intertwined with flesh and blood and stone. But when God wants something done? Intention isn't enough. As far as I can tell, God can't pick up a single stone without a human hand to lift it. When God desires direct action in the world of matter, She must inspire and cajole, adapt and orchestrate, trust and yearn. God too, I suspect, finds it occasionally frustrating.

Consider how much time the Torah devotes to describing God's efforts to conscript humans for specific, necessary tasks. Moses and Aaron take on the hard work of speaking to Pharaoh before they guide the Israelites out of Egypt and through the wilderness, toward the promised land. The people build the *mishkan*, the portable wilderness sanctuary, to God's exacting standard, following precisely the plans that God reveals. The Torah is a chronicle of divine delegation. God needs human hands to lift and build, to make and hold.

It isn't always easy. Beneath the confident surface of divine command, the Torah gives us glimpses of a God who is often frustrated and irritable. There's a famous scene in Numbers 20:11 when Moses strikes a rock to bring forth water, in response to God's command. In Numbers 20:12, God is incensed with Moses and decrees that the prophet will not enter the land. Why? Because Moses lifted his hand against the stone. He was supposed to *speak* to it, to draw forth water by word alone.

The commentators make much of the discrepancy between God's instruction and Moses's action, fashioning this verse to argue that God prizes gentleness over violence, that Moses missed an opportunity to show the people that the very stones themselves are attentive to the word of God. But when I read this passage? It's a scene that reminds me of my own worst moments when directing others to accomplish the physical tasks I can't do for myself. It reminds me of the way it feels to relinquish control over and over again. To have someone else position my things on a high, unreachable shelf. To have someone else arrange the heavy flowerpots on my balcony. To have someone else pick out the produce or select the groceries or do a thousand other things that I want done in a certain, specific way. Even though it's almost always *good enough*, it isn't quite the way I want it done.

Let's go back to Exodus 4:14, the words that describe God's anger with Moses. What if this isn't the anger of the superior, one who commands from a position of mastery? What if it's an anger that arises out of deep dependency? We are so used to assuming that God can do *anything* that it's easy to miss the constraints that govern God's own life. God cannot speak to Pharaoh. God cannot marshal the Israelites or lead them out of Egypt. For all of this, God needs a human messenger, a human mouth. And when Moses turns God down? God is angry. God is frustrated. God's desires are stymied once again.

Yet God adapts. In a quintessential disability pivot, God reworks the plan to take into account Moses's skills and capacities, pairing him up with Aaron so that Moses can get the job done. Even before Aaron arrives on the scene, God is sensitive to Moses's disability. In Exodus 4:1–9, when Moses and God first discuss the sacred work that God wants Moses to do, God offers Moses certain signs that will help convince the people that he has indeed been sent by God. The signs are an extraordinary offer of access. God gives Moses an alternative mode of communication, one that does not depend on words. When

Moses asks, "What if they do not believe me and do not listen to me?"
God instructs the prophet to show them a set of visual signs.[7]

What are the signs? A series of uncanny happenings that each have
some evocative link to the landscape of disability. In the first, Moses's
staff is transformed. At God's instruction, he throws it to the ground,
and it becomes a snake—and then, when he grasps it again, it changes
back into a staff.[8] The Torah tells us nothing about the history of this
staff or why Moses could be counted on to always have the staff at
hand. Perhaps it is nothing more than a walking stick, a shepherd's
crook, a matter of comfort or convenience. But Jewish sources gives
us a more evocative answer. Mishnah Pirke Avot 5:6 describes Moses's
staff as one of the final things God made, right before twilight on the
last day of creation. Midrash Pirke de-Rabbi Eliezer imagines it passed
down through the generations since the very beginning of time. The
staff was given first to Adam in the Garden of Eden, who passed it to
Enoch, on down to Noah, whose son gave it to Abraham, who passed
the staff to his own son. It was taken down to Egypt, where it was kept
in trust, one generation to the next: Jacob to Joseph, Joseph to Jethro,
until it came at last to Moses's hand.[9]

Perhaps because my own disability has led me to a close, intimate
relationship with assistive technology, I've always imagined Moses's staff
as a kind of companion, a friend for the journey. It is his crutch, his
partner in the dance. Each time I read, I shiver when God tells Moses
to throw it down. I want Moses to say no. I want him to keep hold of
his staff, or if he does release it, I want him to lower it gently. To lay
it down with love. And when Moses picks the staff back up? It's hard
to explain the visceral relief I feel, the ease I know in my own bones.
Moses is braced again, as he should be. He's supported, bolstered,
anchored to the solidness of earth.

The second sign God gives to Moses also resonates with an evo-
cation of disability. The skin of Moses's hand undergoes a transformation: first marked with snowy scales, then returned to its original
form. For a moment, Moses bears the marks of *tsaraat*, the biblical
skin affliction sometimes mistranslated as leprosy.[10] Leviticus lays out

the laws associated with this contagious eruption. A person whose skin suddenly breaks out in white scales must undergo a ritual of cleansing and then a period of quarantine: they stay outside the camp for seven days.[11] While tsaraat itself is not described as having a physical effect on body or mind, the stigma it carries and the isolation it brings resonate powerfully with the social reality of disability. Moses's tsaraat is different because it appears and recedes entirely at will. The sign on his skin is meant to be recognized as the mark of God.

If neither of these signs satisfies the people, Moses is granted the power to make one final visual display: to pour water from the Nile onto the ground and have it turn to blood.[12] Here, the divine touch has expanded beyond the visceral physicality of Moses's own body, to offer a sign that makes the water itself bleed like a wound. I'm not sure why these signs have been chosen, or why they all in some way riff on imagery associated with disability. Perhaps they are meant to suggest God's presence as an invitation to see beyond the surface of things, to witness a different kind of truth: a truth told through the crutch, the stigmatized skin, the turning of water into blood.

But the most important thing? The signs are a form of language that does not depend on words. Moses need not speak in order to evoke their power. Between these visual signs and his partnership with Aaron, God has orchestrated a potent set of accommodations for his disabled prophet. With the signs in his arsenal and with his brother at his side, Moses has the tools he needs to communicate with the people in a way that suits his own strengths.

There's a famous midrash about Moses that links his disability to an incident in his childhood, one that's worth examining as an important dimension of how traditional Jewish sources have imagined the possibility of a stuttering prophet. Midrash Exodus Rabbah 1:26 provides us with an origin story for Moses's disability, one that claims his physical difference as a sign of divine protection. To understand this midrash, we have to know something of Moses's own life story. Moses was born during a time of terrible persecution, when the Egyptian Pharaoh had decreed that all male infants born to the Israelites must be killed. After Moses's birth, the Torah recounts how his sister Miriam placed her baby brother in a tiny ark on the river and waited and watched until Pharaoh's daughter found him, took him to the palace, and raised him as her own child.

Now, the Torah tells us nothing about Moses's childhood in the Egyptian palace. But the midrash offers an imaginative glimpse of Moses in Pharaoh's court. As the midrash tells the story, Moses was an indulged and pampered toddler, a child who used to reach for and play with his grandfather's crown. Pharaoh himself was delighted by the antics of the little boy, but his advisers grew suspicious. Did the young Moses's play foreshadow a devious heart? Was the child revealing an inclination to overthrow the king, to seize power for himself? Ultimately, the advisers devise a test. They set before him a bowl of gold and a bowl that held a glowing coal. If Moses reaches for the gold, he will reveal himself as one with a desire for kingship—one destined to take Pharaoh's throne for his own. If he reaches for the coal, then they will acknowledge he is just an innocent child.

Moses, so the midrash goes, does indeed reach for the gold. Our midrash imagines Moses as marked for greatness from even the earliest days of his life. But because the child could not yet afford to reveal himself, because the proof of his future ascension would prove disastrous while Moses was but a boy in Pharaoh's court, an angel intervenes. The angel knocks Moses's hand toward the coal instead. Like any toddler might do, Moses grabs the glowing coal and puts it in his mouth. He burns his tongue and the coal leaves a lasting mark. As a result of the injury, Moses's mouth is permanently changed. But the brand itself? It is no mark of shame. Quite the contrary. As the midrash tells the story, Moses's tongue stands as a reminder of the prophet's path, a witness to his strategically concealed destiny.

I've never been quite sure what to make of this story. On the one hand, I suppose, it's reassuring to see the story of Moses's disability told in a way that has nothing to do with his own culpability. There's

no indication here that disability is a consequence of sin or some mis-
deed on Moses's part. If anything, our midrash relishes the baby Moses
reaching out to claim Pharaoh's crown. We're meant to delight in the
child's antics, to glimpse a promise of Moses's future greatness. We
know the wicked advisers are right, at least in this one respect. Moses
will one day overthrow the Pharaoh who oppresses his people, and the
people will one day be brought out of enslavement with his aid. Our
midrash fashions Moses's disability as a mark of his spiritual affinity,
a visceral proof of his destiny, a physical remnant of this encounter
with the angel. It's a powerful sign, pressed into his flesh.

Maybe you're thinking that's something I'd celebrate. In truth,
there's something about this story that gets under my skin. I chafe at the
way this midrash makes Moses's disability palatable, the way it explains
his disability as a consequence of the angel's touch. It suggests that Moses's speech disability comes about because of divine intervention, and
it claims his physical difference is a direct consequence of his spiritual
greatness, his God-given mission. By telling this story of the angel and
the coal, the midrash catapults disability out of the realm of ordinary
life. It perpetuates one of the most pervasive assumptions I encounter
in religious spaces: that disability needs a God-given reason for being.
That disability has to come with a story. That it requires an account,
an explanation, a spiritual frame that makes it comprehensible.

The Torah says God made Moses's mouth; the midrash says God
made it for a reason. In the midrash's telling, disability becomes an
act of divine providence, an expression of divine care. God is looking
out for Moses, an innocent child in Pharaoh's court, and arranges for
the angel, the coal, and the burned and disfigured mouth—all as a
way to protect him from a greater danger.

But we need to be careful here.

Sometimes disabled folks choose and cherish these kinds of spiritual stories about our disability experience. Sometimes it matters to
us deeply to recognize the way our disabilities unfold with religious
meaning or connect to our own sense of spiritual call. Sometimes we
draw a sense of empowerment or comfort or solace from these ways

of understanding disability as part of God's plan. If that's true in your own life, then carry that insight close. Let it strengthen you.

But here's the other thing I want you to know: I don't believe any of us should be in the business of applying these kinds of stories to someone else's life. The desire to find a *reason* for disability is a powerful desire for many religious folks, especially for those of us who have been trained to look for a hidden divine hand in every aspect of our lives. But to script a story onto someone else's life, to explain their disability as a spiritual gift or a burden to bear, as a divine message or an occasion for sanctified suffering? Reader, I ask you. Steer clear.

The temptation is strong. When the presence of disability stirs up our own feelings of anxiety or grief, when we're feeling bowled over by the unexpected, when we're reaching out for words of comfort, these kinds of spiritual explanations often help us to staunch our own fears. In moments of difficulty, in moments of loss, they allow the speaker to affirm the goodness of God. They affirm that everything, no matter how difficult or incomprehensible it appears, is all unfolding as part of some intricate divine design.

Now I don't know about you, but nothing quite gets my hackles up like being told that everything happens for a reason. Almost every disabled person I know has heard some variation of that line, whether from family, friends, or well-intentioned strangers. It's one of the most common reasons why many disabled folks stay far away from religious spaces. These spiritual meanings get scripted onto our bodies, pressed onto our skin by others as a way to make disability more religiously palatable, to render it God's will, or our special burden, or our divine gift.

Here's why that troubles me. This kind of spiritualizing hijacks my own life story, using it for someone else's ends. All too often, these kinds of stories fashion disabled folks as two-dimensional characters: the suffering saint, the misunderstood genius, the plucky kid who overcomes adversity to demonstrate the triumph of the human spirit. These roles cast disabled folks as teaching figures who model spiritual virtue for others, displaying our gratitude, our acceptance, our patience, our spiritual strength. But playing those parts leaves us with little room to inhabit the actual complexity of our own inner lives. I've watched these kinds of narratives slip like a straitjacket around people's hearts, constricting the range of emotions we're allowed to feel. I notice how the spiritual trope gets used to blunt the force of disabled people's frustrations, to silence our grief, to overwrite the fullness of our humanity.

I've lived my entire life in a world where disability demands explanation. Everyone wants the story of how or why disability comes into this world. I wonder, sometimes, how it would feel to answer those questions with a shrug, to resist allowing them to always claim center stage. Disability is part and parcel of this life, an ordinary fact, just one more element of what it means to be human. Like any part of our experience, disability can be a rich source of spiritual insight and understanding. But those spiritual implications aren't predetermined. The meaning that disability brings to my life is complex and multifaceted, as deep as bone.

As we hold the complexity of Moses's disability story, let's turn toward another truth that shapes his mouth, his tongue, the tenor of his life. Moses grows up bicultural in Pharaoh's court, a reality that Amanda Mbuvi argues is central to his role as prophet.[13] Moses was born during a great persecution, when the ruler of the land had decreed that all Hebrew boys should be slain at birth. He was born to parents who were forced to give him up, to set him adrift in a little ark on the river. When Pharaoh's daughter finds the child, she recognizes him as "one of the children of the Hebrews"—and her heart is moved to compassion. The Torah never grants this woman a name of her own, but in Jewish sources, she is known as Batya, the name by which I'll call her here. Moses's sister, Miriam, offers to find Batya a Hebrew woman to nurse the child and thus manages to arrange for Moses to stay with his birth mother until he his weaned. But after? Moses is taken from his people. Batya names him; Batya raises him as her own. Moses grows up in the Egyptian palace, a child of two cultures who has lost the connection to his mother tongue.

Moses's life story is an intimate history of state violence. We must not tell his history without recognizing that his original surrender, his eventual adoption, the grief, the love, the longing—all of these are shaped by the hard truth of Pharaoh's decree. Pharaoh judges the Hebrew people a danger. He marshals the power of the state, and he commands his people to drown every Hebrew boy who comes into this world. And Pharaoh's daughter? In some ways, hers is a story of resistance, a story of a daughter's power to undermine the cruelty of her father's house. When Batya lifts Moses out of the reeds, she recognizes him as a Hebrew child. She knows the subversiveness of her act, her choice to ensure his survival. But there are also other truths we must remember. Pharaoh's daughter saves the child by invoking her privilege to take him and make Moses her own. Her act is not simply a rescue. It is also a kind of plunder, an act of compassion that is also a claim to ownership.

Moses grew up speaking and writing Egyptian. The New Testament book of Acts describes Moses as having learned "all the wisdom of the Egyptians," as "powerful in his words and deeds."[14] The latter phrase makes a striking contrast to Exodus 4:10, where Moses describes himself as "not a man of words." Is it perhaps *Hebrew* words that fail to flow from Moses's tongue? Perhaps his uncertainty as a speaker is the anxiety of one who has come to a language later in life, who has never quite learned to be at home in the language. It may be that Moses did absorb some Hebrew in his earliest days. Maybe his earliest memories are bound up with his birth mother's voice, the household banter, the Hebrew cradle songs. But I also wonder: Did his lack of fluency cause him shame later in life, when he was reunited with the people of his birth? Did he carry the scar of that absence, like so many children who were denied access to the language of their heritage? Did he hesitate to speak, in part, because his tongue always felt like a stranger?

While Moses grew up in Pharaoh's court, he spent the bulk of his adult life in Midian. It was in Midian where Moses met and courted his wife, Tzippora, and where his first son was born. But when Moses is first introduced to Tzippora's father, as biblical scholar Amanda Mbuvi points out, he is seen indisputably as an *Egyptian*.[15] His Hebrew identity is entirely illegible. Moses stays for years in Midian. We can imagine, surely, that he learns the language, that the traditions of his wife's family and culture become an important strand of his own identity. But Moses also knows himself as a sojourner, a man who is far from home, always somehow out of place. When Tzippora brings their first child into the world, Moses names him Gershom, a name drawn from the Hebrew that was Moses's own mother tongue. It means *stranger there*.

For some traditional commentators, Moses's complex ethnic and linguistic history becomes a way to deflect the association with disability. Consider the commentary of Rashbam, a celebrated rabbi who lived in northern France in the twelfth century. Rashbam cannot stomach the notion that Moses has a speech disability. "Is it possible," he asks, "that a prophet who could communicate with God freely—face to face—and who received the Torah from him and communicated it to his people should have been afflicted with a stutter?"[16] Rashbam cannot square the notion of Moses's stutter with his role as prophet. Instead, he argues that Moses's protest stems from his own sense of linguistic inadequacy. He feels ill prepared to go before Pharaoh, to be God's spokesman. Why? Because he isn't fluent in the Egyptian spoken by the upper classes. Moses does not have a courtier's tongue.

I reject Rashbam's assumption that prophecy cannot coexist with a stutter. On the contrary, I wonder if Moses's stutter isn't somehow bound up with his affinity for prophecy, with the very possibility of revelation. I don't mean to suggest that one *must* be a stutterer to speak prophecy, but it seems perhaps to help. Many of the Hebrew prophets experience an obstruction of some kind with their speech.[17] It's not only Moses who has a slow tongue. Isaiah, too, has "unclean lips." Ezekiel is made mute by God for years.[18] In rabbinic literature, stuttering also plays a powerful role in the transmission of prophecy. The rabbis understand themselves as no longer inhabiting a world of true prophets, but they frequently turn to Torah for divine guidance. Their favorite form of prophecy? They would go to a place where young children were reciting their daily Bible verses and take meaning from the specific verse of scripture that was being recited that day. In many accounts, the meaning of the verse takes on particular poignancy and prophetic meaning when it is spoken by a child who stutters—whose distinctive tongue changes the meaning of a word and thus inadvertently delivers an oracle meant specifically for the sage.[19]

So, yes, I think it not just possible but perhaps even desirable that a prophet might speak face-to-face with God and also stutter. Rashbam projects his own assumptions about desirable bodies onto God. But God seems to me entirely uninterested in the task of fashioning humankind to fulfill some artificial notion of perfection. Is God's sense of self so fragile that it needs bolstering at every turn? I find it hard to imagine that God would be any more troubled by Moses's stutter than by the efforts of any other human speaker. It seems to me that all our human language, all the fluency and poetry of our speech, no matter its form, is but a little playful ripple on the infinite lake of the divine utterance. Everything is but a shadow of that great presence, that speech which is also silence.

But if I have no patience for the assumption that drives Rashbam's question, I savor the insight it yields: the image of Moses as a man juggling language, a man whose Hebrew is halting and awkward. Rashbam's commentary presents it as a choice: either the prophet is a stutterer, or he is a man of mixed heritage who fears to misstep in his non-native language. But that's a false dichotomy. Might we not imagine Moses as a man whose life spans both/and? Might we not know the prophet as a disabled man who is also bicultural, whose stutter spans all of the languages he has learned to speak?

This is the Moses who brings liberation: the Moses who has crossed borders, who is a migrant, an exile, a refugee. This is the Moses whose voice invokes the word of God: the one whose speech still holds an echo of his own immigrant journeys, the brilliant complexity of more than one accent, language, culture, consciousness. This is the Moses who speaks face-to-face with the Infinite: the one who stutters, the one who has learned to ride that bright rush of shame, the one whose speech has long been mocked and maligned.

In his powerful essay "Moses' Tongue," Marc Shell writes about his own experience as a stutterer in Hebrew school, and how large Moses's story loomed in his own life. Hiding out from teachers and fellow students, hoping to avoid that excruciating moment at the start of class when his name was called and he couldn't force out a response, Shell recalls reading over and over again the passage in Exodus where God calls to Moses from the burning bush. Shell knows that "Moses had a severe speech impediment of his own. Yet somehow Moses managed to get out a magnificent answer, *hineni* ("I am here"), when called."[20]

Shell's story haunts me. In it, Moses is not a confidant. He does not reach out a hand in empathy, across the generations, one stutterer to the next. Instead, the prophet becomes an indictment to work harder, proof that it's possible and also desirable to minimize one's disability, and to prove oneself capable according to the dictates of the nondisabled world. The one command Shell internalizes from Moses's life? *Do not stutter.*

Let me tell you a thing that pains me about Moses, a thing that hurts my heart. Even though Moses speaks about his disability to God, we see no other human acknowledge what God knows: that Moses has a disability that shapes his spiritual leadership. In Exodus 4, as we have seen, God affirms the significance of Moses's experience and provides him with accommodations. But once that access has been offered? It's as though Moses's disability no longer matters. It is stripped from his story, no longer a recognized part of his repertoire.

In fact, the Bible offers ample grounds to read Moses as a classic exemplar of a tiresome trope: the hero who "overcomes" his disability, who triumphs over the very thing that nearly prevented him from taking up the task of leadership. At the start of Exodus, Moses describes himself as a hesitant speaker, one who is ill-equipped to carry God's word to Pharaoh or to the Israelites. But by the end of his life? Moses has delivered an exquisite, stirring oration before the gathered nation. Moses's words form the entirety of the book of Deuteronomy, an epic retelling of the people's sacred history.

The classical midrash picks up on this incongruity. In Midrash Tanhuma, the rabbis note the striking difference between Moses's later life and the way he describes himself in Exodus, when God first asks him to speak. They imagine the people of Israel pointing out the inconsistency, wanting to know what prompted the transformation. Here is how the midrash answers:

> These are the words which Moses spoke . . . (Deut. 1:1)
> The people of Israel said:
> "Yesterday you said, 'I am not a man of words'
> and now you speak so much."
> Rabbi Yitzhak said:
> "If you are a stammerer, learn Torah and you will be healed."[21]

If I could, I'd blot these words out of the book. The midrash assumes that Moses's stutter has been cured, transformed by the prophet's contact with Torah. Not only that, it takes this assumption about Moses's own experience and fashions it into a remedy for anyone with a speech disability. Torah becomes a tool for erasing disability.

It's a shaft to my heart. I think of all of us who've found ourselves lured, for a moment or a lifetime, by the hope of healing. I think of all the pain that curls inside that promise, when healing does not come our way, or when it does not look the way that we'd imagined. I think of what it means to internalize so deeply the desire that we be healed: that sense that our own words don't measure up, that our own bodies, our own selves require repair.

I want to spit it out, that bitter lie.

I want to teach it new. I want to upend the assumption that lies beneath our midrash, the assumption that when Moses delivers the words of Deuteronomy, he speaks with flawless fluency. Why should we imagine that Moses has lost the distinctive quality of his own speech? Why should we imagine his mouth remade?

When I tell this story, there is a healing at the heart of this tale. But it isn't the healing that Rabbi Yitzhak assumes. This is the Torah I offer you, the Torah of Moses told in his own truest tongue. Moses becomes a man of words by claiming his place before his people as an unabashedly disabled speaker. Moses has learned to take his time. To claim his space. To claim his own disabled voice. When I read the book of Deuteronomy, I hear him speaking in my heart. I hear him stutter through the long, beautiful recitation of his own life's story. I hear him stutter without flinching. I hear him stutter without shame.

CHAPTER SEVEN

The Land You Cannot Enter

Longing, Loss, and Other Inaccessible Terrain

There's a curious incident that shapes Moses's story, an incident that ostensibly has nothing to do with disability. It unfolds during the wilderness period, during the forty years Moses led the people through the desert, on their way to the promised land. It was no easy journey. The Israelites are fractious and irritable, full of strife and fearful. They pine for the fish they used to eat in Egypt while they were enslaved; they long for the cucumbers, the succulent onions. They weep, they cry, they grumble. They ask Moses for a thousand things.

The incident begins in the Wilderness of Zin, at a place that comes to be called the Waters of Meribah, the water of quarrel. It is the first new moon of their fortieth year in the desert, and Moses's sister, Miriam, has just died. Now the people are without water. As the midrash tells the story, Miriam was the one who made it possible for the people to drink. She had been gifted with a miraculous spring, a source of fresh water that traveled with the Israelites on their journey through the desert. And when she dies? The well dries up. The people are mourning and their throats are parched. They're alone and afraid.

So they turn to Moses. They turn on Moses, banding together against him and his brother. They argue with him, with words that rip his heart. They tell him that they hate the desert. They're tired of this interminable journey. They wish they'd died already. They want to know, "Why did you make us leave Egypt to bring us to this wretched place, a place with no grain or figs or vines or pomegranates? There is not even water to drink!"[1]

God tells Moses and Aaron how to bring forth water. When the two brothers gather the people round, Moses speaks sharply. "Listen, you rebels," he tells them, "shall we get water for you out of this rock?"[2] Then Moses raises his arm and strikes the rock twice with his staff. The water flows and the people drink. But after he strikes the rock, God tells Moses that he will not enter the promised land.

The commentators struggle to explain the crime. Rashi says that Moses *struck* the rock, when he should have spoken to it. For Rashi, this is a matter of hewing precisely to the specific words of divine command. Other commentators draw different lessons from the incident, poring over the spare details of the exchange to understand the error. Nachmanides, another great medieval interpreter, argues that Moses errs by saying "we," by asking the people whether *he and Aaron* should bring forth water from the rock. By attributing the power to himself, Moses implies that the ability to sustain the community lies in his own hands and not in God's. For Maimonides, Moses's sin lies in speaking harshly to the people in calling them rebels. He should have been patient; he should have been forgiving. Instead, Moses gives in to his own frustration and anger.

Behind all of these explanations lies a powerful assumption. There must be a reason for Moses's disappointment. Moses must have done something wrong in order to justify this bitter fate. As they probe the details of this story, medieval and modern interpreters alike are all obsessed with the question of why. Why can't Moses enter into the land? What has he done wrong? If we look hard enough, we'll find the truth: a neatly calibrated connection between deed and consequence that justifies the inscrutable decree. The question presumes a tidy economy of divine justice, a world where every misfortune has a reason.

Disability has taught me to be suspicious of this impulse. As a disabled person, I feel the force of this question in other people's gaze, in their insatiable interest. Grown men stop me on the street to ask, *What happened to you?* Grocery checkers want to know, *Why do you use a wheelchair?* I'm buying shoes, and the clerk asks, *How long you been like this?* Waiting for the bus one sunny afternoon, a woman lays it plain: *What's wrong with you?* There's something about disability that makes perfect strangers suddenly think themselves entitled to the intimate story of a life.

It's not just prurient curiosity that drives my interlocutors. It's a desire to grasp the reason for disability. In religious circles, the desire to account for disability and explain its *why* has particularly pernicious consequences. There's an old canard, rarely spoken so explicitly these days, that understands disability as a consequence of sin. Theological opinions vary. Maybe it was my sin, or maybe that of my parents, or maybe it hearkens all the way back to the beginning of the world, to that first taste of sweet fruit in the garden where some folks say it all went wrong.

I guess at this point I don't need to tell you that my patience for this kind of theology is fairly thin. But you don't have to settle on sin to go looking for a reason. The question *why* has a powerful hold even on communities that would never dream of associating disability with personal wrongdoing. Disability is a test of faith, those folks like to tell me, or maybe it's an opportunity. Disability is an occasion for spiritual growth, the very thing my soul needs in order to learn the lessons of this life.

It's easy to get trapped inside that endless circle, trying to fashion a more palatable accounting of my life. But in truth? I want out of this whole line of thinking. It's not enough to substitute one answer for another, to swap out one explanation for a different one that I prefer. I want to change the very terms of the question. I want to strike it from the lexicon.

What if there is no reason why?

What if we take Moses's inability to enter the land as a simple fact, a fact without a reason? He cannot enter. It is one of the limits that contours his life, an elemental truth, as firm and solid as the stone.

And if he asks? If he pleads? The desert answers as it always does. The desert does not care for his desire. It is beyond him. Amidst the elemental forces of this world, a single human life is small. Our want is insignificant, our yearning ephemeral. The wind doesn't care about our longings. The mountain won't remake itself in answer to our need. We cross this life like wilderness. It offers passage, but it does not yield to want or whim.

We cannot always have what we desire.

The Torah doesn't help me much when it comes to releasing the search for a reason. The Bible returns again and again to the fact that Moses will die outside the land, laying down reminder after reminder that the prophet is shut out from the place of his yearning. After Numbers 20 recounts how Moses struck the rock, the narrative concludes with a definitive statement attributed to God. "Because you did not trust Me enough to affirm My sanctity in the sight of the Israelite people, therefore you shall not lead this congregation into the land that I have given them."[3] In Numbers 27:12–14, the Torah recalls that trouble. God tells Moses that his death is near, that he will soon be gathered to his kin. But first, God tells him to ascend a mountain, to view the land that God has given to the Israelite people. Here, too, the text returns to the familiar theme. Moses will not enter, God explains, because "in the wilderness of Zin, when the community was contentious, you disobeyed My command."

Moses's inability to enter the land surfaces again, at the start of Deuteronomy. As he offers the people a final account of their history together, he suggests a different reason for his own exclusion—one that traces back to a much earlier incident in their journey through the wilderness. In the second year, not long after the revelation at Sinai, twelve scouts venture out and make a first foray into the land.[4] But when the scouts return? They are crestfallen, afraid, sure they will never be able to conquer the giants who live there. God is outraged. A harsh decree comes forth: the faithless people will wander for forty years; they will die without seeing their destination. None of the first generation, save two faithful men, will live to enter the land.

And what of Moses? The prophet's own fate is left oblique in Numbers 14. He is not singled out for punishment or praise. Is he included in the divine decree? When Moses recalls this moment at the beginning of Deuteronomy, he traces his own inability to enter the land back to that experience. Moses says, "Because of you the Lord was incensed with me too, and God said: You shall not enter it either."[5] If that was the moment when the truth settled into his own bones, then Moses has lived with this knowledge for decades. It is no recent decision, no sudden announcement. It's a truth that Moses has carried for most of the journey. He will die in the desert. He will never lie down in the sweet land of promise. He will not come to the place of his heart's home.

But Deuteronomy offers us another truth, a glimpse of how Moses felt when he first learned he would not enter. Moses confesses that he pleaded with God. He cried out to God to reverse the decree. Deuteronomy 3:23–27 reads:

> I pleaded with the Lord at that time, saying,
> "O Lord God,
> You who let your servant
> see the first works of Your greatness and Your mighty hand,
> You whose powerful deeds no god in heaven or on earth can equal—
> let me, I pray, cross over
> and see the good land on the other side of the Jordan,
> that good hill country and the Lebanon."
>
> But the Lord was angry with me on your account
> and would not listen to me.
> The Lord said to me,
> "Enough! Never speak to Me of this matter again.
> Go up to the summit of Pisgah and gaze about,
> to the west, the north, the south, and the east.
> Look at it well,
> for you shall not go across yonder Jordan."[6]

In this passage, Moses bares his heart. He asks that God let him cross over the river, to see the good land that God has promised his people. In Deuteronomy 3:24–25, Moses makes two requests: that he be allowed to cross and that he be allowed to see. These two verbs will recur throughout the Torah's telling. The Hebrew verb "to cross" is connected at the root to the name of the Hebrew people, who are *Ivrim*, the ones who have crossed over. We are boundary crossers, border walkers. Our name as a people is bound up with this passage, with the dare of transformation. We are the ones who have crossed the desert, the ones who have crossed a life of enslavement and been birthed into a more expansive world, the ones who have crossed into freedom. If the name *Ivri* means anything in my own life, it is a call to solidarity, a reminder of all the ways this story is still being told. I cannot write of *crossing* without thinking of those who cross the desert in our own days, from Mexico and Central America into the American Southwest, on the run from violence and violation, from a gunman's bullet, from a life pressed so hard that they can barely breathe. I think of the desperation that drives them, fist in glove with hope. I think of walls. I name the barbed wire and the cages, the detention centers, the deportation, the return: all the ways the crossing is denied, refused.

The story of that crossing is not mine to tell. I will not take it, claim it, fashion it into a tidy moral tale. But I evoke it here—a few spare words, like breath, the barest gesture—because it changes for me the force of these ancient words. It grounds the imperative, the urgency, the drive, the need.

Moses gives his life to this crossing. Forty years he labors, so his people can enter the land they long for. The ones he left with? The ones who first followed him, whose bodies he first guided, hesitant and halting through the split open sea? Almost all of them are buried in the desert. It is their children who press around him now, who will inhabit the dreams of all the ones who raised them, the dreams of the mothers and the aunties, the artisans and the woodcutters, the teachers and the storytellers. Now, on the very precipice of this transition, Moses grapples again with the truth he does not want to take into his heart.

He will not cross. He cannot enter.

In Deuteronomy Rabbah, the midrash recounts that Moses pleads before God, not just once but 515 times. He appeals to divine emotion, he marshals logical argument, he pours out the whole of his heart. "If you will not let me enter the land," Moses says to God, "then let me be like the cattle of the field, who eat grasses and drink water and live and see the land—make me one of them." When that plea does not receive the answer he desires, Moses tries again. "If not, then let me be like the birds who fly on the four winds of the world, who go forth to gather food each day and who return by night to their nests—make me one of them."[7]

There is a part of me that flinches from this plea, from the yearning laid so plain. I want Moses to let go of this desire, to steer clear of this limit, to avoid coming face-to-face with this terrain. It's dangerous to voice desire, a risk to let it be seen. There's a part of me that wants the prophet to deploy the strategies I know so well: the cheery reassurance, the summoned smile. Will he shrug and say it does not matter? Will he say it does not hurt?

The truth is harder than that.

I'm thinking of a moment, years ago, when I was out with friends one evening at the ocean, on the boardwalk. Someone suggested that we ride the Ferris wheel, that we look out at the sea and the stars. But once we drew near, we found the ride was full of steps and inaccessible to wheels. So of course I said I did not mind and stayed behind.

Dear reader, I will tell you this: I lied.

I rolled alone, back to the boardwalk. I turned away from the glitter and the giant wheel and cast my eyes out to the ocean, to the sand, another land on which I cannot stand. And there, in the darkness, I cried.

Was it the heartbreak of a lifetime? Surely not. It was a fleeting thing, a momentary hurt, an utterly irrelevant desire. But it taps into a truth I rarely name. Disability has shut me out of certain things I've wanted.

Having told you that truth, though, I need to tell you another. Of all the stories I have crafted in this book, of all the carefully curated glimpses of a life? This is the one that feels the most dangerous. This is the one I'm still not sure I dare to tell.

To speak of disability loss risks amplifying the one story most non-disabled people tell about my life. To acknowledge grief means stoking ableism's fire, feeding fuel to the assumption that my disabled life is a tale of sorrow and sadness, grief and lament. Everywhere I turn, that story gets broadcast. The trope of disability as tragic suffering is on parade in popular culture, from literary classics to the blockbuster disability drama of the moment. I hear it on the streets, from strangers who see my wheelchair and then tell me that they'd rather die than be disabled. My seatmate on the subway has known me for five minutes but spends the next three stops offering a soliloquy on the courage it takes to live like I do.

By this point, I've mostly learned to shuck off these public inter-actions, to block them out, or armor up, or gently smile and extricate myself from awkward moments. But disability sympathy is harder to handle, especially when we're in ongoing proximity. An acquaintance at synagogue wants to strike up a conversation. "It must be so hard," she says, with a knowing look at my wheels. And there we are, that old story like a wall between us, blocking out the possibility of something more.

My new friend's gesture is a different kind of problem than those brash interactions with strangers on the street, because it isn't thought-less. It isn't cruel. Quite the contrary. It's a surfeit of kindness, an em-pathy misfire, a good intention gone awry.

That response is so widespread that virtually all my public and private interactions are shaped in some measure by the effort to avoid it. Whether or not I'm talking about disability, I'm always assessing how to avoid entanglements with the feelings my disability summons up in others. These calculations aren't a matter of rational thought, and they're usually not even a deliberate choice. They've sunk so deep into my marrow that they shape my words before I even speak. My body knows that certain truths aren't safe to share. My body knows that certain stories are too dangerous to tell. My body knows what causes yours to flinch. I've learned to guard myself against disclosure that might stir up someone's pity, that might kindle someone's fear.

The basic rule is simple: never let them see you grieve. This isn't about putting up a stoic front, and it's got nothing to do with being brave. It's a strategic choice, a political one. To give voice to pain is to feed ableism's arsenal, to open myself up to the assault of those assumptions: that disability is unendurable, that my life is unrelenting loss, that the world would be better off without my presence. Like many other disability activists, I refuse to play into the trope of disability as tragedy because of the way it has been used against us—to declare our lives not worth living, to defund disabled people's health care and our in-home support services, to justify inequitable access to education, to consign us to the margins of politics and policy, to push our bodies out of public space, to figure us not worthy of time, investment, care, or love.

Most disabled folks I know spend a vast amount of energy managing the feelings of nondisabled people. We've honed our capacity to disarm anxiety, to soothe uncertainty, to smooth everything along. We've got different strategies, of course. Some of us know how to turn on the charm. Others tend toward the self-effacing joke, the shared laugh. There's an artistry here, an art built out of hard necessity. These kinds of gestures aren't particular to disability. These are tools honed by many members of minoritized communities, the tools you use to gentle the fears of the people who hold your life in their collective hands. Learning to read and ease the emotions of majority culture is a survival skill.

Here is what I've learned: Loss is a dangerous country. Show even the slightest hint of sadness, and my interlocutors will never let it rest. Touch even for a moment on a story that hints of regret, and empathy will rise up like a tidal wave. It's all disabled people get to hear: how sorry you are, how terrible it is. The tragic story is always waiting in the wings, ready to swallow up my life and all its intricate, complicated pleasures.

It's not precisely that I want to hide the *fact* of pain. It's that I don't trust what people will do with it. Any grief I show gets weaponized,

turned back to cut me twice. Ableism has narrowed the range of emotions I can safely show you. It contours what I feel, and whether I will
ever give it voice. I speak of loss only in my most intimate relationships,
with the friends and kin who are my bedrock.

But this time, friends, I want to try it differently. This time, I want
to trust you. I want to tell you about my own moment with this mountain and what it means to look upon the lands I cannot enter. I want
to tell you how the Moses story curls inside my heart and what unfolds
for me, both generative and difficult, when I root deep into that place
of wanting. It is a telling that holds loss. But loss is not the only thing
that lives here.

Can you hold this story? Can you braid it together with the beauty
of my life?

The Hebrew Bible is famously laconic about matters of the heart.
While divine feeling is often on full display, the emotional lives of its
human figures are often sketched in the sparest of lines. In Deuteronomy 4, Moses returns again to the fact that he will not enter the land.
The repetition of this theme recalls for me the way we often linger
with certain hurts, the way our thoughts and our speech circle back
again and again to the site of our heartbreak. But the text offers no
key to Moses's feelings. Does his jaw clench with the memory of an old
frustration? Does his voice waver in the telling? Are the words stoic,
dispassionate, resigned?

Let's look more closely at those words. In Deuteronomy 4:21–22,
Moses continues his speech to the new generation, the ones who are
poised at the threshold of the crossing, about to enter the land. He says:

> Now the Lord was angry with me on your account
> and swore that I should not cross the Jordan
> and enter the good land
> that the Lord your God is assigning you as a heritage.
> For I will die in this land;

I will not cross the Jordan.
But you will cross and take possession of that good land.[8]

The beginning of the passage lands hard on the familiar notion that Moses's inability to enter the land is a consequence of divine anger, a response to a vow made in the heat of frustration. God was angry with me because of *you*. But Moses's charge is, in this moment, not entirely on target. The people to whom he speaks this day are the children and grandchildren of the older generation, their nieces, nephews, and nestlings. The ones who sparked God's anger on that long-ago day have already passed into memory, their bodies buried in the desert, in the wilderness.

But let us lay aside, for a moment, the fixation on causality. Let us leave behind the fight over fault, the question of why. Let us consider what else we find, if we still for a moment the assumption that Moses's inability to cross is a kind of punishment, a divine response to his own misdeeds or the people's failings. Let us linger with the next verse, a verse that speaks more powerfully to my own disability experience. "I will not cross," Moses says, in Deuteronomy 4:22. "But you will." The people will enter the land, and Moses? Moses will stay behind.

Traditional commentary has understood this verse as a missed opportunity, a moment when Moses hoped to spark the people to action on his own behalf. Deuteronomy Rabbah 3:11 uses this verse to launch a midrash that imagines Moses waiting for the people's prayers, prayers that never come:

When they came to cross over the Jordan,
Moses reminded them of every plea that he had made on their behalf,
because he thought that now they would pray on his behalf,
that he should enter the land with them.

What is the force of "You are crossing over?"
Rabbi Tanhuma said:

Moses prostrated himself before Israel and said to them,
"You are to cross over, but not I."
He gave them the opportunity to pray for him,
but they did not grasp his meaning.[9]

The modern commentator Aviva Gottleib Zornberg reflects on this midrash, writing about the powerful way that Moses lays plain "the geography of his pain." The midrash lingers on the juxtaposition, the contrast between the promise laid before the people and the wall set before Moses. *You are crossing over*, Moses says, *but I am not crossing over*. Why, Zornberg asks, "can the people not hear the appeal hidden within the words?"[10] Why don't they speak up for Moses? Why don't they cry out on his behalf? For years and years, Moses has come before God to plead on the people's account, to advocate for them, to fight for their survival, and for second chances. But now, when he needs an advocate? There's nothing but silence. No one prays for Moses. No one even thinks to ask.

It's an evocative midrash for me, and also a dangerous one. As a disabled woman, I find myself in a very different position, a position where people are ready and eager to pray on my behalf, regardless of what I myself desire. I'm at the grocery store, reaching for the frozen peas, when a lady wants to know if she can pray that I will walk again. I'm with my mother, at a concert, and a young man approaches, asks if we can pray.

It's a thicket of prayer, undesired and unasked for. I can brush off the brash and the bombastic. I have a withering retort at the ready for folks who touch my arms, my legs, my wheels without consent. But I find it strangely awkward to turn away from some of these requests, the shy ones, the tender ones. Even now, from the remove of years, I hear their voices: the child of a friend who told me that she prayed for me when our synagogue recited the healing prayer. I flinched inside, but when I spoke, I spoke to her with gentleness.

Prayer dogs me, even when I'm living my ordinary, lovely life—all the more so, if I give some hint that I'm in need. Like many Jewish disabled folks I know, I won't go near a synagogue's Mi Shebeirach list, the list of names that are recalled "for healing of body, mind, or spirit." Once, after a surgery, I benched gomel in synagogue, making the public affirmation of gratitude that Jewish tradition calls us to recite after recovering from a serious injury or illness. For years after, folks from that community would ask me, solicitously: Was I feeling all right? How was I doing? Did I need anything?

Unlike Moses, I can't get people to *stop* praying for me.

If you've followed me this far, I imagine you already know I'm not interested in those kinds of prayers, the kind that strip away my wheels and fashion me into an effortless strider. But there's a different kind of call, a call to action that I long for. So much of my disabled life has been shaped by physical architectural barriers, by the stairs that shut me out of scenic vistas and student lounges, by design that hasn't made a place for me. I hold in my heart the frustration, the stark truth of that disparity: You can enter. But I? I cannot.

I think of all the Shabbos lunches I've said no to, all the invites I've declined. I think of all the times I've never been invited because it's already clear: I cannot cross the threshold. I can't get in the door.

There's a call there, a call to action. But most times, people miss the meaning.

Many years ago, I lived on a street without a curb cut, the small entry and exit ramp that lets wheelers and stroller pushers and delivery folk glide easily and seamlessly from the sidewalk into the street. Every time I wanted to head westward—toward the city, toward the university, toward a sweet little café—I had to take a circuitous route that snaked some distance out of my way. Of course, my housemates and I called the city to complain, to ask for access. But the official wheels of change turn slowly, and it was fast becoming clear that I'd have moved out of that house and out of that town long before the city got around to fixing my path. One day, when a truck came out to fix a pothole? My housemate grabbed a shovel, asked the workers for a bit of asphalt, and made me a little ramp down from that curb so I could finally wheel free.

That's the kind of prayer I'm looking for, the kind of solidarity that's simultaneously bold and imminently practical. The kind of solidarity that refuses to accept unequal access as fixed and certain truth. That bears witness to the wrong and commits to reconfiguring the facts of exclusion. The kind of solidarity that won't let go until we *all* cross over.

But not all the lands I want to enter can be reached with asphalt. Sometimes I'm denied a crossing because of human choices: because of poorly fashioned paths or failures of architectural imagination, because of assumptions and projections other people lay upon my life, because we have forged violence and inequality into our culture's bones. But if I tell the truth about my life, I must also tell you this: there are other crossings that disability has cost me. I am a woman who loves wild places, the rough-hewn textures of a granite crag, the soft embrace of fern and moss. There's a pull inside me to that wide open ridge where the sky touches down against the scraggy, highland grasses, to the rocky hillside, to the hike that winds deep into solitude. I want to step off the paved path and unfold into the mystery of a forest, to step between two trees and feel uneven ground beneath my feet.

I've shaped my sweet disabled life to meet this love, to seek this wildness. A beloved housemate used to lift me up on her back and trundle me across the sand so we could get down to the ocean and lap our toes into the waves. I have a hiking wheelchair, and I've trained myself to lever and to pull, to ease my wheels through forest floor and dirt track, over stick and stone. I've spent more time in wilderness than most nondisabled folks. I've taken wheelchairs to the Alps and to the Arava, forded an unexpected rush of high water in Venice in the old ghetto, rolled into the sweet silence of a South Dakota cave. Even so, I land time and time again against the sharp limit of the thing, the truth of wheel and bone. There are some rivers I will never cross, some lands I cannot enter.

I know the ache of wanting.

Moses does not get the wings he longs for. Moses never lays his body down in those sweet grasses or savors the scents of that good land. God grants him only this: the chance to climb the mountain, to gaze from the peak and let the sight of that long-deferred promise unfold before his eyes. In the last chapter of the book of Deuteronomy, right before Moses dies, God tells him to climb the mountain, to look out upon the land. Deuteronomy 34:1–4 lingers over the land, allowing the listener to hear the contours and cadences of the hills, the heights and the valleys:

And Moses went up from the steppes of Moab to Mount Nebo,
to the top of Pisgah, which faces Jericho.

God let him see all the land,
from the Gilead as far as Dan,
and all Naphtali, and the land of Ephraim and Manasseh,
and all the land of Judah, as far as the Hinder Sea, and the Negev,
and the plain of the Valley of Jericho, the town of the palm trees,
as far as Zoar.

God said to him:
This is the land that I swore to Abraham, to Isaac, and to Jacob.
I will give it to your descendants.
I have let you see it with your eyes,
but into it, you will not cross.[11]

God's last words to Moses name the limit of his life. It seems a cruel choice, an unnecessary repetition. Why speak again this painful fact? In this final, intimate moment, just before the prophet passes into death, why turn again to disappointment?

Might it be to make repair?

Each of the earlier passages that speak of Moses's inability to cross bind that fact with cause and consequence. The reasons differ. Sometimes it is Moses's failure, sometimes the people's sin. But the theme of divine anger runs through each of these accounts. Only in the last is it absent. Only in the last is there no reason given, no blame to be assigned, no lesson to be drawn. Here, in this final moment, it is simple, elemental truth. This one body cannot ford the river. It will not cross into the land it sees.

When we let go of asking why, then we can ask a different question. What is it like for Moses? Once the knowledge is absorbed, once he has acknowledged grief and disappointment, what does he know? What does he feel?

It is a question that I ask myself, when I have come to face that impasse.

From a country road that winds out high above the rocks, I take in the northeast coast of Scotland, the waters of the Cromarty Firth lapping against the beach below. Cool summer wind edges through my coat, riffling my half-bound hair. The gulls cry overhead, a braid of wonder and of wind. Far below, a couple walks across the place where land meets sea, a place my wheels will never roll. Watching them, I almost feel the water lap around my toes, the grit of sand against my feet. But I do not, not in the flesh.

How do I allow for hunger, for the hard, sharp truth of want?

This isn't only a truth disabled people know. It is a deeply human story, part and parcel of what it means to be alive. All of us come up against the limits of the possible, the compass of what our bodies or our minds will allow. But acknowledging this question runs against the grain. The culture I was raised in leaves no space for unfulfilled desire. I learned to celebrate the act of overcoming limits, to trust that barriers could always be surmounted. We do not speak of dreams that cannot be achieved. Even now, I hear the voice inside my head, relentless in its cheer: *You never know. It* could *still happen. Don't give up.* And when I did encounter limits, when I did give up on dreams? The story I was taught to tell is that *it doesn't matter.* Dismiss the want. Deny its meaning. Deflect the rawness of the loss. *It isn't important. I didn't want it anyway.* Or better still, try to find a silver lining. Spin a tidy tale that makes denial part of some great good.

None of that feels right to me. None of that feels true.

I want to linger with the fact of want, to dwell there without flinching. To hold this feeling gently, to give it space to breathe. To leave it open, unresolved. To witness this as truth that matters, and to resist the lure of consolation, the platitudes that try to paper over loss. This is part of who I am, one of the truths that shapes my life. I am a creature who cannot always enter the places of my longing.

Secretly, I'm glad that Moses does not enter the land. As soon as the Israelites cross the Jordan, the book of Judges turns to war and conquest, to blood and fear and genocide, to a brittle quest to erase all those who came before. There's a part of me that's grateful Moses has no part in this, that he lies down on that sweet mountainside before the promise turns to violence. Elsewhere, the Torah has made plain that Moses is no pacifist. Moses has led the people in battle before, when facing off against the brutal Amalek at Rephidim. It's a curious story, as Rhiannon Graybill has observed, one that once again links Moses with the experience of disability.[12] In Exodus 17, the Israelites will triumph in battle so long as Moses holds up his hands. But Moses cannot do it. His arms grow weary, and he can no longer stand. So Aaron and another man find a rock for him to sit on, and they raise up his arms. They buttress his body. They lift his limbs.

So when it comes to this final crossing, a crossing that will require force of arms? I like to think there was a gentleness in Moses that could not be reconciled with conquest, that something in him recoiled from the brutality that would follow. Moses never enters the land to possess it. He never claims it for his own. He stands on the heights of the mountain and gazes out upon a vast panorama. He looks and knows this beauty will never be his.

Would the land have changed for him, if he had been allowed to close the distance? Rebecca Solnit writes evocatively of what she calls "the blue of distance," the particular color that arises at the far edge of what we can see. In the fifteenth century, she observes, as European painters were just developing the craft of perspective, they used blue at the horizon to bring this quality into their art. They painted a blue world at the farthest edges of what can be seen, evoking a quality of light and softness, a romance of the distant. "The color of that distance," Solnit writes, "is the color of an emotion, the color of solitude and of desire, the color of there seen from here, the color of where you are not. And the color of where you can never go."[13] It is a color that can never be grasped, a quality that cannot be possessed. It is not anchored to a particular place, not tethered to a specific geography. Arrive at a destination, and it has already moved to a more distant shore. That blue belongs to the horizon.

The blue of distance is a gift to anyone who lifts their eyes toward a distant sky. But to savor it requires us to linger with the truth of unfulfillable desire, to hold open a space for the place we cannot go. To savor the blue of distance, Solnit says, is to "look across the distance without wanting to close it up." Can we learn to acknowledge desire without immediately rushing to satisfy it? Can we learn, in Solnit's words, to own our longing "in the same way you own the beauty of that blue that can never be possessed?"[14]

This is the wisdom that Moses offers, a wisdom that is in my own life intimately tied with the experience of disability. Moses takes one final climb before he dies, and he looks out at the land. He looks out *knowing* that he will not enter. I like to think that knowledge shaped his gaze, that it changed what he could see and how. I do not mean he looked with grief or with a kind of weary resignation. To understand this thing, we must let go of the assumption that it is a kind of loss, a species of regret. I mean instead a different kind of presence, a quality of being with the distance.

When I look out at wild places, I long for elemental connection: for the feel of skin on grass, the touch of flesh against the rock, for a sudden caress of sea, sliding up my feet. But I have learned how to use that longing as a door. I know how to let that distance enter me, how to open breath and heart and bone in invitation.

The ancient rabbis believed that vision was a tangible force, that we see what we see in part because our eyes *strike* the object of our gaze—or because we ourselves are struck by what we see. Grounded in the ancient science of Galen, Aristotle, and Plato, these rabbinic notions of vision indelibly intertwine the act of sight with the experience of touch.[15] The science with which I understand the act of seeing is different, but there's an element of that ancient understanding that speaks to my experience. The act of vision connects the one who sees with the object of our attention. When I look, with a deep and generous gaze, I allow myself to be affected by the sight. Sight is a channel, a road back to the one who regards. That which we see touches us, changes us. Vision is a gate that swings both ways, an avenue of contact.

There's a part of me that hesitates to name the role that sight plays in my experience of wilderness because I'm leery of reinforcing a longstanding cultural trope that privileges the visual as a *necessary condition* for knowledge—an assumption that constructs blindness as the antithesis of understanding. So if I am to tell you about the power of the gaze in my own disabled life, I need some assurance from you. I need to know that you won't take this story and turn it, sharp and hard, against my disabled kin.

I like to sit and watch the land in places where I can feel the wind on my skin, the sun against my hands, the texture of pebbles and stones beneath my wheels or my seat. There's something about these elemental sensations that allows me to feel the whisper of wildness, the invitation. Pinned behind glass, I have rarely found the same doorways. But I imagine that this, too, is a matter of practice, a matter of honing my virtuosity. I used to think I needed to *traverse* a forest, to enter a wood to experience this quality of perception, this kind of knowing. But now I find these hidden paths open to me even when I'm perched on pavement, far from the wild places that call to my spirit.

Disability has sheared away the assumption I was trained to, that wilderness is a summit to be surmounted. My pace is slower now, the distance I can close more minute than before. There are some things

I have lost, some rivers I will never cross. But there are also doorways that have opened, other paths I would have missed before. Drawn into distance through the prism of the gaze, I keep company with wild places. I allow the land to take up residence within my bones.

To behold is to invite in.

CHAPTER EIGHT

The Perils of Healing

Years ago, I was buying a mattress in Missouri. My mother had joined me, doing her best to make the task more palatable. We were in a big box store that must have boasted two hundred beds, all arranged in little clusters of domestic bliss, each of them staged in such a way as to maximize the obstacles for a woman on wheels.

I'm surveying my approach when a salesman appears. He's a young guy, blond and gangly, and at first glance, he doesn't have the look of a man who knows all that much about bedding. But the truth is that I'm tired. This hasn't been the first stop of the day and it doesn't look to be the last. So when he asks, I tell him what I want and let him lead the way.

We're heading to the back. I've resigned myself to the fact that the bed that interests me is always tucked in the deepest corner of the most awkwardly arranged store. My sales guy is rattling off some specs about the pillow top, how it stacks against the memory foam. But as he inches another nightstand out of my path, he turns to me and says, "I know a girl who used to use a wheelchair."

"She's walking now," he tells me. "Because she trusts in Jesus."

I freeze.

He tells me about the accident. And how they used to pray. His face is open, utterly without guile. His hands are a breath from my legs. I'm suddenly afraid he's going to touch me, in front of God and everyone, right in the middle of Mattress Firm.

"Let's go," I say to my mother.

She nods, and we're gone.

I think of that encounter every time I read a passage from Luke's Gospel that tells of another woman who finds herself unexpectedly in the middle of a healing story. It's a story from the Christian Bible, a New Testament story, not a Jewish one. But it ricochets against my bones so powerfully that I know it now by heart. Listen, if you will, to how Luke tells the story:

> Now Jesus was teaching in one of the synagogues on the Sabbath.
> And just then there appeared a woman with a spirit
> that had crippled her for eighteen years.
> She was bent over and was quite unable to stand up straight.
> When Jesus saw her, he called her over and said,
> "Woman, you are set free from your ailment."
> When he laid his hands on her,
> immediately she stood up straight and began praising God.[1]

For Luke, as for most readers of the Gospels, this is a story about Jesus. It's a story that proclaims his power and the power of God, a story that bears witness to the way a touch can transform flesh. Luke uses the bent woman's body to stage a story of liberation, to show that life can open up when all things seem constricted. This is a story of the calcified constraints of muscle and mind suddenly coming unpinned, a story of unexpected possibility. Her body bears his witness. Her straightened spine tells his truth.

Her story, though, remains in shadow.

Luke sketches her in caricature. He paints her as beleaguered, a woman captive to cruel fate. Eighteen years bent over, unable to stand straight. Held hostage by a spirit, by a hidden force or power. She is infirm. She is crippled.

The presumption of it galls me.

Every time I read this story, I am struck by all the things we do not know. Her name, for one. What was she doing that morning, before the healer came? Perhaps she came to synagogue to visit with her neighbors. Perhaps she came to learn some Torah, to stretch her heart and stir her soul. Perhaps she came to pray. But if she'd come to pray, remember this: We don't know what she yearned for or how the words formed on her tongue. We don't know the garden that she tended or if she kneaded dough. We don't know the love she counted or the scars.

I feel the loss like fury in my heart. The eighteen years sloughed off like nothing, as though they'd never been. Her disabled life condensed into a prologue, as though it were a footnote to her own becoming. Disability communities have fought hard against the assumptions baked into stories like these: that our bodies are broken; that we are insufficient and in need of fixing; that we are waiting around for a cure, languishing in pain and misery, pining for the coming of a good man's remedy. I've been caught at the center of that story, and all I can think is this:

Get your hands off my body.

Healing feels like an intrusion, an assault. Everywhere she goes, they look at her. They look, they stare, they reach, they touch. How does Luke say it? *Then he put his hands on her.* Yes, of course he does. That's how this story always goes. The disabled body is an object. The disabled body is a showcase, through which the lesson is played out. If the cruel spirit makes you crippled, Jesus lifts you straight.

Do you think it stops after he heals her? Now she's a spectacle of a different kind. When she lifts her head, they know it for a miracle. They whisper when she passes by. Her name is on their lips, bound up with his. *Did you hear what happened?* It's a small town she lives in. The gossip spreads like fire. I bet the story follows her for days and decades. Even now she's pressed between the pages of the book, nothing left of her but this one telling.

You are set free. This is the story I can't get away from, the story that stalks my body through this world: disability as impediment, the wheelchair as a trap. When Luke has Jesus proclaim freedom for the woman bent over, his words figure her body as a shackle. Disabled flesh becomes a straitjacket for the soul.

Luke's healing story is a twist on the common trope of *overcoming* disability. The secular world likes to figure disability as a story of personal triumph. It celebrates the grit of those who surmount the odds, revels in the dedication of those who push through tragedy or cruel circumstance. But the religious frame draws our eye elsewhere. In this telling, the woman bent over has little power in her own right. She needs another to lift her up and set her free. The drama of the healing relies on her own insufficiency. Because she cannot free herself, she needs rescue from another quarter. And when it comes? Her transformed flesh becomes a revelation. Her body lays plain the power of God.

How does she feel when it happens? That's another thing that we will never know. There's a line in Luke's story that aims to pin her in our minds as overjoyed. "Immediately," he tells us, after Jesus touches her, "she straightened up and praised God." The text makes those two events into a single gesture. She straightens and praises. She rises and gives thanks. In that motion, we are meant to feel her gratitude. We are meant to revel in her celebration. We are meant to savor that heady feeling of relief.

Is that the whole of the story?

I suppose the cynic in me is not entirely convinced. I cannot help but think about the way that you and I have learned to praise a gift, even when it doesn't fit. Even when it wasn't quite the thing we'd wanted, even when it's wrapped with hidden strings.

But let's imagine that it pleases her. Let's say this is a thing she's yearned for, that healing is a dream she's courted all these years. Or if it took her by surprise, let's say it was still welcome. Maybe Jesus asked her with a look, if not a word. When he lay his fingers firm against her skin, perhaps he felt assent. I like to think he waited for her nod. Maybe stillness passed between them, like a breath, a trust.

If it truly was good news, if it was joy, then I am glad for her.

But it does not temper my unease. The power of this story stretches far beyond the personal, beyond this one woman and her wants and dreams. While her assent might soften the presumption of the healing, consent alone can't leach the danger from this tale. Healing has a power that pushes far beyond the individual. The notion of miracle contours our cultural responses to disability, shaping the very landscape of our imaginations. Whether in religious contexts or in the halls of medicine, the power of miracle hangs like a promise, a dream, a shiver of possibility. It doesn't matter if we count ourselves religious, if we ourselves believe. Through science or through spirit, most of us inhabit a world that links disability inexorably to the hope of healing.

The cost of that coupling for disabled folks is high. For years after I started using a wheelchair, I'd come home from college to face the selfsame question: *Are you getting better?* It came from friends, it came from family. It came from neighbors, cashiers, and casual acquaintances. Sometimes it was, *How ya feeling?* Sometimes it didn't call on me to answer at all. *You're looking good today,* a passerby would say. Or, with a wince, *You're in pain.*

The words were almost always kind. Folks treated me so carefully, with gentleness, with love. Empathy was everywhere. Sure, sometimes I encountered prurient curiosity or became a kind of spectacle to a stranger on the street. But mostly I was met with genuine concern. I had fallen out of health, fallen into disability. People wanted me restored. People wished me well.

And every time I answered? I felt like I had failed. I let them down. I couldn't patch my life into a neat trajectory of healing. I wasn't getting better. I was getting tired. Tired of waiting rooms and wistfulness, tired of life on hold until the magic happened, tired of being the sadness in someone else's story. There is a weight to other people's grief, to other people's wanting. Until those days, I hadn't really known.

Once you land squarely in the land of concern, there is no easy exit. Shrug off the questions, and you're rude, belligerent. Say it doesn't matter, and you're in denial. *Getting better* has a force all of its own, a tidal pull.

I built my armor fast. But there was a chink at the core, a devastating weakness. I can raise a withering brow to strangers. I have learned to skewer with a look. But faced with friends and loved ones? The soft place in my heart trips me every time.

Let me tell you another story, this time from the Gospel of John. It's a story that takes place at the pool of Bethesda in Jerusalem. Bethesda was known as a place of healing power. When the spirit moved, when the waters were stirred by the angel of the Lord, the first person to step within was healed of whatever ailed them. Here's how the tale unfolds, in John 5:5–9:

> One man was there who had been ill for thirty-eight years.
> Jesus saw him lying there and knew that he had been there a long time.
> He said to him, "Do you want to be made well?"
>
> The sick man answered him,
> "Sir, I have no one to put me into the pool when the water is stirred up,
> and while I am making my way,
> someone else steps down ahead of me."
> Jesus said to him, "Stand up, take your mat and walk."
> At once the man was made well,
> and he took up his mat and began to walk.[2]

For thirty-eight years, that nameless man lies by the waters. For thirty-eight years, he lay on inhospitable ground. Thirty-eight years of watching someone else slip into the pool, push ahead in the queue. Thirty-eight years without a friend, a companion. John gives us the count, so we will feel the weight of this man's waiting.

Thirty-eight years for want of a savior.

I'm not the one who's meant to tell you this story. I'm not the one supposed to give it voice. It's been twenty years and more since my last casual step, twenty years since the last summer I spent on feet, the last mountain I climbed, the hike, the woods, the walking. Give my life story to the gospels, and I guess you'd have the perfect stage to unfold another miracle, some dramatic restoration tale. But I'm not interested in playing that part. I am not watching the water. I've turned my eyes toward a different promise.

What does it mean for a man to become well and walk, as though they were one and the same? Writ plain here is the assumption that wholeness comes only through physical restoration, that walking is the pillar of normalcy.

When my own body changed, I did my time in waiting rooms. I lay my body down on butcher paper sheets, while doctors scrutinized and measured and manipulated. I lay on tables and in tubes, where I was filmed and photographed and X-rayed. But the scans came back with no answers forthcoming.

How long, friends? How long was I to wait?

I can pinpoint perfectly the day I understood I was supposed to wait forever. I was sitting on another table, while another doctor prodded at my hip. He'd seen me before and wanted to know how the treatment was progressing. The answer wasn't good. My pain was holding steady, and my stride was melting into memory. My world had shrunk. Ten paces walking, two minutes standing. Everything boiled down to calculation and logistics: if I step here, if I lean there, if I rest now, if I sit down.

A few days before, a beloved friend had scored me a red electric scooter, a lifeline. For the first time in months, I could breathe. For the first time, I could fly. So I told the doc about the scooter, how the wheels were saving my life.

"You shouldn't use that," he interrupted. "You'll get dependent on it."

Twenty-five years later, and I still remember that moment. The flush of heat against my cheeks. The anger. The uncertainty. And then the shaft of shame.

In my doctor's eyes, to use the wheelchair was tantamount to giving up. But I had tasted freedom, and I wasn't going back.

My friend had snagged my scooter from the storeroom of a disability organization that recycled mobility equipment, a place that passes on tech to those of us who need it. One thing nondisabled people rarely get to know is how much of disabled folks' lives hang on the vagaries of our insurance information, how much our freedom depends on doctors' notes and diagnosis codes, and our ability to pay.

I was three years into my life on wheels before my insurance bought me my first wheelchair. I got lucky. Some folks spend their whole disabled lives cruising discards and donations, negotiating with Medicaid or some other unseen arbiter of fortune.

Whenever I tell this story, I think of the powerful testimony of Black disabled activist Angel Miles. "Rather than solely working towards wellness or cure," Miles says, "a less ableist goal would be to work towards freedom. A world free of injustice and health inequalities caused by them."[3]

That's the truth I take from this gospel story. Not the mystery of the healing pool, not the miracle of one man's word, not walking as the pinnacle of wellness, the dream that all of us must share. No, I linger longest with the truth told by the man who waits. *While I am making my way, someone else steps down ahead of me.* So much in my own life has boiled down to this: the privilege of skin color and class and friends with good connections. A few of us get what all of us deserve, while most are left to live for years or for a lifetime off of scraps and leavings. We live in a world without equal access to the waters.

That's the thing I want transformed.

When I first came into disability community, when I first began building the politics and relationships that would anchor me through the decades, it felt crucial to root my own identity in that bold refusal of healing and cure. I was emboldened by the example of Deaf activists, who fight for the recognition and protection of signing-Deaf cultures, even as technology and treatment offer increasing entry into the hearing world. My experience, of course, was not the same. I tried therapies and remedies, but everything cost more than it gained.

And when it yielded nothing? I turned away. I said no to all the earnest empathy and to the world of pining. I could have stayed forever in the land of wanting. Instead, I built a fierce and tender bedrock of radical self-love. When I said no to the pursuit of cure, I said yes to my own bones. I said, "I love this body as she is, right here and now, with no regrets. No miracles necessary."

In a brilliant book on the politics of cure, Eunjung Kim tracks the way that longing for a cure fixes our attention on the past or sets our gaze toward the future.[4] Cure keeps our eyes trained elsewhere: either back then, when I could walk, or on some mythical horizon, when I'll walk again. The fantasy evacuates me from my real-time life, makes everything about before or after. Saying no to cure was a way of saying yes to *now*. To this one luminous life, however it unfolds.

In many disability circles, the choice to embrace a disabled body-mind is bedrock: a stance that powers disability politics and drives disability culture. For many activists, embracing disability goes hand in hand with rejecting mainstream culture's obsession with cure. It's hard to separate the ideology of cure from the notion that disabled bodies are inferior, that disabled minds are defective. In writer and activist Eli Clare's words, "Defectiveness justifies cure and makes it essential."[5] While curative thinking aims to correct or repair a flaw in the person, disability movements diagnose the problem differently: in a world that refuses to accommodate difference.

Saying no to cure was political.

Cure locates the problem in the individual body or mind. It trains us to solve the disconnect between person and world by bringing the disabled person into line with expectations. Because it directs our attention to the repair of the body or the disciplining of the mind, the dominant model of cure overlooks and obscures the transformation of social structures and attitudes. Because it mistakes what is broken, it leaves the architecture of ableism in place.

Don't misunderstand. For disabled people today, access to respectful and competent health care remains a critical and life-threating issue. Disability activist communities have been galvanized by reductions in health care benefits, by insurance denials and other failures of access.[6] People living with chronic illness, chronic fatigue, and long COVID call attention to the way their experiences are often dismissed or denied within medical contexts and advocate for more research and better therapeutic options.[7] People living with chronic depression and mental health disabilities likewise press for safer and more effective pharmaceutical and non-pharmaceutical treatments.

Saying no to cure isn't saying no to care. It's saying no to the way that dominant culture sidelines disabled folks by imagining us tidied up and made well, our bodies and minds no longer an impediment or a stumbling block. It's saying no to a world where moonshot medical research to eradicate disability comes at the expense of the everyday supports that real disabled folks need to survive and thrive.

During my first year on wheels, I lived in a spectacularly inaccessible house with three wide flights of broad carpeted stairs between the entrance and my bedroom. I used to drag my body up those steps, my face inches away from the knobbled carpet. I wanted fiercely to skip out on the shame of it, the pain. But I would have taken an elevator, just as soon as a successful orthopedic intervention. Either one would have felt like a miracle.

Here's the thing I know: Some disabled folks would say yes to cure in a heartbeat if we could get it on our terms. Some of us would shrug if it were offered, and some of us would turn it down. For everyone, the calculus is different. The stakes are not the same. Reflecting on her own bipolar experience, the Reverend Dr. Monica Coleman told me once, "I'd like to know who I am without depression. I'd like to get that chance."[8]

I hold that witness in my heart. I honor it.

Disability comes into our lives in a thousand different ways. Sometimes disability is woven through the fabric of a self, inseparable. Sometimes it arrives like an interloper, a tide that pulls us from our mooring. Sometimes disability enters like a haunting, diagnosis a shiver, a promise not yet felt, a slow, inexorable arriving. Sometimes it comes suddenly: an accident, a gunshot, a stroke, a terrible upheaval. Everything changes in an instant.

During the days I've spent writing this chapter, I've been praying for healing for a beloved friend's parents. Their Hebrew names are printed carefully on a small index card I've propped up against my desktop monitor. Every time I pause, every time I look away from my work, I glance down and see their names.

Reader, I don't know what you carry. Each of our lives is an intricate unfolding, each of our hearts a universe. The world outside wants to pare disability to a single story, to simplify, to discard what doesn't fit. But the truths we know elude these easy tellings.

I place no judgment on your choices, or your dreams.

Most of us get no choice at all. While the Gospels' healing stories speak of sight restored and bodies unbent because of a savior's touch, most of us live far from that world. No one stands beside us with the power to transform our bodies or our minds. And if they do? It's never clean. It always costs.

I'm thinking of a story that disabled dancer Claire Cunningham tells in her show *Thank You Very Much*. She was seven years old, in the hospital, with a little boy in the bed next to hers. The boy was in traction, with nuts and bolts and pins in his legs. When the nurses came each day to tend him, they'd pull the curtain closed for privacy. But curtains do not keep out screams. A few years later, Cunningham's doctor said to her, "We'd like to do a little operation on your feet, a little bit of carpentry. We'll put in nuts and bolts and pins." She asked the doctor, "Will it let me walk better?" And the doctor said, "No. But it'll mean when you grow up, you can wear high heels."[9]

It was the memory that dissuaded her, the memory of someone else's pain. When I hear that story, I ask myself: How do we judge what's needful? How do we assess necessity or hold a balance between the promise and the cost? How do we separate the quest for wellness from the cult of normalcy, the generative intervention from the desire to fashion bodies so they turn out standard sized? Sometimes the surgeons' knives will save your life. Sometimes they will break your bones for nothing more than shoes.

But even here, it's complicated. Let's linger with shoes for a moment, with the shape of desire. I'm thinking of a story the disabled artist Riva Lehrer tells in her luminous memoir *Golem Girl*, about the way she used to cruise the aisles of the shoe store. She tells us how she'd "moon over the patent leather Mary Janes, the Red Ball Jets, the sandals with the teensy straps," while her mother marched her "straight to the clodhoppers at the rear of the store."[10] Lehrer is the veteran of many surgeries. She learned young how to interrogate a doctor's promise, how to count the hidden costs. But the day a surgeon promised her the shoes? It was the lure she couldn't quite refuse.

Don't reduce the calculus to nothing more than medical necessity. Sometimes the shoes are a bone-deep want. Sometimes they are someone else's fantasy, just one more way the blade of patriarchy slips beneath our skin. For Lehrer, the shoes stayed always out of reach. That surgeon sculpted and remade her bones, but he couldn't deliver the promise of those lightweight soles.

Alongside that story, though, let me tell you another. Fast forward a few decades, and Lehrer has turned the childhood curse of orthopedic shoes into an icon of crip belonging. When I first met her at a conference full of luminous disabled folk, I knew her by her shoes: distinctive high-laced boots, black and bold with brilliant laces. Her boots are part of her signature. Brazen. Unabashed. Beautiful.

People ask me all the time: "If there was a cure, wouldn't you take it?" I used to pour my heart into those conversations. I used to try each time to fold the fullness of my one wild life into the breath I was allotted, to pack the world within the space of one word: yes or no.

These days, I refuse the question. I won't have that conversation on the street or in the checkout line. I won't give my heart for someone else's idle curiosity. I've learned to turn away from inquiries that cost you nothing and me everything. But that question crops up everywhere. It's a centerpiece of John's account of the healing at Bethesda, the first words Jesus speak to the man who lies in wait. *Do you want to be made well?*

It's a dangerous ask, or it can be. Wield that question like a knife and it turns disability into an indictment, a failure of faith. *Don't you want to be made well?*

I'm afraid that's the question that the lame man hears, the question that cuts into an already open wound. Notice how he answers when Jesus speaks. He doesn't say yes. He doesn't say no. Instead, he tells the story of how the others push ahead and how he has no one to aid him. He tells that story because he knows he must explain. He's answering the question he has faced a thousand times before. *Why are you still lying here? Why are you still languishing? Don't you* want *to be made well?*

So many healer stories come bound up with this message, blaming the unwell for their failure to be healed. If healing is a sign of faith, a testament to love of God or Jesus, then what becomes of those who never stand and walk again? If prayer can heal, what of the times it goes unanswered? Since those of us who pray are mostly disinclined to place the blame on God, we often turn our doubt toward the other party in this enterprise. What did the sick one do to be refused this healing? Was it a faltering of faith? Some failure of the heart? Some lack within?

Christian and Jewish scriptures have both, at times, colluded in that claim. Near the end of John's story, there's a verse that leaves me cold. It comes after the healing at Bethesda, after the man has taken up his mat and Jesus has slipped silently away. John can't quite leave the story alone. So he tells us this:

Later Jesus found him in the temple and said to him,
"See, you have been made well!
Do not sin any more, so that nothing worse happens to you."[11]

With these final words, John's Jesus makes the claim that disability is a consequence of some wrongdoing, that disability comes about

as punishment for sin. I don't know how else to read this verse but
as a bald-faced assertion that we should blame the man for his own
disablement, that we can trace his lameness back to some fault in his
character, some failure of the heart. If the man hadn't erred, he never
would have found himself by the pool of Bethesda. If only he had
been more careful. If only he had been more kind.

That's what Jesus says?

Now, reader, we may differ here. Jewish tradition does not see Jesus
as messiah or the son of God. I cannot speak to the power of his story
as a Christian would. I know his teaching through the long practice of
spiritual friendship, because I cherish the faith that many of my friends
and loved ones hold. Though I do not pray in his name or follow in
his footsteps, I honor Jesus as a spiritual witness, a man of great good
will. I honor his life in the way I honor the lives of all great souls, not
only for the integrity of his being but for the way his presence in this
world has lit a brilliant flame. He has transformed the lives of thou-
sands. He has opened hearts and been their balm.

So it's a shock to hear that claim. It feels like a betrayal.

The link between disability and sin isn't specific to the Gospels.
This kind of thinking crops up in virtually all religious traditions, and
it's alive and well in the secular world too. Fat activists call attention to
the way so many of us sermonize against fat, the barrage of cultural
messages that treat fatness as a failure of will, a condemnation of
personhood. Disability evokes the same kind of moralizing, as though
attributing disability to some personal fault will isolate the danger. If
sin leads to sickness, can good behavior save you?

Elsewhere in the Gospels, Jesus challenges this very claim. A few
chapters later, John tells how Jesus and his followers come upon a
blind man:

> His disciples asked him,
> "Rabbi, who sinned, this man or his parents,
> that he was born blind?"

Jesus answered,

"Neither this man nor his parents sinned;

he was born blind so that God's works might be revealed in him."[12]

In this story, we glimpse again the powerful assumption that disability is a consequence of sin. The disciples don't ask Jesus if the
connection holds. They take that link for granted. All they want to
know is where to place the blame, how to attribute the wrongdoing.

This time, Jesus refuses the connection. The blind man's birth is
no punishment, he says. Sin has no place in this story. But in refuting
the claim that disability is caused by moral failure, Jesus attributes a
different significance to that man's blindness. His sightless eyes become
a staging ground for other people's faith. His blindness exists in order
to manifest the glory and goodness of God.

Is it any wonder that so many disabled folks have little patience
for religion? That we want out from under these assumptions? I'm
not myself categorically opposed to the notion that human lives reveal God's goodness or God's glory. But to single out disabled folks to
play that role? To paint that meaning on our bodies and our minds
without regard for the ways we tell our own stories? That move makes
instrumental use of disability, turning disabled people into nothing
more than raw material for a sermon or a moral story. We get used, in
the words of Muslim Autistic Noor Pervez, as "props at the pulpit."[13]

Don't try to sell me on this revelation, to paint it as a sea change
in the way disability is understood. Jesus's words to his disciples don't
feel much better than the disciples' claim. Neither one affirms my personhood. Neither paradigm allows me space to breathe. As disabled
Christian Amy Kenny says, "My body is not an empty canvas on which
nondisabled people can paint their fantasies."[14] If there's one thing I
want from preachers and teachers, Jewish and Christian alike, it's to
stop the relentless trafficking in disability. Stop using disabled people's
lives as foils for the edification of the faithful. Disabled folks aren't on
this earth to enlighten or inspire. We weren't born to put other people's

troubles in perspective, to cheer you up, to remind you that it could be worse. We aren't exemplars of courage or cautionary tales. We aren't your heartwarming story, your feel-good click.

All those times disabled people's stories get used to bolster someone else's spirits? There's a name for that in disability circles.

We call it inspiration porn.

In the Gospels, healing is a crucial part of proclaiming Jesus's promise. When Jesus transforms the bodies of the lame and restores sight to the blind, it becomes a visceral demonstration of his power and presence: proof positive that Jesus is, as the Gospels claim, the son of God and savior. Miracles fueled Jesus's movement. Healing galvanized a crowd. In the Gospels, to be healed isn't simply a personal matter, an individual transformation. It becomes a religious experience, a matter of faith, a coming to conviction.

Healing is part of the way that Jesus grew a movement. The healing stories were a powerful part of how his story spread, across the Galilee and throughout Judea, then more widely, through the Roman Empire and beyond. For the Gospels, healing isn't simply proclamation. It's also provocation. How someone responds to the healing miracles becomes a key litmus test of whether a person resonates with Jesus and his movement. So it should come as no surprise that the Gospels' healing stories are intimately interwoven with high-stakes questions of belief and belonging, that they are some of the sharpest places of polemic against Jews who are not moved by Jesus's message.

And today? The Gospels' stories about healing aren't just weaponized against disabled folks. These same stories of faith and cure also get turned against Jews and Judaism, often in the very same breath. The deeper I dive into these healing stories, the more I've come to see how ableism and anti-Judaism interlock. We cannot defang one kind of harm without also recognizing and resisting the other.

To take up this work, it helps to know something about history—to recognize how and why the Gospels' writers used the healing stories as a linchpin for defining Christian identity and for distinguishing Christians from Jews. From our vantage point today, we tend to look back on Jesus's life and identify those who believed as Christians. But the history of how Jews and Christians came to be two different religions is vastly more complex. The Jesus movement began within the Jewish community. Some Jews followed his teachings; others did not. Some Jews saw him as the messiah, the one long promised by God. Others did not. It will take centuries before the split between Jews and Christians is clear and certain. Three hundred years after Jesus's crucifixion, many Christian monastics in Egypt and Palestine still observed the Jewish Sabbath on Saturday, along with a second holy day on Sunday in celebration of Christ's resurrection, a fact that provoked the ire and frustration of the Christian writer Eusebius, who campaigned hard against what he saw as utter heresy.[15]

Jesus was a Jew. He lived and died embedded within Jewish community, teaching Torah as a Jew, preaching as a Jew, working for justice and for kindness as a Jew. Jesus argued over tradition as a Jew, debated the law as a Jew, taught compassion as a Jew. When I read his words as the Gospels record them, I recognize him as a man whose spiritual insight has deep roots in Jewish tradition.

But the Gospels' writers aren't looking to emphasize continuity. They're invested in distinction. They're looking to make a difference. For them, healing wasn't just an occasion to express religious conviction. It was also a powerful catalyst for controversy.

When Jesus heals? The Gospels' writers almost always fashion "the Jews" as critics and naysayers. When Jesus heals the woman bent over, and when he tells the man at the pool of Bethesda to pick up his mat and walk, both acts provoke the ire of the synagogue leaders, who castigate Jesus for healing on the Sabbath. In Jewish practice, Shabbat is a day of rest, a day of letting go of labor. It's a day of honoring the world that is, a day of desisting from all our building and creating, from the hubris of human transformation. When Jesus heals on the Sabbath, he enters into a long-standing Jewish debate over the limits and bounds of Shabbat practice.

In Luke 13, the leader of the synagogue protests, "There are six days on which work ought to be done; come on those days and be cured, and not on the Sabbath day." But Jesus isn't moved. "You hypocrites!" he says. "Does not each of you on the Sabbath untie his ox or his donkey from the manger, and lead it away to give it water? Ought not this woman, a daughter of Abraham whom Satan bound for eighteen long years, be set free from this bondage on the Sabbath day?"[16]

For many readers today, this text seems like an argument between Jews and Christians, a moment of conflict between two traditions. But that's an anachronistic move. This kind of debate is a familiar practice among Jews, a way of taking seriously a sacred charge not just to keep the law but to interpret it. Rabbinic Jewish texts are built on arguments like these, arguments that grapple with the ethics of right action, that ask us to consider how to put our values into practice, how to live our obligations to each other and to God.

Luke's story paints the law in caricature. If all you knew of Jewish law stemmed from this moment in the Gospels, I imagine you might think of law as bludgeon or as relic, as hidebound cruelty, a blunt instrument of authority that will not yield or budge. But that's a narrow view of law, one that fails to hear its heart. Law is love, or it can be. Law is care. Or in our hands, it might become so.

It's a cornerstone commitment of Jewish interpretation that the purpose of the law is to serve life. Healing on Shabbat? Permissible, when life is at stake. But for a chronic condition, a familiar reality? That's the question that drives the debate in the Jesus story. Whenever I read Luke's account, I imagine the way Jesus's parents might have shaken their heads, half with pride, half with chagrin. "Is the rest of the week no good for healing, son? Do you have to do your thing *today*?"

In truth, I have no way of knowing what was in the healer's heart. Did Jesus want to spark debate? Did he orchestrate the scene and wait until the time was right so he could force the question? If so, it would be well within the bounds of how Jews argue over law: find a test case, raise the stakes, and probe the borders of permissibility. But

I tend to think it's the writers of the Gospels who are drawn to drama and controversy. They use these stories to fashion a split, to force the reader to take sides.

To tell you what I mean, I want to pick up the story of Jesus's encounter with the man born blind, a story that appears in John 9. It's a convoluted story, one of longest and most complex of the Gospels' accounts of healing, and it makes plain the way that healing gets intertwined with anti-Jewish sentiment.

In the first scene of our story, Jesus and his disciples come upon a man born blind. While the disciples ask their question about *who sinned*, Jesus turns in a different direction. Jesus speaks to the man, describing himself as "the light of the world." He spits on the ground and lifts the moist mud up to the man's blind eyes and then he tells him to wash in the pool of Siloam. The man goes and washes and when he returns, he can see.

The neighbors are flummoxed. Those who had seen him before as a beggar asked each other if this was indeed the same man. Some say yes, and others say no. It's a moment that many disabled folks will find familiar. We become known by our white canes or our wheelchairs, the distinctive markers of our disability. But the specifics of who we are as individuals turn strangely interchangeable. I once traveled to Norway and was greeted effusively by a passing car of strangers, "recognized" in an unfamiliar country as the one wheelchair user I guess they know. In my own neighborhood, I go incognito if I change my tech. When I switch from wheelchair to scooter? The only folks who greet me are the dogs.

In John 9, the scene unfolds like this:

The neighbors and those who had seen him before as a beggar
began to ask, "Is this not the man who used to sit and beg?"
Some were saying, "It is he."
Others were saying, "No, but it is someone like him."
He kept saying, "I am the man."
But they kept asking him, "Then how were your eyes opened?"

> He answered, "The man called Jesus made mud, spread it on my eyes,
> and said to me, 'Go to Siloam and wash.'
> Then I went and washed and received my sight."[17]

As the debate continues, the neighbors bring the once-blind man to the Pharisees. As any biblical historian will tell you, the Pharisees are one of several different identifiable groups in the early Jewish world. "Pharisee" is a loaded term in contemporary culture. Most folks who use the term today use it as an insult, a history that dates back to its use in the Gospels. To call someone a Pharisee is to call them a hypocrite, a close-minded person who chooses law over love. The Pharisees appear in the Gospels as rule-bound bigots, whose miserly approach to matters of faith has them turn away goodness and kindness, generosity and grace.

It's no objective report. Amy-Jill Levine, a prominent Jewish scholar of the New Testament, argues that the Gospels' portrait of the Pharisees is not a historically accurate account.[18] The writers of the Gospels are invested in growing the Jesus movement, and the Pharisees are their primary rivals. The Gospels treat the Pharisees the way modern-day politicians tar their opponents, accusing them of all the things they know their base will hate. Facts are fungible. Hyperbole is everything.

But hyperbole has consequences.

The figure of the Pharisee is steeped in anti-Jewish stereotype. The Pharisees are recognized as the precursors to rabbinic Judaism, and in the Gospels, the Pharisees often appear as representatives of Jewish authority. When the Gospels castigate the Pharisees, those notions get transferred all too easily to the Jewish community as a whole. Bound by tradition? Sticklers over detail? Legalistic? Oppositional? Cruel? As Levine explains, "We are heirs of two millennia of negative stereotypes of Pharisees and, by extension, of Jews."[19]

Notice what happens next. John 9:18 reads, "The Jews did not believe that he had been blind and had received his sight until they called the parents of the man who had received his sight."

It's a curious verse, because as far as I can tell, everyone in this story is Jewish. Jesus, the disciples, the neighbors, the parents, and the man himself. John deploys "Jew" not as a marker of heritage, ethnicity, or religious belonging, but as a negative descriptor. "Jew" becomes a stand-in for hostility, for belligerence, for refusal to believe. A few verses later, the rhetoric gets sharper. When the parents are called before the tribunal, they profess ignorance. They say they have no knowledge of how their son regained his sight. John 9:22 explains: "His parents said this because they were afraid of the Jews; for the Jews had already agreed that anyone who confessed Jesus to be the Messiah would be put out of the synagogue." What's lost in this telling? The parents *are* Jews, and so is the son. Once again, the term "the Jews" applies only to the cruel authorities, not to the family who fears losing their place within their synagogue community.

While his parents equivocate, the man born blind speaks the truth of his experience. He testifies, telling them how Jesus gave him sight. The elders call Jesus a sinner, and they drive out the man who defends him. Afterward, when Jesus finds the man again, the man declares his faith and trust. Then Jesus lifts the experience of blindness and of sight into a final teaching. John 9:39 reads:

Jesus said,
"I came into this world for judgment
so that those who do not see may see,
and those who do see may become blind."

In this verse, blindness as metaphor is on powerful display. Blindness doesn't function here as a neutral description of a bodily reality. It denotes those who fail to comprehend the truth. Disability becomes shorthand for describing spiritual insufficiency. The metaphor expands the meaning of disability so that it no longer speaks solely of specific bodily identities. The category "blind" expands to encompass anyone who fails to measure up to the speaker's religious ideal.

But notice what that sleight of hand takes as a given. The metaphor takes for granted that disability is a negative category. Without that baseline assumption, the metaphor itself falls apart. Blind only works as an insult if we all agree that blindness is undesirable, that blind people are less astute than sighted ones.

The metaphorical use of blindness is so deeply embedded in our cultural lexicon that it's almost impossible to find words for blindness that *don't* signify spiritual incapacity. Darla Schumm, a blind scholar of disability and religion, points out that the phrase "blind Christian" is practically a contradiction in terms. Christians, according to the metaphor, are the ones who have by definition shed their blindness and embraced the truth of Christ. To be a Christian is to see the light.[20]

Not so, when it comes to Jews.

The trope of the blind Jew has a long and difficult history. In medieval Europe, many cathedrals and churches boasted a pair of large-scale statues of Ecclesia and Synagoga, allegorical representations of Church and Synagogue. Both are portrayed as beautiful women, but Ecclesia wears a crown and holds the chalice of Christ. She stands with her head held high, gazing out benevolently upon the people. Synagoga, by contrast, has a bent head and downcast eyes. Many sculptors endow her with symbols meant to evoke the replacement of her law with a new order. Her crown slips from her head; the tablets of the law fall from her hands. But her most iconic feature? A blindfold, meant to evoke the sightless eyes of the Jews, a spiritual blindness, a staunch refusal to see and embrace Christian truth.

It is a risk to speak of this. There is a hard history that binds us, a history of Christian violence, of forced conversions and pogroms, a history of Talmuds burned and bodies brutalized, a history of Jews forced from home and made to wander, a history of Jewish pain and bitter anger. A history of blood.

But I do not think that history is destiny, that Christians and Jews must be forever locked into this story. I believe we can unbind these bitter chains. I believe that you and I can do the work to lay a deeper trust between us, to forge a different future.

May I tell you one more thing?

Among disability theologians today, it's become common to distinguish healing from cure. Kathy Black argues that while preachers and believers alike tend to use these terms interchangeably, there is a world of difference between them. Cure points to the elimination of disease, or at least the eradication of its symptoms. But healing? Healing has a much wider valence. We speak of *healing* presence, recognize *healing* moments, and understand healing as a process: a movement toward greater wholeness, well-being, comfort, and ease.[21] This distinction between healing and cure affirms that healing can unfold for us, regardless of whether we experience physical change in our bodies or minds. It decouples healing from a specific medical outcome. And it allows us to call for the promise of healing without insisting on the eradication of disability. Healing can happen for all of us.

But what does healing look like? There's a powerful resonance here between this call for healing and the vision of disability movements. Some Christian preachers have begun to use the healing stories to echo the call for social transformation, shifting the focus from broken bodies to broken societies. Rather than focus narrowly on the physical fact of cure, this understanding of healing affirms that the "problem" of disability lies not with our bodies but with disability stigma and with ableism. Rather than focus on the physical act of healing, these readings draw our attention to the social transformation Jesus inspires.

It's a powerful message. But it also comes with a danger. If Jesus becomes the great revolutionary? If he's the one who brings a radical new social order into being? What does he transform?

The Jews.

All too often, the message of social change and radical solidarity with disabled people ends up casting Judaism as the oppressor. Jews and Jewish tradition get positioned as a bitter, repressive force—the "old order" that must pass away so that Jesus can usher in a new age of kindness, compassion, and liberation. In affirming Jesus as the symbol of all that is good and just and right, Levine explains, Christian preachers and teachers have often cast "his Jewish background as the epitome of all that is wrong with the world." To make this contrast, Levine observes, they have tended "to map onto Jesus everything good and onto Jesus' Jewish context everything bad."[22] Rather than recognizing Jesus's commitment to justice as a part of his Jewish tradition, rather than hearing in his call to liberation an echo of the Hebrew prophets and a Jewish commitment to transformation of the world, Jesus becomes a radical exception. But Jesus, Levine reminds us, does not have be utterly unique in order to be profound.

Think back to the scene in John 9 when the disciples ask Jesus who sinned, the man born blind or his parents? Whenever I recount that story, someone in the audience is quick to explain how Jesus's words are revolutionary. In their telling, the disciples' assumption that disability is a sign of sin becomes a widespread Jewish belief, one that Jesus rejects and transforms. But that's a dangerous misunderstanding of the text. As we've already seen, the association between disability and sin surfaces in both Christian and Jewish traditions. When Christians push those undesirable ideas away by scripting them solely onto Judaism, they disown a crucial part of the work. I want Christian and Jewish communities alike to contend with the way our texts and traditions have been used to do harm to disabled folks. I want us both to do the long, hard work of reckoning. I want us both to take up the mantle of interpretation, the responsibility to repair. I want us both to strengthen and build upon the resources in each of our traditions that align with principles of disability justice. The work of liberation belongs to *all* of us.

Each of our traditions pulse with potential: to draw us toward the source of life and love, to draw us with humility toward the work of justice and generosity. I want to live in a world where the beauty and power of the Christian promise isn't built on the backs of my beloved community, where Jesus's stirring call to social transformation doesn't depend on turning my kin into caricature. I want to live in a world where Christians listen to and love the riotous diversity of contemporary Jewish practice, where Jews aren't frozen in time, cast as relics from the days of Jesus. I want to live in a world where Jews and Christians are both invested in each other's flourishing, a world where we commit to helping each other thrive.

What does it mean to flourish? What does it mean to thrive?

To consider that question through the lens of disability, I want to turn back again to the story of Bethesda, to the encounter that happens by the healing waters. When Jesus bends toward the man who waits, Jesus asks, "Do you want to be made well?"

The question changes if we admit we do not know what wellness means. Can the man be well even if he never walks again? I know some folks who are traveling that road. I remember the day I understood that health and wholeness were not dependent on driving out my disability, the day I understood I would *be well* with wheels.

The story of Bethesda takes a different tack. Whatever else unfolds by those stirred up waters, the healing that Jesus brings about includes a transformation of the body, a restoration of the physical capacity to stand, to walk.

But the moment that matters most? For me, it's not the moment when the man lifts up his mat or the moment when he leaves the pool behind. It's the moment when Jesus offers him a choice, when he lays out the question.

When Jesus asks the man by the waters whether he wants to be healed, I take him at his word. I hear him say, *Your wishes matter.* I hear him pause. I hear him check himself. Rather than assuming he can identify candidates for healing at a glance, Jesus asks. He pushes back presumption. His words affirm the disabled man's agency at a time when circumstance has narrowed his choices. The question becomes a request for permission. "Do you wish this healing? I will do nothing without your consent."

We are so rarely asked.

Yet the question itself is not enough if the answer is a foregone conclusion. What remains absent in the Gospels, as in so many religious and secular portrayals of disability that emphasize the promise of healing, is the robust recognition that disability does not foreclose a good life. We need to see that, to know that, if we want to make the question matter. To grapple with consent in a way that is true, we must ask in a way that makes "no" a viable answer.

When Christian theologian John Hull became blind, he came to read the Bible with newfound insight. In his "Open Letter to a Sighted Savior," he offers a powerful account of how the Gospels' presumption of blindness as a negative condition fails to speak to his own spiritual need. "On an individual basis," Hull writes to Jesus, "you are sensitive and tactful towards blind people, and while acknowledging their condition of economic deprivation, you insist upon their inclusion. Nevertheless, you did not include a blind person in your closest circle."[23] That absence cuts, especially because Jesus so often interacts with blind folk. Especially because Jesus so often transforms blindness. For Hull, it is not enough to offer hope only by restoring people's sight. Hull wants a savior who can be "a companion during blindness,"[24] a scripture that does not demand we leave disability behind.

This, too, is my desire. I want the Healer to travel with a blind disciple, a beloved friend who knows disability from the inside. Just once, I want the one who can give sight to affirm that sight is not the only way. And when he offers healing? Just once, I want someone to decline. Not in disgust and not in rage but with a gentle explanation that there is no need. Just once, I want to see someone turn away from the water's edge, to leave behind the waiting. Just once, I want the limp to linger. I want the Healer to stay his hand.

I want a story where the man stays blind.

CHAPTER NINE

Isaac's Blindness

The Complexity of Trust

One of the best known stories of disability in the Hebrew Bible is the story of Isaac's blindness. Isaac is the father of two men, twins who come into this world mere moments apart. As he grows old, as his eyes dim, Isaac prepares to grant his blessing to one and only one son so that his eldest will go forth secure in his inheritance. Isaac calls his older son, Esau, to his side. He asks his firstborn to hunt and prepare for him a favorite dish so that he may eat the fruit of his son's hands and grant him the blessing before he dies. But Isaac's wife, Rebecca, overhears their conversation. She takes advantage of the moment to advance the fortunes of her other son, Jacob, the one she loves best. Her instructions are precise. Jacob should fetch two goat kids from the flock so that she can prepare Isaac a dish, and he should take it to his father, wearing the clothes of his brother and the skins of slain animals.

When Rebecca first lays out her plan, Jacob protests that the scheme will never work. Despite being twins, the brothers are very different. Esau is a bold hunter, a rugged man of the fields, while Jacob is more inclined to stay close to the tents. "My brother is a hairy man," Jacob says, "and I am smooth-skinned."[1] Surely Isaac won't need sight to discern the difference between his sons!

But Rebecca reassures him. If Isaac discovers the ruse, if he curses his younger son instead of blessing him, Rebecca will bear the curse herself. So Jacob does all that she asks. For a single moment, when Jacob comes before his father, it seems his voice might betray the truth of his identity. But Isaac does not give credence to what he hears. Instead, he reaches out to touch, and he's fooled by the hides that Rebecca has wrapped around the hands of her youngest child. "The voice is the voice of Jacob," Isaac says, in Genesis 27:22. "Yet the hands are the hands of Esau."

A different set of clothes, a scrap of goat skin? Is this all it takes to assume the semblance of another, once the father is blind?

Our text presents Isaac as fooled by the barest of effort. It isn't that Rebecca's scheme is so good or that Jacob has a true rogue's heart. It's that without sight, Isaac seems to have no senses on which he can rely. He does not trust the testimony of his ears. And when he tries to rely on touch? His own hands betray him.

Only later, once the blessing has been irrevocably bestowed, does Isaac realize that he has given his patrimony to the wrong son. After Jacob departs from his father's side, Esau returns from his hunt. He, too, prepares a dish, and he brings it before Isaac. When he asks his father for the blessing, the moment is charged with pathos. "Who are you?" Isaac asks. And when Esau answers, Isaac begins to tremble. He tells Esau the terrible truth: that his brother has come before him, that Isaac has already given the blessing, and that Jacob will remain blessed. Esau weeps, in bitterness and pain, with the cracked open voice of a brokenhearted child.[2]

Let me tell all the things I hate about this story.

Let's start with the meaning it scripts upon the disabled body. Isaac is a tragic figure—or a fool. Blindness makes him helpless. He is incompetent, a bumbler, a man who is susceptible to every trick in the book. He cannot even tell the difference between his own two sons.

When I said I wanted a blind man in the book, this wasn't what I meant.

Isaac's blindness is a prop, a way to propel the story forward. It's because of Isaac's blindness that Jacob, the underdog of the Genesis story, can overturn the misfortune of his birth and escape the bitter lot of the second son. It's because of Isaac's blindness that our hero can seize the blessing God intends for him, fulfilling the prophecy God had granted to his mother.

Blindness makes great plot. But the blindness on display in Genesis has little to do with the actual embodied experience of blind folk. It holds none of the keen attention to sound, touch, or texture that I might expect from a blind narrator, none of the discernment or the ingenuity I encounter among blind communities. It reads like caricature, like a sighted person's nightmare of sightlessness as utter incapacity.[3]

I could stop here. I could leave you thinking I dislike this story because it gets disability wrong. It does, of course. It does. But there's another story to tell, a story that comes closer to the bone. Whenever I read Genesis 27, I am confronted with Isaac's inability to manage as a blind man, his failure to perform disability well. I come to the verses where Jacob stands before him, when the son allows his father to feel his wrapped up hands, when the son lets the father breathe in the earthy scent of his stolen clothes. I come to the verses where Isaac hesitates, and then I'm drawn again into his choice to trust.

For sure, I'm angry about Jacob and Rebecca's deception. I hate the way Isaac is manipulated, the way he is used. For sure, I'm angry about the lies, about the way his family takes advantage of his blindness. But beneath that easy anger, I need to tell you something else. I'm also angry about Isaac's incompetence, about the fact that he fails to discover the ruse.

This is one of the ways that ableism cuts against my heart. It has made me demand perfection of myself and other disabled folks. It has taught me to allow myself no failure, to afford myself no weakness.

How can I trace what this demand has cost me? Some years ago, I decided to run a benefit race. It was a strictly amateur affair. Most folks who took part considered the run a fundraising challenge, not an athletic event. Not me. I trained for weeks, building up my stamina, taking the measure of my pace. I scouted the course. I planned my route. Why?

Because I knew that out there on the street, I wouldn't be just any other runner. I'd be the woman in the wheelchair. Maybe the rest of you can afford to dial it in. But if I flagged before the finish, if I dragged myself across the line, miserable and wheezing, I'd give credence to the doubters. I'd make us all look bad. I'd be subjected to some stranger's saccharine assessment of my performance, all those patronizing compliments with their backhanded sting: "So good of you to get out, dear. At least you tried!"

Excellence became my shield, my protection against pity. But it makes a brittle armor, and the cost of carrying it is high.

The pressure to prove the haters wrong is hardly unique to disability. It's something a lot of minoritized folks know, the urgency of excellence, the way it seems to promise some protection, even while it fails in practice. But there's something quite distinctive about the way this pressure plays out for many people with disabilities. We often have times in our lives where our bodies or minds change, where our old strategies prove insufficient, where we need to learn new tech, new tools, new modes of adaptation. At those moments, we're acutely vulnerable to the undertow of ableism.

Acquiring a disability or experiencing significant disability change often means a period of adjustment, a period of devising new ways of being in the world. When I first got my electric scooter, for example, I was a terrible driver. I got stuck backing out of elevators, with the alarm beeping all the while. I once wedged myself between bathroom stalls in a public restroom, and three women I'd never met before offered useless advice while I slowly, painstakingly eased my way out. After I started using a manual wheelchair, there were a whole host of other hacks to learn. Over time, I devised my favorite strategies for carrying luggage and discovered exactly how much water I could safely carry in a cup pinned between my knees. I watched other wheelchair users, checking out how others in the club made their way. I leveled up through trial and error, through experimentation, through ingenuity and creativity over time.

I think of those early days when I read Isaac's story, those days when my walking life had crumbled beneath me but I hadn't yet acquired my expertise with wheels. Is that the moment when we're seeing Isaac? Does this story capture him in the awkward time before he learns the ropes of being blind?

If it were me, I'd want to blot those memories from the book. I had no patience for my learning, no tenderness toward my fumbles. Some of it was pure frustration. When my body changed, I stared down the sudden imposition of incapacity, the loss of things I used to do without a second thought. But some of it was a different kind of fear.

If I was going to be disabled, I wanted to be smooth. Elegance offered some thin protection from the weight of the world's disdain. I knew it wouldn't spare me the stares or the scorn, but I thought it might blunt the worst of the blow. I had taken ableism's measure, and I figured speed and skill might save me from the knife.

Let me tell you what I mean. When my insurance finally agreed to buy me a fancy set of wheels, I sought out a rigid-frame wheelchair. Unlike the common sort of wheelchair that folds in the middle and jiggles a little with every bump in the road, a rigid-frame chair is solid at the core. To stow the chair in a standard car, the back snaps down and the wheels pop off with a quick-release twist. It's a sweet arrangement, and a much smoother, gentler ride. Only problem was, I'm no genius with mechanics.

They delivered my wheelchair, and I fell in love. But then I realized I couldn't work the release. It wasn't a matter of physical limitations. These days, they make quick-release wheels for folks with impairments far more significant than mine. This was an ordinary incapacity, a very familiar story. Faced with a twist of the wrist and certain kind of pull, I had a tough time working the mechanism.

There are a whole lot of folks in this world who can afford to bumble a bit with their keys, for whom the inability to work the car radio is a kind of charming endearment. Not me. I can feel the press of seconds hot against my skin: how long a taxi driver would grant me before slamming the door in disgust, how long I could take before becoming a burden, before becoming a cog in a fast-paced machine. I practiced, over and over, until I had it all down cold.

Of course, it didn't spare me. Some drivers still pull away before I open the door. Mockers still mock, and haters still hate. But the lesson of excellence is deeply ingrained. This is one of the ways that ableism scours me: this relentless pressure to be competent, to give no credence to naysayers, to have it all together, always.

Consider how the Genesis story changes if we read it as merely the beginning of Isaac's life with blindness. What if this scene were the catalyst for Isaac to grow into disability experience, to hone the tricks of the trade, to develop expertise and acuity as a blind man? If I were given free rein to spin out this fantasy, I'd imagine Isaac with a friend in blindness, a mentor, someone who has traveled the road and knows its contours. But even if he were alone, I'm sure he would have learned to find his way.

We don't usually consider this possibility because we're trained by narrative and culture alike to imagine disability as the end of the road. But there's a curious fact tucked into the chronology of Isaac's story, one that most of us miss. Most readers think of Genesis 27 as Isaac's deathbed scene, his final hour. The arc of the narrative guides us here. Isaac himself introduces the theme of impending death. "I am old now," he says in Genesis 27:2, "and I do not know the day I will die." As the chapter unfolds, Isaac passes his blessing on to the next generation. His trickster son now stands at the center of the Genesis story.

But Isaac lives another twenty years or more.

I think it's no coincidence that most readers miss that detail. All too often, disability gets imagined as though it were the end of life. Midrash Tanhuma is blunt in its assessment: "One who is blind is like the dead."[4] According to the Bible's own chronology, Isaac has decades before he passes from this earth.[5] But the scene that describes his blindness is that last episode told from his perspective. Once sight slips from his eyes, he will no longer be the agent of his own story. The midrash makes the logic plain: to be blind is to have no future.

In popular culture, the link between disability and death is profound. Consider the fate of most characters who become disabled on screen or on the novelist's page. More often than not? Before the final scene rolls, they're either healed or dead. To keep a disabled character alive on stage, on screen, or in the world? To keep their disability intact, without neutralizing its power? It's the rarest of choices, a thing we almost never get to see.

I'm thinking of a beloved character in a long-running fantasy series who acquired a disability near the end of a novel, one that would have real consequences for her character. I was shocked but also eager. I wanted to see how she grappled with genuine limits, with the loss of physical prowess that had shaped her character thus far. I wanted to see how the other characters responded, how her injury and its aftermath got negotiated within the complex tenor of their relationships. I wanted to see her come to terms with difference and to watch others recognize that her valor hadn't ended. But I shouldn't have gotten my hopes up.

She was dead before the end of the next book.

In another novel, postapocalyptic this time, the brother of one of the main characters is a wheelchair user. At first I thought it was going to be okay. The brothers hole up together, hunkering down. The main character has stockpiled toilet paper and provisions. They're in the apartment, and I allow myself to believe the author is committed to the guy on wheels, that we're invested in his story, that he matters. When the time comes for our two characters to venture out into the dystopian streets, the brother doesn't know how they'll make it in this harsh new world, how his sibling will manage in the wild. But the disabled guy has already thought it through. He kills himself to give his brother a chance to survive.

It makes me rage. It makes me want to weep. I suppose I could let it go if it were just a matter of artistic license. But the message is everywhere: in fiction, in film, in debates about public policy. Advocates for physician-assisted suicide bank on the public assumption that disability is an unlivable life, an appropriate reason that people want to kill themselves. While individual disabled folks hold a range of different views about autonomy and choice in end-of-life decision making, disability advocates have fiercely contested the underlying assumption that disabled lives are not worth living. We know ourselves already at the precipice of risk: that our lives are already judged too difficult, too burdensome. How easy might it be to figure our deaths a kind of benevolent act, a greater good, a kindness for all involved?

Disability is the thing most people despise about aging, the thing that most of us fear. It's not growing old that folks resent; it's that age goes hand in hand with impairment.

Isaac grows old, and his eyes begin to dim. It's a familiar reality, a fact that makes disability a near-universal experience for those who live long enough. In disability circles, it used to be commonplace for activists to refer to nondisabled folks as "temporarily able-bodied." Whether through age or accident, we will all eventually lose physical strength and sensory capacity. Nondisabled folks like to treat their ability status as secure and stable. But the truth is plain. Even if you aren't born disabled, even if you haven't become disabled over the course of your lives, you'll likely acquire disability as you age.

It's a simple fact, a shared experience of flesh. But the desire to push it back, to hold the truth at bay is everywhere. Whether it's anti-aging eye creams or adventure advertising, we're bombarded with products and services that sell us an illusion: that aging happens only to the unwary, the unlucky, or the unprepared.

Consider another famous biblical example of aging: that moment when Moses climbs the mountain for the last time. Deuteronomy 34:7 describes Moses's final days as days unmarked by disability. Moses was 120 when he died, but the text hastens to tell us that his vigor was undiminished, "his eyes were undimmed."

It's a Jewish custom to greet friends' and loved ones' birthdays with a wish for those 120 years, but the unspoken implication is clear. May those final years be like the years of Moses, rather than the years of

Isaac. Live long *without* disability, lest becoming old become a curse instead of a blessing.

But I wonder what we've missed by lifting up this image of the elder Moses as robust in every way, in refusing to imagine him as touched by the years. I ask myself: Must he stay Superman until the very end? Must he do it all alone? I hold a different set of questions in my heart. Who looked after Moses when he tired? When his bones ached? When all he wanted was to lay himself down, in the sunlight in springtime, to savor the warmth against his face, to close his eyes?

When I read over the Bible's account of Moses's last days, I let myself dream. What if we were not invested in this notion that the hero's strength never waned, that he was vigorous and fresh even in his final days? What if the Bible had let Moses become old? Would it have been Joshua, his chosen successor, who helped him up the mountain, who settled him at the vista and then backed a few steps away to give him privacy for one more whisper with his God? Or would it be a person whose name we do not know, someone who tended Moses as he aged, who bathed him with warm water and a soft cloth, who washed his hair and cut his food, the small and intimate gestures of care?

I think of the love we lose by snipping this end from the story. I think of the doors we close by setting ourselves up to imagine that the only way to age well is to remain strong and independent in our elder years, our body robust, our mind sharp as a tack.

What would we need in order to trust that we could rely on another's care?

I think of the gentling it would take, the inner work we'd need to do. A loss of strength often demands a widening of the heart, a release of attachment to the way things used to be. But it isn't simply a spiritual change we need; it's also a political one. We'd need a better system of providing care, of protecting those who give it and receive it. We'd need to ensure that those who did the raw physical work of washing, dressing, lifting, and turning were honored and paid for their labor and their love, that they were paid well enough to tend their own bodies, that they weren't forced to endure brutal hours or unsafe work conditions.

We'd need to ensure that access to care wasn't a matter of good fortune or a flush bank account, that it didn't rely on family systems already stretched to the brink. We'd need to plan for it, not just individually but as a society. What if we lived in a world where care was bedrock, where we could trust, truly, that we would receive what we need?

Trust is at the heart of Isaac's story, a trust that is often betrayed. To tell you what I mean, we have to go back to a different story, a story from Isaac's childhood, a story about growing up in the shadow of his father's towering spiritual life, his stark commitment to his God. Isaac is one of the three ancient Hebrew patriarchs, the son of the great spiritual seeker Abraham. Jewish tradition honors Abraham as the first to hear God's call. He leaves his homeland and his father's house, refashioning his life in accord with divine promise. Abraham makes a covenant with God, the covenant that anchors Jewish fidelity and spiritual commitment. And in return for his loyalty? God promises him as many descendants as the stars.[6]

Isaac's life was indelibly shaped by his father's spiritual striving. One fateful day, when Isaac was still young, he and his father went together up to the summit of Mount Moriah.[7] And at the top of that mountain? Abraham drew a knife, prepared to sacrifice Isaac in obedience to what he thought was God's command.

God intervenes, calling off the sacrifice at the last second. An angel's voice cries out in protest and in pain. A ram appears, a substitute. Isaac is spared the cut of the blade, unbound from the altar. Somehow the man and boy make their way back home. But the scar remains, in myth and in memory.

Through the centuries, Christian and Jewish interpreters alike have praised Abraham as a spiritual hero, a man who proved willing to surrender to God so deeply that he would give up even his beloved child. In Søren Kierkegaard's famous telling, Abraham's act signals the deepest faith—faith that God will intervene, faith that God will save.[8]

I cannot countenance that tale. Like many Jews today, I regard this story as one we must tell and retell to remind us of a great ethical failure: a moment when Abraham should have protested against authority. I read this story and I think of all the ways that humans have picked up that knife, all the ways we have rationalized cruelty. I think of what it means to refuse to follow orders, even if they come wrapped in the voice of God.[9]

And Isaac? When I think of Isaac, I think of how it feels to be a survivor of intimate violence, to have been betrayed by those you trusted. I think of what it means to make a life *after* brutality. To insist that we aren't only the sum of the worst that's been done to us.

I think of Isaac after his innocence shatters, his eyes drawn again and again to the distant horizon, to the peak of the mountain. I think of Isaac, the quiet one, the one who learned to watch and wait. I think of Isaac, slowly finding his way to the pulse of his own breath, to a different kind of trust. I think of Isaac, standing in the field at twilight, praying in the language of silence and shadow.[10]

The trauma of that moment on the mountain lives for a lifetime.

A famous midrash traces the onset of Isaac's blindness to the very hour when he was bound. The textual hook for this idea rests on an ambiguity of Hebrew grammar in the first verse of Genesis 27. Most English translations begin like this: "When Isaac was old and his eyes were too dim to see." But the original Hebrew text could mean either that Isaac's capacity for sight dimmed or that he became blind because of something that he saw. His eyes dimmed *from seeing*. Our midrash takes the second tack, asking what Isaac saw that caused his eyes to change. One of the proposals? Genesis Rabbah 65:10 reads:

At the hour that Abraham our father
bound his son upon the altar,
the angels wept. . . .
The tears from their eyes fell into his,
and they left traces in his eyes.[11]

The midrash ties Isaac's blindness back to that moment on the mountain, to the terror of his binding. But it isn't so much what Isaac sees as what the angels witness. The angels watch the father prepare to sacrifice the son, and they cry out. Their tears fall into Isaac's eyes and cloud his vision. The angels' grief leaves its mark on Isaac's sight.

It matters to me that the angels weep. I've always recoiled from a straight reading of Genesis 21, in which God tests Abraham's faith by telling him to kill his child. I refuse to picture God as catalyst or goad to the abusive father, as coconspirator to brutality. Every year I read this story, and I reaffirm: the voice that Abraham hears, that tells him to betray his child? To violate trust? To prize faith or principle over bonds of responsibility or love? That is not God.

I read this story as a warning, a reminder to beware the fantasy of clear instructions, the brutality that follows when we think ourselves compelled by God. We have seen this tragedy, have spooled it out a thousand times in politics and in the private dramas of our lives: the knife held against the neighbor's neck or plunged into the child. I do not need a text to tell me it is right to weep, to rage, to demand a different answer to this age-old story. But I am glad to know the ancient rabbis shared something of my own disquiet, that they too felt heaven's heart lament.

Disability is often intertwined with trauma. In our desire to tell a powerful story about disability, in our desire to push back the relentless tide of tragedy that surrounds disability in popular culture, disability activists have sometimes given short shrift to this truth. Sometimes impairment is an ordinary fact of life, a consequence of genetics or of happenstance. But sometimes it is produced by violence. Sometimes it is ground into our bones, the long, slow brutality of living in a system that turns some people's bodies into discards. Sometimes you can trace it back: To a raging father. To a gun. To poison in the groundwater. To long hours for shit pay. To food stretched thin, over and over again.

That is not my own story. But it is a story that many folks know well. I think of the powerful prose poem "Dirty River Girl," where the brilliant disabled writer Leah Lakshmi Piepzna-Samarasinha tells a story of growing up working class along the banks of the Blackstone River in Worcester, Massachusetts. They track the pollution that travels across bodies, making visible the way poison seeps into the water and leaches seamlessly into flesh. They recount unflinchingly the harm that exploitation and profit-seeking has wreaked on both body and land: the lies of the city fathers who deny the thirty-three cancer-causing compounds in Worcester's water, the tentacles that touched their mother's uterus "blooming like algae in a polluted lake." They tell the story of the first girl they ever kissed, "who found out she had cervical and uterine cancer at 28, when she went for her first pap smear in ten uninsured years."[12]

This, too, is a disability story, a story of harm done for other people's profit, a story of bodies betrayed. Piepzna-Samarasinha tells this story without flinching. They tell it in a way that holds space for anger and for pain. But they refuse to traffic in the lure of some pretty fantasy of restoration or repair. Rather than imagine the river and the body washed clean and made new, they turn toward the body as it is. What would it take to know and claim the body polluted as a source of beauty, as a site of love? Not beauty like a myth, a dream that never was. Not the beautiful untouched, not beautiful pristine. "Beautiful," they say, "like the weed trees that would take over every abandoned lot in my hometown."[13] Fierce and bent and scraggly. Beautiful, exactly as they are.

As I read this story, I hold two things to be true: First, I know that we must change the root conditions that make disability commonplace. We must challenge the patterns and practices that make asthma rampant in certain neighborhoods, as ordinary as poverty, as racism, as the lure of not-in-my-backyard. We must challenge the patterns and practices that make it a foregone conclusion that some folks don't get preventive health care, that make the emergency room the point of first intervention and the place of last resort.

But here's another thing I know: how easy it is for these campaigns to turn disabled folks into shake-your-head statistics, how easy it is to write us off as the ruined ones, the tragic cases, the bodies already halfway to the grave. I have a fierce love for disabled folks, a love that insists we matter *as we are*. I honor us. I honor how we've learned to take the ripped-up places in our lives and mend them so the seams still show. How we've learned to claim the scar as witness to survival.

I think of that, when I think of Isaac's story: how it feels to live into the aftermath, when everyone you meet knows the story of your wounding. Or how it feels to carry trauma like a secret, how it slumbers underneath the skin until it cleaves through silence like a fissure. I think of that whenever I lay out the link between disability and social violence, whenever I name the way disability is made through war, through racism and white supremacy, through the churn of capitalism. Through the father's knife.

These are lives and stories, each of them a world.

Say Isaac's blindness began the day his father raised the blade. That doesn't mean he must remain forever pinned by that knife, forever trapped in that moment. Trauma winds through our bodies and our minds, our memories and our futures. But we are not caught unending by the harm that has been done to us. Slowly, gently, we can braid other truths alongside those old stories. The meaning of disability is not foreclosed by its beginning. We are all more than the worst that has been done to us.

If we accept the midrash of the angel's tears, we end up with a different picture of Isaac's blindness, one in which disability has been a long companion in his life. The story doesn't speak definitively about the way that Isaac's eyes have changed. We don't know for sure whether the tears bring about blindness immediately. Perhaps the midrash deploys them as foreshadowing, a symbolic gesture that presages how Isaac's sight will eventually shift. But I want to consider how this story might unfold if we let Isaac's eyes change when he's still young, if we allow that some degree of visual impairment begins to shape his perception from an early age.

One of the things we notice is how rarely the Bible associates Isaac with sight. Biblical scholar Rebecca Raphael suggests that, throughout the book of Genesis, the Bible repeatedly figures Isaac as marked by a curious disengagement from the visual.[14] Raphael doesn't argue that Isaac is blind from birth or that he cannot see. Instead, she's interested in the way that the Bible associates Isaac with a curious absence of vision. When Isaac is first born, his mother names him for the *sound* of laughter. When he climbs Mount Moriah with his father, his only words are a question. "Where is the lamb?" he asks, the haunting question of a child from whom so much is hidden, who cannot clearly see. When Isaac meets his wife, Rebecca, the biblical story gives a rich account of *her* visual impressions. She raises her eyes and sees him—and the sight affects her so deeply that she falls from her camel.[15] But Isaac? All he sees are the camels approaching from a distance, the broad outline of their familiar shapes against the horizon. There is no scene where he sees his wife, no moment when he responds to her in visual terms. Later, in Genesis 26:7, Isaac seems to know his wife is beautiful. But beauty plays little role in his own regard for her. While other biblical men are frequently struck by women's beauty, Isaac's response seems different. When he meets Rebecca, Genesis 24:67 tells us that Isaac brings her to his tent, that he takes her to be his wife, that he loves her and draws comfort from her presence. What's absent from the scene? There's no visual encounter, no moment of beholding. Isaac's love is a love that does not rest on sight or seeing.

Of course, there's no definitive claim to be made here about whether or how Isaac perceives during his early years. But instead of assuming that every biblical character senses according to the normative pattern, I'm inclined to let the available evidence invite us to ask the question. What if Isaac has never been secure in his sightedness? What if his vision has always been unreliable?

My first instinctive response is to expect him to compensate, to hone other modes of perception that might guide his way through the world. It's something of an old canard, this notion that disability heightens one's other senses. I grew up hearing stories about blind people with hyper acute hearing, stories in which blind people developed an almost superhuman capacity of auditory discernment. The first blind person I ever met was a piano tuner, and I remember, as a child, watching him work. I watched as he adjusted the tenor of the strings, responding to minute gradations in sound with a sensitivity I did not have. It was the first time I realized that disability could be good for something.

The way I learned that story, though, it made blind people's sensory sensitivity seem like a superpower. Extraordinary hearing became a kind of magical sensitivity, a capacity bestowed benevolently by the fates when sight was unavailable. The story I grew up with portrayed this ability as a gift granted to the blind man without effort on his part, as though it were a natural side effect of blindness.

I think of it differently now. Sensory perception is a quality of attention. Sensory perception is a skill we develop through awareness and interest, a skill that takes practice and care. Disabled folks often develop alternative sensory awareness because certain avenues are closed to us.

Isaac does not display this sensitivity. Quite the contrary. In Genesis 27, Isaac cannot tell the difference between the hide of a goat and the hair of his child. How is it possible that he discerns so poorly? I find it inconceivable. Has Isaac never learned to sense by touch? Has he internalized so profoundly the dominant assumption that sight is best that he discounts the testimony of his ears, that he gives so little attention to the play of fingers over skin?

What kind of a blind man is he?

But as soon as I ask the question, I know. He's a blind man who spent his life grasping after sight, a blind man who internalized so thoroughly the logics of the sighted world that he never learned to know through touch. He's all of us disabled folk who have been taught to prize the patterns of the nondisabled world, to pursue what we do not have. I think of Deaf kids with their hands bound behind their

backs, forced to read lips and navigate auditory culture. I think of
Autistic kids subjected to behavioral therapy, trained to comply with
the norms of a non-Autistic world. I think of all the ways internalized ableism sinks into our bones, the way it teaches us to turn from
what we know.

Is this Isaac's experience? Has he taken into his heart the notion
that touch is an inferior sense, a crippled way of knowing? In several
places, the Bible itself stigmatizes the association between touch and
blindness, portraying the act of knowing by touch as an insufficient
form of sensory knowledge. When the Torah recounts the misfortunes
that God will bring upon those who turn away from the commandments, Deuteronomy 28:29 says they will "grope at noon like a blind
man gropes in the dark," a phrase that appears again in Isaiah 59:10.
The prophet uses blindness as a metaphor for sin, which keeps the
people from true knowledge of God. "We grope like blind men along
a wall; we grope like those without eyes. We stumble at noon, as if in
darkness."

It's a passage that underscores the biblical author's investment in
sight. Sight, these verses assume, is the key to perception and acuity.
Without it, people are plunged into a darkness both physical and spiritual. If you cannot see, you cannot know.

That's a lie, of course. And the notion that blind people are "incon-
venienced" by darkness is likewise laughable. Blind theorist Georgina
Kleege points out that blind people are often entirely accustomed to
navigating without sight, a skill that can be a decided advantage when
the lights go out. Kleege tells the story of an airplane flight where her
neighbor protested to the flight attendant that he didn't want to sit
next to a blind woman lest he become responsible for her in the event
of an emergency. But Kleege defused the awful moment. If the plane
is plunged into darkness, if there's smoke, if visibility is poor? She'll
be in her element. She'll be the one who leads him out.[16]

Rejecting the widespread notion that blindness is an impediment
to perception, Kleege argues that we need a different meaning for the
phrase "to turn a blind eye." Blind perception isn't a deficit, Kleege

argues, but an alternative form of knowing. "Turning a blind eye," she maintains "is to offer a different perspective on the subject, to provide observations devoid of the distractions and manipulations of images, and to foreground other sensory perception as well as knowledge outside the sensory realm."[17] To look with blind eyes is not to *overlook* but to perceive differently.

There's a fantasy I indulge in sometimes, an alternate story where Isaac knows full well that Jacob stands before him. When I tell myself this story, I imagine Isaac as a man who colludes with the ruse, who allows himself to *seem* deceived. When I tell myself this story, all the father wants is for his son to tell the truth about his life.

The Bible itself holds the seeds of this reading. Genesis 27 is charged with tension around perception and knowledge, deception and disclosure. At the very start of the story, Jacob fears discovery at Isaac's hands. When his mother first proposes the deception, Jacob protests: "My brother Esau is a hairy man," Jacob says, "but I am smooth. If my father touches me, I will be like a trickster in his eyes, and I will bring curse upon myself and not blessing."[18] In this verse, touch serves as a way to cut through deception. Jacob fears that his father's hands will unravel the ruse. They will make the truth apparent to Isaac's eyes.

Rebecca does not deny the truth of her son's words. She does not reassure Jacob that the deception will hold. Instead, she doubles down on the deception and accepts the consequences. "Your curse, my son, be upon me," she tells him. "Just do as I say."[19]

Jacob fetches the goat kids and accepts the dish Rebecca prepares. He allows her to dress him in his brother's clothes, to cover his hands and his hairless neck with the hides of the goats who have just been slain for Isaac's supper. She puts the dish and the bread into his hands. Wrapped in animal skins and his brother's clothes, Jacob comes before Isaac.

He says one word, and one word alone: "Father."

Isaac responds with a question, the first of many that he will pose to Jacob. "Which of my sons are you?"

To read these words as a straightforward query, we would have to assume that blindness has blotted out Isaac's other sensory skills, that he has no means to ascertain the truth for himself. Many readers have done that, have followed the cultural script that blindness is the end of perception. But I am not convinced.

Read this question slant, and it opens up a very different moment. It is no longer a simple question of fact, an attempt to distinguish between brothers. It is an existential question, an uncanny one. As a queer reader, I am haunted by Isaac's question. It is an invitation to disclosure, an invitation to tell truth.

Who are you, child? Will you reveal yourself to me?

Jacob refuses the invitation. When he answers his father, he claims to be his brother. He presents himself as if he were the man his father loves. "I am Esau, your first-born," Jacob says. "I have done as you told me. Please sit and eat what I hunted, so that you may bless me with your innermost blessing."

Isaac asks another question. "How did you succeed so quickly?"

When I read these words, I hear the voice of a parent who knows full well that something is amiss but who waits to see whether the child will persist. Isaac faces the lie, and he gives his son a second opportunity to come clean. He holds open the door.

But Jacob doubles down. He does not dare reveal the truth. "Because the Lord your God granted me good fortune," he says, an answer charged with irony. He is the second son by mere moments, a son stripped of abundance by the circumstance of birth.

The third time Isaac speaks, he turns away from questions. He says, "Come closer that I may feel you, son, whether you are really my son Esau or not." And when he reaches out to touch, he encounters the goat skins. He touches the masquerade. "The voice is the voice of Jacob," he says, "but the hands are the hands of Esau."

After this encounter, Genesis 27:23 concludes: "He did not recognize him."

Isaac did not recognize his son because Jacob refused, time and time again, to be present as himself. He buries his own identity, disowns his own truth. He lets his hands be covered, his self be subordinated. His voice peeks through, but he uses it to deny who he is.

I grieve the loneliness that Jacob bears, the way he has to claim his brother's name in order to be blessed. I know something of that pain. I want a different ending to this story. But truth stays beneath the surface in this story, unacknowledged.

After the touch, his father asks again: "Are you really my son Esau?"

Jacob's response is affirmative. The sense of the Hebrew is unambiguous; the Bible clearly means to tell us he answers *yes*. But the phrase itself is haunting. It is a single word, the last word he will say to his father.

When Jacob answers, the word he says is "I."[20]

Even though there are tantalizing verses in Genesis 27 that invite us to imagine that Isaac knows the true identity of the child who stands before him, the overall thrust of the story conveys the idea that Isaac was tricked by Jacob's disguise. While Isaac questions Jacob repeatedly at the start of the story, his uncertainty resolves once Jacob gives his final answer. The act of blessing blots out Isaac's doubt. Isaac calls him close and asks his son to serve him the meal. When the two men embrace, when they kiss, Isaac is enfolded by the scent of the fields: Jacob's scent, verdant and fresh. The sensory experience draws out the fullness of his blessing. Jacob carries the scent of the fields in his clothes, in his hair; and Isaac blesses him to know the goodness of the earth, asking God to grant him bounty from "the dew of heaven and the fat of the earth, an abundance of new grain and wine."[21]

The kiss, the touch, the scent, the word—all of these things seal father to son, confirming not just blessing but social hierarchy. If the beginning of Isaac's blessing speaks of earthly abundance that both his sons could know, the conclusion places one son above the other.

"Let peoples serve you and nations bow to you," reads Genesis 27:29. "Be master of your brothers, and let your mother's sons bow to you."

And it is this imposition of hierarchy, this choice to elevate one child over the other, that results in tragedy. Moments after Isaac conveys the blessing, Esau returns from his own hunt. He, too, has prepared a dish, as his father desired. And when Esau comes to his father's side, when he serves his father food, and offers to help him sit and eat before he blesses, Isaac comes to realize that something has gone terribly wrong.

"Who are you?" he asks. When Esau answers, Isaac begins to tremble. He begins to piece together what transpired. He tells the story to his son. And Esau, the bold, brash hunter, begins to cry. The rugged son weeps, seized by bitterness and grief. He weeps for what is gone, for the blessing stolen, and for the position that he cannot have. But it is more than that, more than the push for dominance, more than desire for earthly goods. Three times, Esau asks for his father's blessing. Three times, Esau asks for his father's hand upon his brow. The words are a shaft to the heart:

"Have you but one blessing, father? Bless me too!"[22]

But Isaac has already given the primary blessing to his other son, so the blessing that remains for Esau is meager. His house will still know the blessing of the land, but he will live by the sword—and be a servant to his brother.[23]

It's a terrible moment—the moment when Isaac realizes the truth of the trick, when he confronts the magnitude of his error, its finality. When Esau declares his identity, the voice is utterly clear. This time, Isaac has no doubts. A single question is sufficient.

When Isaac hears Esau's answer, a terrible tremor runs through him. It is a rare biblical disclosure, a moment when the body's tell is broadcast. Isaac feels the impact of deceit physically. The deception shakes him to the core.

And when his son weeps?

The Bible gives no glimpse into Isaac's heart. After Isaac's tremble and Esau's cry, the biblical tale returns to its familiar spare style, recounting only the words that pass between them. But I need no body sign to recognize this moment or to know its cost. I need no window into Isaac's pain.

As a disabled person, this is the moment I have always flinched from, this moment when disability translates so clearly into vulnerability. This fear has stalked me all my life: The fear that I will need to run but can't. That I'll be too weak, when raw strength could save me. That disability itself will be my weakness, something others will exploit.

Exploitation lies at the center of Isaac's story. His wife plots to take advantage of Isaac's inability to see, while his son persists in deception despite his father's attempts to ascertain the truth. Rabbi Lauren Tuchman, herself blind, offers a striking reading of this scene. The text of the Torah makes it clear that Isaac "knew that something wasn't adding up." But in the end, it doesn't matter what Isaac knows or doesn't know. He is powerless to do anything about the deception.[24]

For Tuchman, Isaac's story recalls a kind of cruelty most disabled folks know well: "That playground bully who delights in disguising their voice as a test, only to laugh at us when we get it wrong." It reinforces the feeling that "we are set up to fail in a system that structurally disempowers us, despite our best efforts to do all of the right things."[25] Isaac's story is a breach of trust, a reminder that disability accentuates our vulnerability, and the world can't wait to take advantage.

But when we talk about vulnerability, we must be very careful.

All too often, we imagine vulnerability as a signal characteristic of disability, a quintessential fact of the body. Of course, there's an element of truth here. Because Isaac can't see, he's more susceptible to a certain kind of trick. Because I can't run, I'm at a disadvantage if survival comes down to a foot race. But framing vulnerability as an inherent property of disabled bodies overlooks crucial questions about the way that vulnerability gets baked into the social structures and systems we inherit, the way it gets intensified by society's choices.

Isaac is locked into a system where only one son gets the blessing, where only one son receives the full measure of the birthright. It's this arrangement that has stoked a long-simmering conflict between the two brothers, this knowledge that only one of them can seize the birthright and their father's patrimony. It's this arrangement that has Rebecca scheming; only the patriarch bestows the blessing, leaving her with no direct agency, no straightforward means to shape the future of her family.

Blaming the trick on Isaac's blindness misses the inequity that drives this story.

The conventional telling of this tale assumes that Isaac gets tricked because he goes blind. To guard against deceit, to protect against powerlessness? The solution is to double down on the capacity to dominate, to wield conventional power. Stay alert. Stay vigilant. Watch for duplicity at every turn. Above all, never become disabled.

But that solution hides another possibility: a story where liberation unfolds when we refuse the terms of the zero-sum game. What if Isaac could have unbound his family from that age-old tale, where one son receives the full measure of blessing and the other gets a belly full of bitterness? What if Isaac and Rebecca could have woven differently the dynamics of their marriage so that both of them shared the task of navigating difficult decisions? What if Jacob had dared come before his father as himself?

None of these things are possible in the story that we have. The very bones of this narrative claim that deception is necessary, that rivalry and dominance are the only way. Jacob's lie is vital, the Bible wants us to believe, not only for his own future but for the divine design. And in the chapters that follow, as God's mysterious plan unfolds, Jacob and his descendants rely on the brash and scrappy brilliance of the trickster, the one whose blessing is always intertwined with the weight of simmering jealousy and old anger.

But I refuse to leave this story without conjuring a different world: a world where two brothers know they're both beloved, a story where sons can tell the truth before their fathers, where all of us might be seen and loved for who we are. Perhaps the seeds of that new story are present, even in these ancient words. Perhaps they linger in the silence that trails each of Isaac's questions, like an invitation.

Who are you? Will you reveal yourself to me?

CHAPTER TEN

Jacob and the Angel

Wheels, Wings, and the Brilliance
of Disability Difference

What is the catalyst that transforms our life? What is the moment that changes the way we know ourselves, that brings us closer to the heart of things? For Jacob, the catalyst is an unexpected encounter with a powerful stranger. In the dark of night, Jacob stands alone on a river-bank, preparing in the morning to reunite with his estranged brother. I imagine him in that moment: each error in his history running its claws against the tender insides of his conscience, each regret sitting like a stone in his gut. I've known that night. Maybe you have too.

By the banks of the river, a man appears from out of the darkness. He is an uncanny figure, one who Jacob will later recognize as divine. The two of them wrestle, the man and the angel. Here is how Genesis 32:25–27 describes their meeting:

Jacob was left alone
and a man wrestled with him until the break of dawn.

When he saw that he did not prevail over him
he touched his hip;

Jacob's hip was wrenched, as he wrestled with him.

He said, "Let me go, for dawn is breaking."

He said to him, "I will not let you go, until you bless me."[1]

It is a scene charged with power and potency. Two figures grapple by night: arm on hip, hand around thigh, breath against skin. And when Jacob emerges? He is physically and spiritually changed.[2]

That meeting transforms Jacob from wayward son into powerful patriarch. When dawn breaks, when he will not let go, he once again wrests a blessing for himself. The angel grants him a new name, a powerful symbol of rebirth. Jacob becomes Israel, a name drawn from the Hebrew verb "to struggle." The name pins Jacob into place as the progenitor of the Jewish people, the one in whose image we see our own spiritual journey. The tradition calls us "children of Israel," evoking our spiritual kinship with this moment, this man. We are the ones who wrestle with God.

The meeting with the angel isn't only a spiritual catalyst. It also sparks a physical transformation. As they wrestle, Jacob's hip is wrenched at the socket. In the words of Genesis 32:32, he emerges from the struggle "limping on his hip." The wound has a long afterlife in Jewish tradition. As Genesis 32:33 explains, it is because of this that the children of Israel do not eat the muscle that crosses the hip. One of the formative practices of keeping kosher, of asserting and affirming Jewish difference, is bound up with the memory of Jacob's wound.

Disability enters Jacob's life in the aftermath of his encounter with the angel. It is part and parcel of his experience of drawing near to the divine. As a disabled reader, I savor the fact that Jacob gains his limp during this moment of meeting, a moment he will later describe as "seeing God face to face."[3] It is a moment charged with spiritual potency, a moment the Bible associates with struggle and with blessing.

Of course, there's a danger here. There's a danger in expecting disability to have spiritual import, to carry the weight of the angel's touch. Human beings acquire disabilities in all sorts of ways: through accident or illness, through violence or malice, through the blueprints of our genes or the hand of our creator. I don't want to lift up the spiritual frame as a necessary or ideal paradigm for naming how a disability comes into our lives.

All the same, it matters to me that Jacob's limp is no tale of tragedy, no story of woe. The story of how the patriarch acquires his disability is inextricably entwined with his spiritual unfolding, with the way he acquires his true name and the fullness of his adult identity. In a few spare lines of prose, the Torah whispers a thing I know well. Disability can be bound up with transformation, with our own becoming. It can be a catalyst, a place of possibility. Those who wrestle with the angel will be changed.

It's a path most commentators decide not to pursue.

Instead of treating Jacob's encounter with the angel as a lasting reorientation of his person, traditional Jewish interpreters maintain that Jacob's disability is not permanent. Take a well-known midrash, Genesis Rabbah 79:5. The midrash interprets a verse that describes how Jacob finally returns to the land of his birth. After he meets and reconciles with his brother, Esau, he settles in the land of Shechem and builds a home there. "Jacob," Genesis 33:18 tells us, "arrives safe in the city of Shechem." The Hebrew word for safe is *shalem*, a word that also means peace and wholeness. It's that final meaning that our midrash picks up, imagining Jacob arriving "whole" in the city—restored to right relationship with his family, restored with regard to his learning, and restored in body. His wound, the midrash maintains, is no more.

That claim was canonized by Rashi, a medieval scholar whose commentary on the Torah is the go-to reference for traditional Jewish readers. Describing the conclusion of the patriarch's extraordinary journey, Rashi comments that Jacob arrives "whole" in body, in his finances, and with regard to Torah. He has reconciled with his brother and regained the cattle he relinquished at the river. His mind is also honed; he has become "perfect in Torah."[4] His fortune, in the full sense of the term, has been restored.

And his limp? His limp is gone.

It's classic disability denial. These readings minimize the wound to Jacob's flesh, figuring it as a fleeting injury, nothing more. Neither Rashi nor the midrash tell us why. They take it as self-evident that wholeness is a desirable quality in a hero, and they both assume that to be whole requires physical restoration. They refuse to consider disability as a lasting part of his personhood, as a significant dimension of his mature adulthood. Jacob's limping body becomes an impediment to his heroism. To arrive whole and victorious, the wound has to be erased.

I read Jacob's arrival differently. Rather than imagining Jacob acquiring wholeness by shedding his limp, I like to think he became whole by incorporating these physical and spiritual changes into his sense of self. Something happened on the journey, something that left its mark on flesh and soul. To imagine him as shrugging off that moment? To erase the impact of that meeting? I say no. Jacob arrives whole in Shechem not because he strides in, unaffected by his encounters on the road, but because he has integrated disability into his identity, because he has allowed himself to be changed by the angel's touch.

While Jacob's experience is the obvious place to engage disability, there's another dimension of this story that speaks to me: the figure of the angel. Alongside this story of how the patriarch got his limp, I find a powerful disability kinship in the other body who wrestles at the river's edge—in the uncanny, unexpected stranger, the one who is no ordinary man.

Let me be clear: I don't mean to say disabled folks are angels. That notion has a long and dangerous history. There's a tendency in some quarters to imagine people with disabilities as spiritually gifted, as "blessed" with a particular closeness to God. In American popular culture, this notion burst into popularity with the 1953 publication of TV star Dale Evans Rogers's *Angel Unaware*, told through the voice of her daughter Robin Elizabeth, born with Down syndrome. Her parents call her their "little angel." The best-selling book, written after Robin's death at an early age, lays out a powerful account of Robin's divine mission—framing her life on earth as part of God's plan to transform human hearts.[5] Andrew Walker-Cornetta, a scholar of American religion who has studied the impact of Rogers's book, observes the way that Rogers's testimony tapped a powerful nerve in American culture. He argues that the book offered many parents a compelling way to recognize and name their children's abilities, to shake off narrow notions that judge people's capacities solely on the basis of their verbal communication or their IQ.[6]

But I am uneasy about this deployment of the spiritual, uneasy about what it means to imagine disabled people as somehow inherently closer to the divine. I'm uneasy about the way that this notion has been used to script a certain kind of "sweetness" onto disabled bodies, the way that it demands a certain kind of embodiment that couples spiritual wisdom with worldly naivete. I'm thinking about Ashley X, a young woman with significant mental and physical disabilities from static encephalopathy, whose parents call her their "pillow angel." When Ashley was six years old, they sought elective surgery to remove her breast buds and inhibit her growth in order to keep her body small and childlike forever.[7] I'm thinking of an insight I learned from Rabbi Ruti Regan, about the way assistive communication devices for children with disabilities are often programmed to afford the user a narrow range of approved emotional responses. "How are you feeling about your bar (or bat) mitzvah?" isn't a real question if the only potential replies are "Excited!" and "Happy!" If you want people to make a genuine spiritual choice to praise, she argues, you also have to equip them with the option for blasphemy.[8]

All too often, the idea that disabled people have a special affinity for the spiritual gets used to deny the complexity of our stories, to overwrite our very humanity, to cover over our feelings of anger, frustration, or malice. To all of that, I say no.

When I evoke a resonance between disability and the angel, I mean something very different. In ancient Jewish tradition, angels are strange and powerful figures whose presence provokes a kind of rupture in the ordinary. When an angel appears? It's a moment when the unexpected breaks through, a moment when the uncanny bursts onto the scene. That's the connection I'm interested in, the kinship I'm after. It isn't so much the facts of the body or a shared physical experience. It lies in the reaction of the onlookers, the response of the witnesses. It's what the angel stirs up, what the angel's presence uncovers. It's the trail the angel leaves behind.

One of the most distinctive characteristics of angels in the Bible is that people *don't* always recognize them as different. Biblical scholar James Kugel notes that biblical encounters between humans and angels are often built around a "moment of confusion," a moment when the human partner suddenly recognizes that they have been in conversation with a divine being.[9] When the angel is seen? When their otherness is actually perceived? People respond with fear and awe.

Consider the angel who appears to Manoaḥ's wife in Judges 13, a perfect example of this combination of misrecognition and fear. The story begins when an angel of the Lord appears to the childless wife of Manoaḥ, promising her that she will bear a son. When the figure returns, Manoaḥ treats him as an ordinary man, asking him questions and offering him food. Manoaḥ recognizes him as an angel only when he disappears in a blaze of fire. Once he understands the truth, Manoaḥ is overcome by fear. "We shall surely die," he says to his wife in Judges 13:22, "for we have seen a divine being." Manoaḥ's wife reassures her husband that God does not intend to strike them dead. But she, too, feels the impact of this brush with the uncanny. When she first sees the "man of God," she describes him as *nor'a*, a Hebrew word that holds both fear and awe.[10]

These twin responses—the failure to recognize the angel as different and the fear prompted by an encounter with the uncanny—also mark the Jacob narrative. Genesis 32 begins with Jacob wrestling with a man ('ish), a figure he eventually comes to recognize as God ('elohim). Like Manoaḥ, Jacob first seems to mistake the identity of the stranger. And when he recognizes the truth? His brush with the divine provokes a combination of fear and awe, a recognition that death was very near.

After the angel departs, Jacob names the place Peniel, "for I have seen God face to face, yet my life has been preserved."[11]

These same dynamics surround disability in contemporary culture. Nondisabled folks often don't account for disability and fail to notice disabled people in their midst. But when the presence of disability becomes undeniable? It often provokes anxiety or dread.

Let me explain what I mean. Disability stigma often exaggerates the impact of a disability, heightening other people's perceptions of the way disability affects a person's life. But this tendency goes hand in hand with another: the tendency to *not see* disability, to deny its presence and significance. "I don't think of you as disabled," folks often tell me, despite the obvious presence of my wheelchair. Why not? Disabled scholar Rosemarie Garland-Thomson argues that these denials of disability represent a desire "to rescue people with disabilities from a discredited identity."[12] If people consider disability a negative state, then calling someone disabled seems akin to an insult. In other words: "To be disabled is to be incapable, but I don't see *you* that way."

It's meant as a compliment, but it feels like a slap. That claim shears away a crucial dimension of my experience in the world. It also reminds me that I'm here on sufferance. My life is seen as meaningful only insofar as it matches a nondisabled norm.

The failure to perceive disability also stems from a strong cultural presumption that everyone's bodies and minds operate within a narrow range of what we consider "normal." It's a laughable claim. But we persist in expecting people to match a single standard, to fit within conventional norms. What's the default setting when we meet someone new? Most of us assume they're *not* disabled. Faced with evidence to the contrary? We hold it at bay, shear it away, or attribute it to personal failings. Couple disability with other minoritized identities and the tendency to misattribute disability becomes especially stark. Black disabled activist Leroy Moore recounts how the distinctive limp and slurred speech of his own cerebral palsy often gets read as drunkenness or drug use. Denial of disability runs hand in hand with the racist imagination to misread the truth of Moore's body.

And when disability difference *is* recognized? It often provokes fear. Disability activist Harriet McBryde Johnson describes her own disabled body as a "death totem," one that thrusts the complacently able-bodied into sudden encounter with their own mortality.[13] Like many wheelchair users, Johnson finds that her visibly disabled body and her striking physical difference causes people to grapple with the recognition of their own vulnerability, their own finitude. It's a lot to carry: the weight of other people's projections, their dread, this resurgence of suppressed knowledge.

The Bible never tells us how the angel feels, what it's like to be on the other side of that gaze. We see the meeting only through Manoah's eyes. We watch him shear away the angel's difference. We see him refuse to notice the signs. We see him persistently mistake his visitor as an ordinary man, turning away from the clues that might alert him to the fact of difference. And once he *does* recognize the angel as an uncanny body? The knowledge hits him hard. He's convinced that the angel has come to herald his own death, that he will not survive the aftermath. The encounter is a provocation, one that forces him to recognize his own mortality. Manoah sees the angel and knows that he will die.

Freud famously uses disability to illustrate the quality he calls "the uncanny."[14] The uncanny, Freud maintains, is unsettling not so much because it is strange—but because it confounds expectation, troubling the distinction between the familiar and the unfamiliar. It brings us into encounter with something we think we know but then discover is slightly off. Things that blur the lines between animate and inanimate are a prime example. As a child, I flinched from the husks that cicadas left hanging in the eaves of my climbing house, the way their discarded exoskeletons preserved the contours of the living insect body but were hollow inside. Dolls likewise blurred the lines between the living and the lifeless. I felt the uncanny like a haunting.

The angel that wrestles with Jacob? The angel that foretells the child to Manoah and his wife? Each of these sightings ripples with the uncanny. The angel's body looks like an ordinary human form, until some aspect of the encounter forces the observer to look and look again, to reconsider what they think they know. There is an elusive quality to the angel's otherness. The difference hovers just at the edge of perception. Now you see it, now you don't.

Artists looking to represent angels in visual form gave these figures a distinctive difference: They painted them with wings. Calling on a motif that appears elsewhere in the Bible, in the visions of Ezekiel and in the descriptions of Isaiah, the wing developed into a definitive marker of the angelic body. The wing breaks decisively with the expected human form. It signals clearly to the viewer that the angel belongs to the heavens, not the earth.

Western culture has a love affair with wings. We commonly associate wings with freedom and flight, with the promise of transcendence. But what if we saw the wing as a congenital difference, as a birth anomaly? Or, as they said when I was born, "a birth defect"? Might we use that kinship to look anew at disabled bodies? To see our difference as a mark of beauty, as a rare and lovely form? Irish artist Mary Duffy, who was born without arms, created a performance piece in which she displays herself nude, in a posture that evokes the classical *Venus de Milo*, the famous ancient Greek sculpture whose armless form is often evoked as the height of feminine beauty. Duffy asks the viewer to recognize the kinship between the Venus and her own body, to come into encounter with her own beauty.[15]

How thin the space between the sublime and the stigmatized.

The angel is often seen as an ethereal figure, a being whose body is insignificant and insubstantial. But to understand the disability kinship with the angel, to feel the textures of Jacob's own encounter with the angel, we need to reckon with the angel's physicality. We need to let our attention lodge in the interplay of muscle and bone.

Wings are a challenge that way. When artists represent a winged form, they fail to grapple with the mechanics of flight, with the visceral implications wings pose for a human body. The English poet Edward Carpenter recalls how as a child, fascinated by the question of how angels disrobe, he spied Piero Della Francesca's *Baptism of Christ*, with its angels portrayed as "three stout country girls looking on at the ceremony."[16] But those Renaissance angels did not pass muster. "The wings," Carpenter recalls, "came straight through the pink gown without the least little hole or wrinkle."

And to fly? To actually, not just miraculously, fly? Carpenter calls attention to the musculature such lift would require, the way the traditional artistic choice to set the wings into the human shoulder blade "would paralyze the wing and also paralyze the arm in a way that no Archangel even could surmount."[17] For angels to fly in truth, their bodies cannot mirror the normative human form. They will be changed, reshaped, restructured by the demands of the wing.

My muscles know something of that transformation. For more than twenty years, I've used a manual wheelchair. My legs are spindle thin. But my mode of moving through the world has built the muscles in my shoulders and across my chest. Over the years, I've ripped the seams in fancy tailored blouses so often that I know my own body doesn't match the stereotypical expectations of the feminine. The athleticism I've gained through disability strains at the confines of conventional gender. I know something of the angel's strength. My wheeler's body has a muscled chest. These arms are built to lift a body's weight. The knowledge whispers in my bones, a secret that I almost know: the physicality of flight.

W hat happens if we let the angel carry the presence of disability? To affirm disability in and through the body of the angel is to recognize disability as a meaningful difference in the world, to recognize it and to celebrate it. To honor the brilliant peculiarity of bodies that cannot be assimilated, that refuse the cover of the conventional.

I first asked this question during a summer spent working with disabled dancers, an exhilarating immersion in the world of disability arts. Most folks think of the relationship between disability and the arts in terms of therapy, as a practice where art becomes a vehicle for healing the body or the psyche, for strengthening muscles or releasing trauma. Art therapy can be a powerful tool for personal transformation. But it isn't what I'm talking about here. By disability arts, I mean the work of professional performance makers whose artistry is rooted in lived disability experience. I mean the making of art that illuminates the power and promise of disability politics and culture.

For years now, I've been working with Claire Cunningham, a critically acclaimed disabled dancer, choreographer, and performance maker. Claire uses crutches—both in everyday life and as a catalyst for art. Claire's crutches are material expressions of support. She needs them. She depends on them. And over the years, she's built up knowledge about what they can do and what she can do with them. Through expertise and kinship, she has fashioned her crutches into dance partners. They are the medium through which her artistry emerges.

As a dancer on crutches, Claire has a repertoire of movement all her own. I've watched her use her crutches to spring over cracks and crevices, to explore the nooks and crannies of a rocky overlook by the sea. I've watched her use her crutches to vault herself over a curled up human body.

Consider, through Claire's artistry, the relationship between the crutch and the wing. She can launch herself into the air—her body held horizontal by the crutches, one breath of perfect suspension, before she sweeps her legs into a slow, deliberate curve that brings her feet back to the ground. The crutches offer lift, height, suspension: all qualities I associate with flight. But this is no flight *from* disability, no escape from the body. There's a popular trope, a fantasy that flight will bring release, that it will let us leave the constraints of the body behind. Yet Claire's artistry suggests the opposite. Disability is the very quality that makes her movement possible. It's not just the moves themselves but the skill that guides them, the expertise honed over the course of a lifetime. If this is flight, it is a flight that's born of disability embrace.

It's this embrace that draws me to disability arts: the choice to say an unabashed *yes* to disability and what it offers, the choice to center what disability brings into the world, what it makes possible, without flinching from its costs. It's this embrace that draws me time and time again: to venues where disabled folks have claimed the stage, the page, and the imagination, because it feels to me like this is one place liberation lives. This is one way we get free.

Now, to be clear: I'm no professional dancer. Claire and I have built collaboration around a kinship in our ways of thinking about disability—a resonance in the kinds of questions we're asking, the kinds of politics we're forging. I turned to disability arts because I was frustrated with the limits of the conventional religious canon. I needed to shiver something new into the familiar constellations of biblical and rabbinic texts about disability, something that would speak to my own heart. I wanted a way to name the sacredness I've found in disability circles: the ethics embodied in the practice of access, the recognition of radical interdependence, the beauty and the care.

That night, when it all began?

I was sitting in a Berlin dance studio, watching Claire work with the nondisabled dancer and choreographer Jess Curtis. They were sharing glimpses from the piece they were creating together, a brilliant duet called *The Way You Look (at me) Tonight*. The audience was scattered throughout the space, arranged on chairs and cushions that brought us very close to the action—close enough that we could see the performers' faces and hear their breath. We were right there, feeling the timbre of their muscles, their presence, their sweat.

It was dark, and it was late, and I was watching them move. I was watching them move, but it was more than that. I was watching two people who have honed very acutely their capacity to pay attention to each other, who have built together the ability to listen to and through the language of the body.

There's a moment in the performance when Claire begins walking on Jess's prone body, traversing his feet, his sides, and his chest. The score is made possible by the specifics of their physicality. Jess is a lean, athletic six-foot-tall man with a shock of white hair; Claire is a small woman, muscled and slender; she uses forearm crutches. She walks carefully, deliberately. She walks across his flesh. As the piece unfolds, she begins to move among the audience, her bare feet touching our shoes, our socks. The piece, Claire tells me later, is "about taking time. Reading permission. Some people will put their feet out there, inviting contact." Other people tuck their feet away, their gesture saying no without words.

That night I watch Claire move through the space, coming to rest on other people's feet. I watch them look up when she lands. I watch them soften; I watch them start to smile. There is an intimacy here, all unexpected. An invitation. Then Claire spins on her crutches. She propels herself into the air and touches down on my knees.

It's like a breath, an extraordinarily delicate contact.

Maybe that would have been unremarkable for you. But as a wheelchair user, that kind of touch is rare. When I'm out in public, people either treat me as an object—a parcel to move, a piece of ungainly furniture—or they keep their distance, afraid to hurt me, hesitant to get too near. I can count on one hand the times when someone I don't know well has reached out and offered physical contact, has brought our bodies close in a way that feels generous, careful, and bold. This is not the invasive touch of a stranger on the subway, who grabs my chair to steer me out of his way. It is not the touch of a doctor, professional and probing. It is not the touch of a beloved.

It is a crip touch. A meeting. A recognition.

A life with crutches has allowed Claire to develop a specific set of skills. She knows exactly how to land on an object, how to touch it without pushing hard, without knocking it over. She can hover in the air, bear her weight through the crutches, rather than her feet. This is a crutch user's artistry, a particular expertise. Claire lands with infinite lightness. When she touches her toes against the join of my thigh and my knee, one of the places where my own limp lives?

I feel something open inside my skin.

That's the moment I remember every time I tell the story of Jacob and the angel. The memory makes me wonder: how the angel bursts into the scene with the whisper of an unexpected touch, how surprise and recognition ripple through bone. To recognize disability in and through the angel's body is to know difference as a site and source of beauty. I think of how the angel lands, how the unexpected splits through ordinary time, how wonder cuts against familiarity, about the brush of awe.

What happens when these bodies touch? Some readers imagine the wrestling match as a barely restrained site of physical violence. Other readers have found in the story a luminous invitation to recognize the sacrality of queer eros.[18] In *Soulfully Gay*, Joe Perez writes of "the implication that Jacob discovered a profound truth that night in an unexpected grip and toss, pinned to the muscular body of another man," while queer Jewish poet and liturgist Andrew Ramer uses the encounter to claim gay men's sexuality as a site of blessing.[19]

I'm drawn to an old tradition, a reading that likewise recognizes the potent charge of that touch. The medieval commentator Rashi considers the significance of the unusual Hebrew verb *ye'aveq*, translated here as "to wrestle." Maybe, Rashi says, the word was chosen to evoke the dust (*'avaq*) the pair raise with their feet. But he favors another interpretation. He suggests that the Bible uses this word to echo the Aramaic expression "they became attached." Rashi writes, "For so is the habit of two people who make strong efforts to throw each other down—one embraces the other and attaches himself to him with his arms."[20] To wrestle, Rashi suggests, isn't merely an exertion, a way to throw another to the ground. It is also an embrace, a moment that binds bodies together.

That notion of *embrace* gives the meeting a very different tenor. When I first learned this tale, the scene seemed simple: Jacob wrestles with the man and nearly overcomes him. But at the final moment, as dawn breaks, the angel realizes that he cannot win—and so reaches out to strike Jacob's hip, leaving him with a limp that will mark this moment of spiritual encounter.

But there's something curious about this story, a detail that doesn't quite cohere. "While it is Jacob who is wounded," the literary critic

Geoffrey Hartman observes, "it is his antagonist who immediately pleads for release."[21] The logic doesn't scan. If the angel has triumphed over Jacob, if he has achieved a physical victory, why must he ask Jacob to let him go? If the angel struck a victorious blow, he could have slipped away without a word. What would hold him past the dawn? What would stay his flight?

At the end of our passage, it is Jacob who controls the terms of their encounter. It is Jacob who refuses to release the angel until he receives a blessing. That leads Hartman to ask: Is it Jacob who is the unidentified actor in verse 26? Is it Jacob who realizes he cannot overcome the one he wrestles? Is it Jacob who touches the hollow of the angel's thigh, who scores the low blow and achieves an underhanded victory? It would not be entirely out of character.

I lift up Hartman's reading not to argue that it is definitive but to illuminate the way the biblical narrative resists framing the wrestling as the simple triumph of one body over another. In blurring the certainty of the biblical scene, Hartman forces us to imagine the angel's body, pinned and pressed by human flesh. Both bodies in this encounter face risk; both are vulnerable to the other's grip. Perhaps violence is not essential to this tale. To wrestle, after all, is not to kill. When athletes wrestle, both parties agree to hold back, to affirm the boundaries of acceptable risk, to arrest the possibility of real violence. To wrestle is to grapple with another body; it is not a deliberate, intentional attempt to harm.

Might we read that recognition back into the biblical tale? The injury to Jacob's hip is certainly a site of pain, a rupture. But it need not stem from an intent to wound. The Hebrew word the Bible uses to describe the act that causes injury is *naga'*, a word that can mean "to touch," "to reach," or "to strike."

How do we understand this gesture? There could be violence here. *Naga'* is the verb Boaz uses when he tells Ruth he has ordered his men not to molest her.[22] But there are also other possibilities. *Naga'* also conveys the reach that lets us to grasp something we desire. This is the verb the serpent uses in the garden: Adam and Eve shall not touch the fruit.[23] It evokes the touch of body against body, the proximity of flesh; it is the verb Leviticus uses to describe the consequences of coming into contact with a corpse.[24] That's the kind of touch I mean when I describe the angel's contact with Jacob's hip. The contact brings Jacob into charged proximity to the divine body, one that ricochets against his human flesh.

After his brush with the angel? Jacob's hip is wrenched. It's a word that captures dislocation, a word that tells of life pulled out of joint. After the angel comes, after that night, after they grapple, when the morning breaks?

Everything has changed.

Does the aftermath go hard with Jacob in the days that follow? The biblical story gives no hint about this landscape. Those emotions live entirely at the margins of our tale. But that silence covers over crucial questions, human questions. Bodies know this, or they learn: how to grapple with limit, how to tangle with finitude.

To examine this terrain, I want to turn back to my dancers—to Jess and Claire and *The Way You Look (at me) Tonight*. At the beginning of the piece, I suspect most audiences read Jess as an unequivocally able body: athletic, masculine, hyper-capable. But over the course of the performance, that reading begins to fray. In one particular score, Jess probes his own changing physicality, the way arthritis is reshaping the contours of his hip. Claire sets the instruction for his dance, telling him not to do movement that hurts. It's a striking limit, one that over-turns the usual injunction to overcome disability, to work through pain.

Jess explores the landscape of the changed and changing body, letting us look while he probes the question. What can be done, here and now, in *this* body, without pain? It is a difficult thing, to trace the contours of memory. I watch him flinch. I watch him learn the limits and decide to work within them. This is a different kind of wrestling: the wrestling that happens after the angel has come and gone, when the limp remains.

It is no easy embrace. At times, Jess works slowly, turning toward muscle and joint with gentleness, with tenderness. But that isn't the whole of it. In the middle of the piece, he roars—giving animal voice to frustration, to limit and loss. I know that truth. I need it, and I need what follows. After his raw voice splits the silence, Jess spins out into a brilliant solo dance. It is the movement of a dancer who knows what it means to limp, who has refused to leave the body behind for some idealized image of the perfect form. It is the choice to turn toward disability, to examine what it offers, to consider what is lost and what is new and what remains.

It is the artistry of the actual, the truth of breath and bone.

Jacob's limp lingers for me as a powerful reminder that disability is an essential part of what it means to be human. Rosemarie Garland-Thomson calls disability "the etchings left on flesh, as it encounters world," a phrase I love for the way it names disability as an ordinary consequence of living, a register of our experiences.[25] To think of disability this way reminds me of the wear my favorite prayerbook has acquired over the decades, the scuff marks along the spine, the places where the pages are creased and the edges are worn. Those marks hold an entire history. To swap them for a clean, crisp binding? To change them out for a perfect cover, pristine and neat and smooth? No thank you.

We often treat disability as an aberration or imagine it as exceptional. But that's a strange way of thinking. Disability is a ubiquitous part of human experience, an ordinary part of our existence. The particulars differ for all of us. But the fact that disability will enter our lives? That it will change us and our loved ones? It is a universal truth, a truth that is as inevitable as our mortality.

Yet even as I affirm disability as a fundamental aspect of what it means to be human, I'm not content to *only* universalize. There's another dimension to disability that matters to me: the recognition of disability as difference. Some disabilities are commonplace; others are very rare. It's that rareness that I think of when the angel comes: the way the strange and unexpected breaks into our lives, the way it blossoms through us, how it steals our breath.

I feel it in the brilliance of the angel's body, the way it sparks both fear and awe. Disability is like that. Disability is a wild, uncanny presence that rips through norms and shatters expectations. There's a part of me that revels in the difference that will not be assimilated, the otherness that will not bow before convention, that will not be subdued. There's a part of me that fears it.

To meet the angel in my own life is to cross that threshold. To be thrown out of ordinary time, thrust into a place where the customary norms no longer hold sway. When I think of the angel, I think of those who have embraced the brilliance of otherness—who have chosen to move, to think, to see, to know according to the dictates of their nature, not the expectations of the world. This is the quality that makes me call the angel crip—the brazenness, the utter unabashedness of how the angel lives into difference, the choice to unfurl it like a pair of powerful, luminous wings.

The first time I saw disabled dancers? The first time I watched wheelers spin across a stage? The angel shivered down my spine. It was a gift, a revelation.

Afterward, a friend said, *I bet you'd never imagined.*

But I had dreamed of this. I had known deep within my bones that disability could pour out possibility, that wheels could crack open a whole new world. I had *always* known. But I'd never thought I'd see that vision in the flesh. I never thought I'd see it realized. I never thought I'd see it shared.

That's what happens when the angel comes. When Jacob meets that stranger in the dark, when their bodies intertwine? The man comes into contact with the crip. I locate the sacred in the sinews of that charged embrace: the press of chin against cheek, the touch of hand on hip, the breath that hovers there, the sudden whisper of the wing. The touch will change him. It will leave its mark upon his flesh. If he lets it, it will set fire to what he thought he knew. It will change his world.

CHAPTER ELEVEN

The Politics of Beauty

Disability and Desire

Disability is a creative force, a provocation. When I tell the story of Jacob and the angel, that's the place I always land—with the way the angel's brilliant strangeness opens like a revelation, the way the touch of the uncanny shakes up what we thought we knew. When I invite you to imagine the angel as disabled, I'm asking you to see disability as shot through with the sacred. I'm asking you to recognize the angel's power, to feel disability as a catalyst for transformation. But more than that, I want to claim that moment when the angel holds your gaze. When awe catches hold. When the luminous shivers down your spine. When you are set alight by beauty.

Disability often gets positioned as the antithesis of beauty. Beauty, we are told, lies in symmetry and harmony of form. It is bound up with grace and elegance; a matter of lightness, the capacity to fly. Even when we can't quite pin it down, it seems we know what it is not: clunky, awkward, disabled.

Remember that story I told you from the Talmud, the one I learned my first year in rabbinical school? There were two famous rabbis whose students were debating how to praise a bride. Shammai says you praise the bride "as she is," while Hillel says you praise her beauty and her grace. To which Shammai retorts, "What if she is lame? What if she is blind? Doesn't Torah forbid you from telling a lie?"[1]

As a disabled woman, I have an uneasy relationship with the beautiful. Beauty has been weaponized against me, against so many of us. Conventional notions of beauty feel impossibly intertwined with the norms of whiteness, with the policing of gender, sexuality, decorum, and class. I live in a world that fashions fat into a moral failing, a world that teaches girls to pluck and primp and tuck their elbows in. Accolades go to bodies that are lean and limber, toward faces that are symmetrical and smooth. No one ever had to tell me that disability disqualifies. It was the subtext of the movies I watched and the books I read. It was in the advertisements I flipped past, in the magazines I browsed in waiting rooms and doctors' offices. It was a palpable force, on the street and in the high school cafeteria. A girl with a limp learns to face a different kind of gaze.

There's a cultural story we tell—that aesthetic judgments are arbitrary, that beauty lies in the eye of the beholder. But within a given culture, at a particular moment in time, our notions of beauty are remarkably consistent. People judge the same types of bodies as beautiful, and they agree on which bodies fall short.[2]

If you've felt that lash, you know. To be perceived as ugly leaves a person vulnerable to hatred and disdain. And simply to be seen as plain? That too can cost. Economists Daniel Hamermesh and Jeff Biddle have studied the impact of beauty on the labor market. They determined that people judged "plain" pay a significant penalty in terms of employment and advancement in the workforce.[3] Looks play a powerful role in friendships, romantic relationships, and the snap judgments strangers make on the street. If beauty is a quality that smooths our passage in this world, then beauty's absence is a slammed-shut door.

Beauty and ugliness aren't simply deployed as physical opposites. We also use them to map out strikingly different moral terrain. We attribute goodness and kindness to beautiful faces, a move psychologists call the "halo effect."[4] Ugliness, by contrast, gets taken as a sign of moral deviance. Classic cinema tropes depend on disability to flesh out the visual portrayal of villains, a move that uses disfigurement and deformity to map out the terrain of moral monstrosity. Consider the common turn of phrase *ugly as sin*, or the assessment that someone *looks like hell*.

The politics of beauty are no superficial concern. Disability theorist Tobin Siebers argues that judgments about beauty and ugliness serve as key markers of cultural value, assessments by which we frequently measure social worth. When we judge someone or something *not beautiful*, we contribute to the process of social disqualification, a process that "removes individuals from the ranks of quality human beings, putting them at risk of unequal treatment, bodily harm, and death."[5] These aesthetic determinations go hand in hand with our assessment of the quality of people's lives. Judgments that disabled people are incompetent, inferior, or pitiable are driven, in part, by our response to appearance, by visceral feelings of disgust, aversion, anxiety, and fear that certain bodies stir within our own. "Aesthetics," Siebers explains, "studies the way that some bodies make other bodies feel."[6] Beauty is a magnet, a lure, and a draw. Revulsion has a different power. When a body generates discomfort? When its presence makes us recoil or flinch? Those are the bodies most likely to be rejected from the human community, to be judged not worth our time, our love, our care.

Name this problem out loud and watch how quickly people disown beauty. *Beauty doesn't matter*, we like to tell ourselves. *It's what's inside that counts*. In some respects, I agree. Were I in the business of assessing human value and determining who merits particular acclaim, I would make those decisions on the basis of character, on the basis of heart. But the tendency to dismiss beauty as irrelevant fails to account for the powerful role that aesthetic judgments play in people's lives. It fails to account for the way that beauty or its absence affects a person's embodied experience. It fails to account for the power beauty has, the way it shapes our everyday interactions, the way that we're perceived.

Implicit in all this is the notion that disability is obviously, inherently unbeautiful. While it's crucial to recognize the long cultural history that has associated disability with ugliness, I don't think this claim is actually objectively true. When I first began engaging with disability, my instinct was to turn away, to overlook, to flinch from otherness and difference, my own included. But over time, as I've immersed myself in communities where disabled folks are commonplace, my perception has shifted. I've come to associate disability with a particular kind of beauty: intricate, complex, and visually satisfying.

It feels like a tangible change in the mechanics of perception, an actual reworking of how and what I see. At first, I didn't really know how to look. Like most of us, the cultural repertoire I had received for looking at disabled folks shuttled between averted eyes and a rapt stare. It took time to hone other ways of seeing. It took time to learn where to let my eyes land, how to linger visually in a way that felt apprecia- tive and appropriate, how to acknowledge difference, how to enjoy it.

Tobin Siebers argues that body forms that evoke disability are ac- tually central to the aesthetics of modern art. While we think we like symmetry, it's often the off-kilter that draws our gaze. Contemporary artists and critics alike are drawn to compositions that eschew neatly centered, symmetrical figures. Modern art gravitates, Siebers shows, toward the misshapen, the twisted, the partial. Disability pulses with vitality and dynamism, while pristine perfection ends up looking more like kitsch.[7] It's a provocative argument, one that turns on its head what we think we know about the location of the beautiful.

But there's a gap, somehow, between theory and life. There's a gulf that separates Picasso's Guernica from the enfleshed disabled body, a disconnect between the visual pleasure of the celebrated artistic form and what many of us see when we look in the mirror, what we feel reflected back to us in the supermarket or the street. This isn't just a story about disability. It's also a story about fat hatred and femme hatred. It's a story about whiteness and lightness and all the ways our bodies fail to measure up.

When it comes to liberation, I want two different things. I want us to reclaim beauty, to take satisfaction and pleasure in the body forms we have, to root ourselves fiercely and unabashedly in the joy of our own flesh. I don't mean beautiful *in spite of* disability. I mean beautiful *because* of it. I want a world that knows how to look with pleasure at disabled folks, that knows how to appreciate us without trading in spectacle, without trafficking in freakery. I want a world that knows how to look without colonizing and commodifying. I want a world that knows how to savor the sight of us, a world that relishes us.

But I also want to unbind the connection between beauty and worth, to recognize that beauty makes a poor measure of value. My own thinking on this question is indebted to queer Korean American disability justice activist Mia Mingus, who calls us to move beyond the search for beauty and the quest to be desirable. "We all run from the ugly," Mingus writes. "And the farther we run from it, the more we stigmatize it and the more power we give beauty."[8]

The ugly that Mingus evokes looks different in each of our lives. By "ugly," she means the things we fear, the things that pulse with shame, the things we try to tuck out of sight. Sometimes it's about the physical body; sometimes it's the way we move through the world. My ugly is the drool that trickles at the edge of my lip, the way my foot spasms unexpectedly, the way I look when I'm bone-tired and sloughing myself on my butt up some unavoidable flight of stairs. It's the things we hide, the aspects of ourselves we'd rather deny or keep from view.

"Our communities," Mingus says, "are obsessed with being beautiful and gorgeous and hot." Rather than chasing after beauty, Mingus calls us to embrace our own magnificence, the truth of who we are, the spitfire, rough-cut, edgy actuality. "There is magnificence in our ugliness," she tells us. "There is power in it, far greater than beauty can ever wield."[9]

What would happen if we turned toward the ugly? The risk feels visceral and sharp. I pluck the small dark hairs that curl along my chin, even though it hurts my bones to brace myself against the bathroom sink, even though I pay for vanity in pain. What would it mean to be done with that foolishness? What would it cost? What would it cost to let the drool linger? To let the spasm show?

The dimensions of my ugly are things the world judges harshly. While I still can, I hide them. I deny them. I have seen how judgment cuts, how it disqualifies. To turn toward the ugly is to shoulder that disdain, to embrace it and to alchemize it, to let it roar inside me. I fear that move. And I am drawn to it.

"What would it mean," Mingus asks, "to acknowledge our ugliness for all it has given us, how it has shaped our brilliance and taught us about how we never want to make anyone else feel?"[10] This is the very question I have tangled with for decades, the question that has powered so much of my work with disability. Disability has enriched my life; it has shaped and honed my spirit. Disability pulses through my deepest joys, my love, my pain, my knowledge of this world. Disability has taught me viscerally about structural violence, about the brutal ways we devalue people and deny their personhood.

And yet. I still divide the palatable parts of disability experience from the ones that spark my shame. I curate the parts of my life that I will make visible on the speaker's podium or the street. I cringe when some ungainly aspect of my disabled life rips unexpectedly into public view. Even here, I split the pretty from the ugly.

Let go of beauty, Mingus tells me. Embrace magnificence.

When I think about beauty and the Bible, I think of Leah's story. Leah is the first wife of Jacob, the ugly one, the one who wasn't desired. Leah's sister, Rachel, is the beauty in the family, the one who captures Jacob's heart. The Bible portrays their meeting as a great romance. Jacob has left his family's home, on the run after deceiving his father and taking his brother's blessing. After a long journey to the land of his mother's kin, he comes upon a beautiful woman at a well. Rachel is tending her father's sheep. Smitten, Jacob helps her water the flock. He kisses her and bursts into tears. By the time they return to her father's home, he's sure that he has found his wife.

Leah is the wife Jacob gets instead, the one he never loves. The one who isn't beautiful.

Here's how the story unfolds: Jacob has agreed to work seven years to secure Rachel as his bride. But Rachel has an older sister, and her father is determined to see his eldest wed first. He sends Leah to Jacob on their wedding night—and Jacob does not discover the truth of his bride's identity until morning breaks. The deed is done, the marriage sealed.

Devastated, Jacob agrees to labor another seven years in order to win Rachel's hand. In the end, it is a complicated, fractious family that Jacob forms. Because Rachel and Leah both bring an enslaved woman into the marriage, Jacob ends up taking four wives. For each of the women, the marriage is a site of trouble. Bilhah and Zilpah are denied their autonomy, their presence barely acknowledged in Jewish tradition, save when they bear a child.[11] Rachel struggles to become a mother, giving voice to the pain of infertility. Leah herself bears seven children, but she never feels assured of her husband's love.

Is disability a part of Leah's story, a part of why Jacob does not desire her? Jewish tradition suggests it might be so. When the Bible introduces the two sisters in Genesis 29:17, the text waxes poetic about Rachel's beautiful form and lovely appearance. But when it comes to Leah? It tells us only that Leah's eyes are *rakot*, a word that is usually translated as "weak" or "delicate." Because it is never elsewhere used to describe eyes, commentators puzzle over its precise meaning. Were Leah's eyes unusual in appearance? Was she nearsighted? The Talmud explains this phrase by claiming that Leah's eyes became weak from crying. In the Talmud's telling, people used to say that Leah and her sister would be married to Isaac's two sons. As the elder daughter, Leah would be given to the wicked Esau, while her sister would marry Jacob. Leah was so distressed by the thought of marriage to the evil brother that she wept until her eyelashes fell out.[12]

Other commentators assert that Leah's weak eyes reflect a visual impairment. Perhaps her diminished vision is why she stays close to home, why she does not tend her father's flocks. Perhaps she cannot find her way across the stony slopes or see well enough to take care of the sheep. So it is the younger sister who becomes their father's shepherd.[13] When the medieval Jewish commentator Abarbanel reflects on Jacob's desire for Rachel, he stresses that Jacob is not judging simply on the basis of beauty. Jacob was worried that Leah's eyes might have been as weak as his father's, Abarbanel tells us. He feared that she, too, would eventually become blind.[14]

I'm not really interested in the question of whether Leah actually had a visual disability. What strikes me about this story is the way disability gets intertwined with Leah's undesirability, the way her potential blindness lives alongside the notion that she is an inferior bride. In Abarbanel's tradition, Leah's disability masquerades as an acceptable reason for Jacob to disfavor her. Jacob's turn away from Leah isn't an arbitrary choice, Abarbanel reassures us. Jacob's concern isn't simply a matter of beauty. He's concerned for his children, for the future of his lineage. This isn't an unfamiliar story. In some Orthodox Jewish circles today, where families still arrange and negotiate marriages, the presence of disability among one of the prospective partners commonly serves as a reason to avoid a match.[15]

The Talmud tries to fashion Leah's unconventional eyes into a mark of moral sensitivity, making her weak eyes a consequence of grief at being promised to a wicked man. But it feels like a thin attempt to salve the raw biblical story, to cover over the fact that Jacob doesn't find her beautiful. While Rachel's appearance catches Jacob's eye and opens the door to his heart, Leah is unlovely. It is one of the first things we learn about her, this business about her eyes, this public judgment about her appearance. It is a powerful witness to the way of this world. Beauty gets positioned as a measure of a woman's worth, the most crucial fact to understand about her personhood.

How do we undo this knot? One answer is to claim that beauty does not matter, that aesthetic judgments are only skin deep. It's Leah's heart that counts, the Talmud reassures us. Only a boor would judge on the basis of her beauty. But there's something unsatisfying about this response, something that concedes to Jacob's initial judgment. I don't want a world where we *look past* her eyes. I want us to savor the shape of her—her skin, her face, her very particularity. I want her to savor that herself. I want her to own her own splendor, to know her own magnificence.

But the path of reclaiming beauty is fraught with its own risks. It rests on retraining the heart and the mind. It requires us to *feel* a certain way, to look and then to love. What happens when we can't or don't? Have we betrayed ourselves?

A few years ago, after a significant surgery, the shape of my body changed. At first, I thought everything was golden. I was buoyed by relief that the surgery had gone well, that everything had been success-ful, that the worst-case scenario had not been borne out in the flesh. But over time, that feeling slipped into the background. I'd find myself looking down, looking a bit critically at the new terrain.

A broad scar now traces its way across my abdomen. But the cut my surgeon made was not precisely centered. I'm sure there were good reasons for that decision. Since I don't know the first thing about surgery, I cannot tell you what they were. All I know is that when I looked in the mirror, those first months after, I felt a tremble of regret for that slightly left-of-center scar. I thought it made my belly look off-kilter. There was a rise in one spot, a little concave tuck in another. My stomach sunk a bit and then jutted out, where it hadn't before.

For much of my adult life, I have built an embodied spiritual prac-tice around a commitment to loving my own bones. I have taken pride in that embrace, in the choice to honor and cherish my actual body-mind—even when it's complicated, even when it's painful, even when it's the cause of other people's unease. To tell you this story makes me feel a bit ashamed. Not of my body itself, but of that little hitch in my own self-love.

In the months that followed, I built a new aesthetic appreciation for the belly that is mine: for the rise and for the hollows, for the swell and for the scar. When I look now at my flesh, at the curve and the cleft? Most days, I recognize myself as beautiful.

But I no longer think *reclaiming beauty* is the crucial revolutionary act.

I want to unbind the spell that beauty holds, to root myself in tenderness. This is how I practice: I run my hands along the surface of my skin, letting my eye follow the press of my thumb. I let touch become my guide. I let my gaze go soft, soft as the stroke of my own fingers. I let my senses sink into the substance of myself: the viscera, the cradle of my fat, the skin that holds me. I teach myself to look, to look simply and softly. To look at what is, without assessment or judgment. To approach with gentleness. To linger with the intricate.

This capacity for tenderness feels more durable than beauty. When I'm rooted in that place, wonder lives everywhere I cast my eye: in the thick ridge of veins that run through the back of my own hand, the curl of joint and knuckle, the play of tiny, cross-hatched lines along my skin. Against the marvel of that making, conventional beauty is a meager measure. It cannot tell the truth of us. It cannot hold our splendor.

"What would happen," Mia Mingus asks, "if we stopped apologizing for our ugly, stopped being ashamed of it? What if we let go of being beautiful, stopped chasing 'pretty,' stopped sucking in and shrinking and spending enormous amounts of money and time on things that don't make us magnificent?"[16]

When I ask these questions with my mind on the Bible, there is a woman who answers: the prophet Miriam. Miriam is the woman who led the Israelites in song and celebration when they first crossed the sea of reeds, the sea that split to open up a path to freedom. The Bible describes her as a prophetess, a title confirmed by the Talmud, which counts her among seven biblical women to be so named.[17] Tradition has it that Miriam's merit calls forth a well in the wilderness, that this miraculous flow of water follows her through the desert to sustain her people until the day she died. Miriam nourishes an entire generation. But she is no man's wife. She is no one's mother. She is a sea unto herself.

In "Songs of Miriam," the Jewish feminist poet Alicia Ostriker summons forth the prophet woman's voice, imagining Miriam standing on the banks of the sea. In Ostriker's poetic voice, the Prophet Miriam says:

> I lead the women in a sacred circle
> Shaking our breasts and hips
> With timbrels and with dances
> Singing how we got over.[18]

The ambiguity of that final line calls to me, the way it not only evokes the Israelites' liberation from enslavement but also invites us to consider our own. How will *we* get over, you and I, to set ourselves free? What must we release? What must be left behind?

In the Exodus story, the armies of the oppressor chase the Israelites right up to the edge of the waters. The story could so easily have ended in catastrophe, the bodies of the enslaved shattered by the hooves of the horses and weapons of their enslavers. Instead, the sea splits and the Israelites cross, and when the army follows in pursuit, the waters close over them and swallow them whole.

The Bible records one of Miriam's songs, how she sings in praise of this most unexpected rescue: "The horse and his rider / have you thrown into the sea."[19] Ostriker lingers on that verse, calling it Miriam's "unended and unfinished prophecy." In Ostriker's poem, the horse becomes *captivity*, its rider *fear*.

You and I have felt that horse and rider at our backs. When we make our break for freedom, they will come for us. Any time we make a crack in the carapace of capitalism, any time we wrestle loose the tight hold of patriarchy or the gender binary, any time we chisel away at white supremacy, fat hatred, or ableism, horse and rider rise in hot pursuit. Horse and rider are the things that bind us: the pursuers at our backs, the structures that constrain us. But they also live inside our skin. Fear makes a prison of my own mind, calls quit to my own daring. Fear bridles me. Fear keeps me in line.

The biblical Miriam is not afraid to speak. Consider the enigmatic scene where Miriam and Aaron rebuke Moses on account of his wife. "Miriam and Aaron spoke against Moses," Numbers 12:1 reads, "because of the Cushite woman he married." Following the lead of an ancient midrash, the medieval Jewish commentator Abraham Ibn Ezra observes that the verb used in our verse is in the feminine, which leads him to conclude that it was Miriam who spoke; Aaron merely went along with her words.[20]

But what did Miriam say? The biblical text gives us no conclusive account. Because the verse lingers on the identity of Moses's wife, referring to her twice as a Cushite, some readers suggest that Miriam rebukes her brother for marrying outside the community. The biblical land of Cush is a territory to the distant south of Israel, an African nation that archaeologists link to ancient Nubia. Biblical translators sometimes translate Cush as Ethiopia, though the territory of Cush extends far beyond the borders of the modern nation. The biblical Cushites were recognized as powerful and striking, with distinctive dark skin. The Cushites conquered much of Egypt, and during the age of the Hebrew prophets, the Cushite dynasty held the seat of Pharaoh. It was Cushite soldiers who stemmed the terrible advance of the Assyrian army, temporarily saving Jerusalem from assault and protecting the throne of King Hezekiah of Judah.[21]

Some ancient traditions hold that Moses remarried late in life, to an Ethiopian princess. Other commentators dismiss that suggestion, arguing that Numbers 12 describes Zipporah, Moses's Midianite wife, who is called a "Cushite" in honor of her beauty.[22] Either way, this line of commentary understands Miriam's rebuke as bound up with the woman's ethnic identity. For some Jews today, Miriam's rebuke to Moses serves as a haunting testament to the corrosive power of racism, to the poison of prejudice. It serves as a call to wrestle with the way we turn against those marked as Other, those we see as different from ourselves. Even Miriam is not immune.

There's another possibility here. Traditional commentators have often taken these verses as a hint that Moses had separated from his wife, that he did not satisfy her sexually. Preoccupied with prophecy, Moses became unavailable to his wife. Miriam, so the story goes, knew Zipporah's loneliness and grief and tried to intervene on her behalf. It is a powerful moment, a story of solidarity and sisterhood, a moment when Miriam uses her position to advocate for a woman made vulnerable.

Rather than resolve that contradiction or argue decisively for one reading or the other, I take this biblical moment as a reminder of choice: that you and I will likewise find ourselves sometimes caught at the precipice between prejudice and solidarity, facing a decision about which way to turn. Miriam's story contains both possibilities, just as our own lives do. Instead of a foregone conclusion, the narrative asks us to recognize our agency, to take responsibility for our choices. Miriam's example reminds us that the work of liberation doesn't simply come about through the dramatic choice to cross the sea. It lives also in the moment by moment work of small, but consequential, choices: the relationships we build that allow us to witness a deeper measure of another person's pain, the choice to speak on behalf of someone who is wronged, the willingness to risk our own tenuous position when we live adjacent to power.

Miriam chooses to speak. And she is rebuked by God.

The portrait of God that unfolds in the Bible's pages is not always a likeness of the God I know and love. Numbers 12 is a case in point. After Miriam and Aaron make their complaint, the Bible recounts how God calls all three siblings to the Tent of Meeting. The divine presence descends in a pillar of smoke, and God addresses Miriam and Aaron. God speaks in defense of Moses, singling out the specialness of God's communication with Moses. Moses isn't like an ordinary prophet who receives revelation in vision and in dream. Moses speaks with God face-to-face. Moses has seen the likeness of the Lord. Why, God asks, would you two speak against him? God is incensed, Numbers 12 reports. And when God departs, Miriam is stricken and her skin is marked with snow-white scales.[23]

The God we meet in Numbers 12 responds to challenge like a bully, using force to impose order, to silence dissent. In this passage, God appears as one who protects the powerful, as one who champions the number one prophet against the complaint of the subordinates. When Moses is rebuked, God responds with fury. God lashes out.

Perhaps the charge the two siblings level against Moses is spurious. Perhaps it is right that it angers the divine. But other aspects of this scene lead me to doubt that conclusion. Notice how God singles out Miriam for rebuke, even though the text describes both Aaron and his sister as sharing the complaint. Notice how God's response insists on the privilege of Moses as prophet. Notice how nothing is said about the matter of his wife.

And when God's anger blazes, when Miriam's skin turns white? Aaron turns to Moses, pleading with him to intercede. Moses cries out to God on behalf of his sister. "Please God," he prays. "Heal her."[24] But God does not remove the marks from Miriam's skin. Quite the contrary. God says to Moses, "If her father spat in her face, would she not bear her shame for seven days? Let her be shut out of camp for seven days, and then let her be readmitted."[25]

Elsewhere, the Bible lays out in extensive detail the community's approach to the matter of *tsaraat*, a skin disease that Jewish tradition takes as part medical condition, part spiritual ailment. Tsaraat discolors the skin and results in patches of dry and scaly skin, not unlike the modern conditions of psoriasis or vitiligo. Biblical texts regard it as contagious on contact, so those who experienced an outbreak of tsaraat are usually required to isolate from the community and undertake a series of ritual practices and sacrifices. Ancient and contemporary commentators alike link the appearance of tsaraat with spiritual wrongdoing. A tradition in the Talmud lists seven sins associated with tsaraat: gossip, theft, arrogance, stinginess, murder, forbidden sexual relations, or an oath taken in vain.[26] Of all these sins, it is the charge of malicious speech that particularly stuck to Miriam, in part because Jewish commentators read her case as a rebuke for speaking badly of

Moses. If tsaraat is a consequence of a wicked tongue, then Miriam's punishment seems to make plain her crime.

But I am not so sanguine. Consider the history of the term "gossip"—not merely the act of gossiping but the figure of "the gossip." In its earliest English incarnations, Alexander Rysman explains, a gossip was originally a godparent—a person who stood in close spiritual relationship to a child. While the gossip was originally a gender-neutral term, it became closely associated with a woman's companions in childbirth—not only the midwife who attended her but also the women who stood beside her at a time of trial and transformation.[27] As the term grew gendered, it acquired a negative connotation. Gossip came to evoke a particular kind of speech among women, a speech that men perceived as dangerous and subversive.

It's not hard to conjure up the dangers of gossip, the way words become a weapon that tears another person down. Gossip can destroy relationships, shatter reputations. In many circles, gossip is part of the architecture of oppression. It is used to reinforce social expectations, to police gender conformity, to check anyone who steps out of line. But when it's turned against the powerful? Gossip can also be a tool of resistance, a way of sharing knowledge that cannot be spoken outright. Feminist cultural critic Reina Gattuso recalls the lists of names that women recorded in the stalls of bathrooms at her university, names of men who raped and bullied. The lists were scrubbed away by janitors, blotted out, painted over. But the names returned, the warnings resurrected. Gossip, Gattuso reminds us, can also be a way for "marginalized communities to build guerrilla information networks to keep ourselves and each other safe."[28] That's what I think of when I think of Miriam. I think about the price that some of us pay when we dare to speak the truth aloud.

The moment when Miriam is struck with tsaraat is the first time the biblical text calls attention to her body, the first time we learn anything about how she looks. When we first meet Miriam, after the birth of her baby brother Moses, it is Moses who is described as beautiful. Miriam's physicality occasions no comment. It's a refreshing absence, a silence that moves me. We hear nothing about beauty when Miriam leads the women in song and dance after the Israelites cross the sea. Her appearance is beside the point, her form and figure irrelevant.

But when the tsaraat erupts across her skin? The Torah's telling makes it plain that Miriam is punished. Her body becomes a text that testifies to her transgression, her sin made manifest in scales and scabs. Her skin becomes a sign, a site of judgment. Miriam is rebuked, and she is meant to bear her shame until the lesions fade.

Yet that is not the only way to tell this story. I gather to myself a litany of Jewish readers who have imagined this moment differently, who have made some other meaning from these words. In 1939, the Russian Jewish poet Yocheved Zhelezhniak turned to the biblical traditions of Miriam as a way to tell her own life story. She lingers with this episode when Miriam rebukes and is rebuked, finding her own history echoed in Miriam's alienation. "I shall tell," Zhelezhniak writes, "jealous and leprous. I shall tell, complaining, of myself." Rather than pushing the tsaraat away, Zhelezhniak sees it as a vital part of Miriam's experience—and a crucial part of her own.[29] To call herself "leprous" is to embrace the tsaraat, not to deny it. To recognize it as the mark of the outsider, the one who has been scorned.

Contemporary Jewish feminists have fashioned Miriam's tsaraat as a site of power, not punishment. Rabbi Wendy Zierler crafts a modern midrash that claims Miriam's changed skin as a mark of prophecy, one akin to the tsaraat with which God strikes Moses, when Moses is first given signs that will allow him to prove himself to the Israelites. In Zierler's midrash, Miriam's tsaraat stands as a similarly potent gift, a moment when God has "etched the power of prophecy onto your skin."[30] Yiskah Rosenfeld's poem "The Murmurings of Miriam" imagines the tsaraat as a potent moment of communication between Miriam and God, a moment when divine presence sears itself into her skin. It is no mark of shame. It is a kiss from God.[31] Rosenfeld's Miriam does not want to be healed, does not want to be stripped of her difference and made ordinary again. Her difference is her power, her testimony. What others have named as tragedy, what others have seen as punishment, Rosenfeld claims as revelation: "G-d writing herself on my body."

This is the Miriam I claim as ancestor, the Miriam I honor as kin.

The Torah gives no accounting of the time that Miriam spends in the wilderness, no chronicle of the seven days before the tsaraat recedes. We are meant to picture Miriam outside the camp, her face turned back toward the familiar, longing for return. But what if those seven days are her crucible of transformation, her initiation? I imagine Miriam's wilderness experience as her entry into disability conscious-ness, her time of psychic transformation. It marks her, more than tsaraat itself. Seven days alone in the desert, outside the camp. Scars like lightning, inside her own skin.

So many of us who live with disability have known this kind of forced separation from the rhythms of ordinary life: the sudden rup-ture of accident or the revelation of diagnosis, the hospital stay, the bed rest, the long weeks of rehab, the institutionalization. If we come home, none of us comes home unchanged.

I fantasize sometimes about the Miriam who returns. I imagine her scoured out, walking back into the camp, her eyes filled with des-ert fire. I imagine her unbowed and unashamed. Nothing left to run from. This is the Miriam we meet in the final stanza of Ostriker's verse, the Miriam who cuts through falsity, the Miriam who shatters illusion. She says:

> I peel the skin off myself in strips
> I am going to die in the sand
> Miriam the leprous, Miriam the hag[32]

My tongue plays over the words of Alicia Ostriker's poem, think-ing about Mia Mingus's call. This is the woman who has turned away from chasing beauty. This is the one who knows magnificence as her own true name.

CHAPTER TWELVE

The Radical Practice of Rest

Shabbat Values and Disability Justice

Two tea lights perch on the balcony rail outside my little rented room, their silver skins nestled atop the green peeling paint. It's Friday night in Berlin, and I watch the sun set through the trees in a quiet part of the city. Spread out before me is my gathered bounty: two luscious sunflower seed rolls I picked up that morning from the bakery just down the street, some hard cheese and tomatoes from the little grocery a few blocks away, and the apricots and berries I tucked carefully into my bag when I happened on an open-air market. I have one plate, one set of silverware, one little cutting board. A book of matches. My own breath.

This isn't the textbook way to usher in Shabbat. I once told this story to a lovely Jewish woman sitting next to me at some synagogue affair, when guests were asked to share a special Sabbath memory. "No one invited you for dinner?" she asked me, plainly scandalized. "You spent Shabbat alone?"

Known as "Shabbos" in the Ashkenazi Yiddish dialect of my own heart, the Jewish Sabbath is a day of rest, a day of renewal. It's a day when observant Jews refrain from thirty-nine different categories of labor, everything from lighting a fire to writing a word. Translated into a modern idiom, those prohibitions mean no electricity, no carrying, no commerce and no spending money, no travel beyond a small area meant to be navigated on foot. Yet if you think all those restrictions translate into a solemn, somber day, you're missing something crucial about Jewish practice.

Shabbos is the pearl at the heart of the hectic press of time. But for most Jews today, it's not exactly a contemplative tradition. The preparations start hours, even days, before—the cooking, the cleaning, the invitations, the plans. Shabbat dinner is a festive affair, time to bring out the fine plates, the beautiful candlesticks. There's meant to be a crowd around the table, with stories and songs and laughter, the kind of love where everyone speaks over the end of each other's sentences. I relish the heady energy of the traditional Shabbat table, the shared meal, the prayers, the tender beauty of singing in harmony. But for me? Those are rare pleasures.

The Shabbos I know best is different. My favorite way to usher in Shabbat is to be outside at twilight. There's a particular moment when the shafts of sunlight slice like dusty gold between the trees. For an instant, each individual leaf turns incandescent. As the darkness comes, it softens my vision, smoothing away the sharp-edged sight of ordinary time. I notice what I've missed before: the sudden flight of birds against the darkening sky, the shimmer of grass in the evening breeze. The calculating gaze of most of my days gives way to a different sort of perception, where I glimpse as much through the wind on my skin as I do through the sight of my eyes. My heart opens up, my mind slows down, and the sweet expanse of stillness sweeps me up in her arms.

I want to tell you about this world I know, this world that lives one breath from the present, one breath away from the press of productivity and the relentless push for more. There are doorways to that world in many different spiritual traditions, a thousand portals that can take you there. It's a world I've discovered through Shabbos practice, a world I've come to know by rooting deep in disability community.

On the seventh day, God finished the work of creating. And God rested from all the work of making.[1] So begins the second chapter of Genesis, the words observant Jews recite each Friday night to bless and sanctify the beginning of Shabbat. In Jewish tradition, Shabbat is a day that recalls God's own rhythm of creation: six days of the week to work, to shape, to make, and to labor, and then the seventh, set aside to rest and savor. When Exodus 31 describes Shabbat as the day on which God rests, it uses a beautiful Hebrew phrase, *shavat vayinafash*. The verb that describes God's act of rest is linked at its root to the Hebrew word for soul, for the spirit of life that breathes through our bodies. God stopped and got Her soul back.

The practice of keeping Shabbat has long been at the center of Jewish religious culture. Reflecting on this weekly commitment to the practice of rest and renewal, the Hebrew writer Ahad Ha'am famously said, "More than the Jewish people have kept Shabbat, Shabbat has kept the Jews."[2] Shabbat has sustained us, through grief and peril. Through crisis and despair. Through joy and celebration.

Rabbis often wax poetic about Shabbat, and I suppose I'm no exception. But rather than extol Shabbat as a foundation for Jewish practice, I want to lay out its political force, the way it resonates with the principles of disability justice. Shabbat isn't just a way of tapping into Jewish culture or tasting a distinctive Jewish joy. It's an invitation to enter into a different relationship with work, with the world, with time. Shabbat is a way of unwinding the lies that make work the measure of our worth, the cultural patterns that tie our basic value as people to our ability to labor, produce, accomplish, and earn. Shabbat is my antidote to ableism.

Keeping Shabbos is a counter-cultural practice, one that flies in the face of my usual habits. In his famous meditation on the significance of the Sabbath, Rabbi Abraham Joshua Heschel names the challenge of this practice:

> He who wants to enter the holiness of the day must first lay down the profanity of clattering commerce, of being yoked to toil. He must go away from the screech of dissonant days, from the nervousness and fury of acquisitiveness and the betrayal in embezzling his own life.[3]

Left to my own devices, I would eat up my life with worry and work and fear. It's Shabbat that reminds me: I am more than my "to-do" list. My work is not my worth. My humanity is not dependent on my ability to get things done.

The tendency to value accomplishment isn't simply a personal fetish. It's baked into the very structures of society, the structures that undergird ableism. Ableism is a complex system, one that works in myriad ways to deny disabled people access, agency, resources, and self-determination. Ableism manifests in the social attitudes that stigmatize disability, the architectural barriers that impede access, the complex set of power relations and structural arrangements that privilege certain bodies or minds as normal while marking others as deviant, dangerous, and despised. One of the ways ableism operates? It fashions speed and stamina as a threshold condition for basic belonging. Ableist values intertwine with capitalist pressures to laud those who work at a punishing pace. One of the lies ableism tells us? You only matter if you can keep up.

Dominant culture tends to rank people's worth on the basis of accomplishment. It prizes forms of doing that are economically productive, that earn money, status, accolades, and all the trappings of approval. But disability justice refuses the assumption that the measure of a person's value lies in what they can do, in how much or how quickly they can produce. Consider the words of Patty Berne, the cofounder and artistic director of the disability justice performance collective Sins Invalid: "We don't believe human worth is dependent on what and how much a person can produce. We value our people as they are, for *who* they are, and we understand that people have inherent worth outside of capitalist notions of productivity."[4]

Berne's words resonate with me profoundly, as a Jew. A cornerstone of Jewish ethical commitment is the recognition that we are all made *b'tselem Elohim*, in the image of God. To be *b'tselem Elohim* isn't dependent on speech or smarts or your ability to work the system. God doesn't see Herself just in the clever or the quick, in the lives we hold up as billboards of accomplishment.

And disability justice? It too demands a place, a future for all of us. When I speak about disability justice, I mean a distinctive form of political organizing and cultural work led by disabled people of color, many of whom are trans and queer. Disability justice calls us to recognize the connections: the way ableism links up with white supremacy, with misogyny, gender violence, and trans hatred, with antisemitism and xenophobia. To challenge the violence and marginalization faced by people with disabilities, disability justice contends that we must also grapple with poverty and racism. To build a world where disabled folks can thrive, we have to challenge the unchecked, turbo-charged productivity culture that keeps all of us racing to catch up.

Even if you're not disabled, the cultural logics of ableism can be deadly. Ableism is part of what drives the brutal, brittle culture of efficiency that makes us to head to work even if we're sick, that imagines the body as an obstacle to someone else's bottom line. Ableism is the fear that gnaws us in the night: that we're only as good as our last accomplishment, that if we're feeling bad, we better fake it—that we only matter if we're healthy, wealthy, and well.

This lie that work is all we are? This is what Shabbos comes to shatter.

I started keeping Shabbat in graduate school, not the time most folks decide to set aside twenty-five hours each week for rest and rejuvenation. I can still remember how scandalous it felt, how subversive it was to come back to my dorm room and begin the ritual of unwinding my mind from the endless clutch of assignments, deadlines, worries, and work. No matter what I had to do, no matter what I'd left undone, on Friday night, I surrendered to the setting sun. I'd set out my tea lights, take a breath, strike the match, chant the blessings, and let the world turn to shadow and to gold. I would sit in the dark for hours, watching the candle flames flicker. Some nights I would read a novel. Some nights I would doze. Mostly I would sing, softly, without words. Sing myself back home.

In the years since, I've lit my travel set of Shabbos candles all around the world: on the sterile tabletops of hotel conference rooms; on my parents' screened porch, while the cicadas sang; by the Sabie River in South Africa, on a carefully folded square of purloined aluminum foil; on makeshift ledges and rickety tables, on cedar chests, and in elaborate dining rooms, on bare rock and holy ground.

Jewish tradition emphasizes the importance of celebrating Shabbat in community. Yet my own Shabbos practice is often solitary. Some of that, surely, is a reflection of my own soul's temper, a measure of the way my spirit seeks stillness, the way I yearn for darkness and the draw of a deep well. But much of it is a matter of disability.

I can count on one hand the number of times I've accepted an invitation for Shabbos dinner. When it comes to synagogue services, at least in the US, there's often some way for a wheelchair user to get into the building. If I want access to the bimah, all bets are off. Most synagogue architecture still assumes that everyone who chants the blessings or lifts the Torah or leads the prayers can navigate a couple stairs. But if it's enough for me to slip into the back, to watch the show unfold, there's usually a way to make it happen. It might be a side door, locked unless I make arrangements in advance; it might be the door through which they haul out the trash.

Private homes are a whole different terrain. There's almost always a step or three to get inside. Once I'm inside, it's a minefield of furniture. Carpets are like quicksand. Rugs are my nemesis. Gathering together around the table in the company of friends and strangers takes a legion of logistical arrangements, none of which most folks are prepared to undertake for a casual invitation. It's no one's fault, in particular. It's ableism in action, constraining all our choices, stripping away possibility before the invite even gets made.

Access isn't just a matter of architecture. If the Shabbat-hosting home is, by some miracle, not up a couple stairs, then I confront the question of how to arrive and how to get back home. Here, too, my access needs run deeper than most people realize. Accessible public transit isn't just about getting on the bus or making sure the metro has an elevator. It's a matter of coverage maps and people-centered design, a question of infrastructure. When I roll to the stop, do all the sidewalks and the curb cuts check out? Is my destination close enough, with traffic lights and safe crossings? Can I do it after dark?

On a weekday, I might chance a rideshare or a taxi. Given the privilege of my own bank account and the particulars of my own disability, I can usually make that work. But on Shabbos, that strategy is off the menu. I don't carry money on Shabbat, and I don't use my phone. I'll confess, I've given thought to shifting that part of my observance. My personal practice when it comes to Shabbat is already a patchwork of contradictions. Most observant Jews don't use electricity and wouldn't drive at all. But I get to synagogue thanks to an electric scooter. At home, I flick on and off the lights without a qualm. I'll accept a ride if someone offers. I just won't pay for transportation. I only travel with friends.

My thinking isn't really rooted in the particulars of Jewish law. It's a buffer against ableism. One of the places I'm most likely to face disability static is when I try to hire a car. Taxi drivers drive off and leave me by the side of the curb. Ride share drivers give me the evil eye. Someone manhandles my wheelchair or complains about having to pop the trunk. Any given weekday, I power through that business like a pro. I've got my strategies in place. I'm girded up for trouble, ready to shrug off the aggressions, prepared to shoulder the frustrations. But on Shabbos, I've taken off the armor. My heart is gentle, my gaze slow. I can't navigate the world that way, with my softness so exposed.

Years ago, I spent Shabbos on the banks of the Sabie River, after spending a pair of weeks in South Africa, working in the company of disabled women activists from many different countries. When I'm among secular activists, I usually keep Shabbat privately. I find a moment to slip away, a quiet place to light candles and mark the moment. But something felt different this time. I was camping with a small circle of folks who had become friends, at a beautiful spot in the countryside, where little rivulets of water ran among the ruddy stones. We'd been talking by night about the things that sustain us, about the ways we draw strength for long and slow work. So when Shabbos came? I wanted to share with my friends a tangible taste of the practice that cradles me, the tradition that anchors me.

There's a traditional custom to welcome in Shabbat by baking two braided loaves of bread. Making challah is one of my touchstones, one of the ways I settle myself into a different kind of time. Making dough is an elemental pleasure, one that takes a different kind of attention. First, I warm the water and dissolve the sugar. I mix the yeast into the slurry and let it start to feast. I blend the dough by hand, my fingers working in the flour. It's physical labor, thick and tangible. Knead dough and let it rise, punch it down, then wait. It takes the time it takes. Once the dough is made, I roll out the strands, pliable and tender. I braid them like a prayer.

As a practice, baking bread crystallizes some of the qualities that most draw me to Shabbat. No matter what, bread will not be rushed. To make Shabbat requires planning and preparation. That afternoon in South Africa, I had no pantry at the ready, no supplies on hand. My friends and I set out together, hunting for eggs, oil, sugar, salt, and flour in the camp store and at local markets. We found a precious packet of yeast. I had none of the tools to which I've grown accustomed—no measuring cups, no kneading board, just a simple stone oven over an open fire. So I laid the loaves in a bit of aluminum foil, nestled them into the flames. That night, as the sun slipped into the river and the brilliant darkness came, I sat with friends who'd never before kept Shabbos, lit the candles, spoke the blessings, and savored the bread that we had made.

Part of what makes Shabbat tick is the preparation. You can't keep Shabbos in the traditional sense and simply drop into rest as the sun sinks beneath the trees. The custom is to cook in advance, to make plans beforehand, to arrange the rhythm of the hours before Shabbat begins. In that sense, Shabbos shares a quality with my own day-to-day disability experience. Very little in my life happens without a lot of planning. Going to an event means calling ahead for access, researching the route, making arrangements for transportation. Spontaneity is a privilege, one I rarely enjoy.

And speed? Disability means I often have to take it slow. When I travel, I'm at the mercy of other people's schedules. Because I don't drive, I usually travel by bus. But like many folks who can't always access traditional public transit, I also get around with Paratransit, a shared-ride van service that picks me up at my door. Paratransit is a masterclass in learning how to wait. Rides are scheduled at least twenty-four hours in advance. Even when everything works flawlessly, there's a half-hour window for pickup times, and there's no one to call when the driver's running late. Once I'm on the van, it's a crapshoot where we'll go and what order we'll each get to our destinations. If I'm heading to a meeting or somewhere else I need to be on time, I build in at least an extra hour, sometimes two or three. Arrival times are out of my control. I'd rather show up early than risk missing my appointment, standing up a colleague, or leaving my students in the lurch. To navigate that system? To learn to wait with grace? For this, I thank the practice of Shabbat.

Keeping Shabbat has changed my relationship with time. Because I set aside my phone on Shabbos, there's no last-minute call to make arrangements, no quick text to update arrival times. If I'm getting picked up, I set a time in advance, and I tell friends not to worry if they're late. It's a familiar phenomenon but with a twist. Shabbat consciousness shifts the way I wait. I'll sit outside, watching the birds or feeling the play of sunlight on my face. I take a book. I daydream, drifting, my thoughts slow and soft. I unwind the notion of *being on time*. In part, it's possible because I've set up the conditions of my Shabbos life so that arriving late is a matter of little consequence. If I'm leading services or speaking at an event, I've already orchestrated the logistics, usually with a generous buffer for the unexpected. And if I'm simply arriving at synagogue or meeting a friend, Shabbat frees me from the pressure of precision. It frees me from the tyranny of the clock.

It would be a lie, of course, to say I'm always blissful when Paratransit's running late. When I'm sitting in the cold, when I'm weary or in pain and I just want to go home? It steams me up to be kept waiting, to be at the mercy of a system that assumes my time is free. But sometimes, I can tap a little taste of Shabbos even in the midst of an ordinary day. Sometimes I can give myself the gift of gentleness. Sometimes I surrender to the slow. When I do, it's like a doorway opens in my heart, a path to the sweet water that lies at the center of my soul. It isn't only Shabbos when I can be refreshed.

Whenever I describe the way I keep Shabbat, when I lay out the specifics of my practice and acknowledge the complexities that come with setting aside my wallet or powering down my phone, someone always asks me why. Wouldn't it be easier to pick up the phone? To just hire a car?

There's no question that keeping Shabbos complicates my life. Because I live and work in communities that aren't organized around Jewish time, I'm always having to negotiate observance, to mark out time and space for my own practice. When I travel for a weekend work trip, keeping Shabbos means I need an extra night in the hotel and other special arrangements. Coupled with the rest of my access needs? Sometimes I fear it's all too much.

But keeping Shabbos has given me a framework for navigating disability, for making arrangements that will afford me access when I travel or teach. Disability means I need to think through a thousand logistics in advance, just as I do to prepare for Shabbat. It means I need to ask for alternate arrangements, often arrangements that will add to my host's expense. Shabbat practice has helped me hone the skill of laying out my access needs forthrightly, without flinching. It's helped me learn to be upfront about complexity, to explain at the outset what I'll need, and then to assess whether the invitation is one I can accept. Ableism puts tremendous pressure on disabled folks to absorb the cost of our own accommodations, whether the cost be financial, emotional, or paid in pain. When it's only disability on the line, I'm more likely to accept marginal access, to make do with paltry accommodations, especially when access gets expensive. I find it easier to insist on keeping Shabbos. Because Shabbat observance is anchored in my spiritual commitments, because Shabbat is rooted in tradition that runs deeper that my own particular life, it's easier to resist the temptation to say yes when I mean no.

But the other side of this story is that I've carefully chosen the practices that will make my Shabbos meaningful, carefully negotiated how much complexity I can stand. When it comes to religious observance, I afford myself a high degree of autonomy, granting myself the right to determine the practices I keep and those I set aside. That's not a posture that's permissible in every Jewish setting. In more traditional communities, disabled folks often get shut out of the most vibrant communal spaces because our access needs are deemed a violation of Shabbat. Traditionally observant communities forbid active engagement with electricity on Shabbat, on the assumption that flicking a switch to turn on the lights is akin to the ancient prohibition of kindling a flame. That prohibition has huge implications for people with disabilities in observant Jewish communities. The same logics that have me turning off my cell phone lead some rabbis to look askance at accessible communication devices, to forbid the electronic tools many disabled people use to communicate. It makes power wheelchairs unacceptable on Shabbat, according to some religious authorities, unless the wheelchairs are equipped with a special Shabbat starter that includes a work-around to avoid making a spark.

Now, it's important to be clear. Jewish law not only permits but actually *requires* a person to violate Shabbat in order to save a life—should they be in that position—or to protect a person from imminent danger. So even in the strictest circles, there are times when these laws are set aside. But this principle is often narrowly understood, and it's rarely invoked to affirm disability access. Observant Jewish communities have evolved all sorts of ways to make Shabbat more pleasurable, such as special Shabbat elevators that stop at every floor so you don't have to press a button. Yet this kind of innovative technology tends to be more available when nondisabled people also stand to benefit. Disabled people's needs are often left out of the calculus.

So it's not inevitable that Shabbos leads to disability paradise. In more traditional communities where the norms and conventions of Shabbat observance often run counter to the embodied needs of disabled folks, Shabbat can be the hardest time to feel fully at home, to be fully engaged in vibrant Jewish life. Sometimes the rules for keeping Shabbat get weaponized against people with disabilities, rendering our electric scooters, our reading devices, our communication tech, our hearing loops and microphones off-limits during Shabbos, a violation of communal norms. All too often, Shabbat becomes a day of isolation, a day of exclusion from community.

Jewish law often gets a bad rap in Christian circles, where it's put down for being legalistic and hidebound. So I'm always a bit hesitant to speak of these matters in mixed company, for fear of reinforcing stereotypes and activating those old familiar tropes. When I say it matters that traditional Jewish communities consider how to negotiate observance in ways that express and affirm a place for disabled Jews as full members of the community, I don't mean to jettison the law or set it aside. I mean I'd like to see a world where more communities commit to including Jews with disability expertise in the process of making halakhic decisions, a world where disabled Jews help shape these conversations and negotiate practice. Communal norms are complicated, and navigating these conflicts over practice takes care and keen deliberation. But my own Jewish values lead me to prioritize building communities where disabled Jews can flourish, where we know that we belong.

That doesn't mean I want to do away with all the practices that mark out Shabbos time. While Shabbat is often described as the Jewish day of rest, there's a lot about the traditional Sabbath that runs counter to ease. It's harder to navigate the world without access to the technology I usually depend on. It makes more work for me. Yet in my own experience, part of the secret of Shabbat lies in the acceptance of a certain set of arbitrary limits, limits that operate beyond my moment-to-moment desires. Figuring out what this means is not

without challenge, especially in community. I'm not lifting up my practice as a recipe, and I don't believe my limits should be yours. I'm not
sure Shabbos works if it's a flat prescription, an unbending set of rules
imposed from high. But I know that my own life needs some combination of flexibility and constraint. If I simply organized Shabbat to
match my own convenience, I would lose something infinitely precious.

Shabbat has given me a framework for acknowledging rest and
renewal not simply as a spiritual good but as a spiritual obligation. Left
solely to my own devices, I'd fritter away the very thing that sustains
me, whittle away the peace my own soul needs. Jewish law, Jewish
custom is part of what I brace against. By taking on certain practices
that extend beyond my own convenience, by accepting arbitrary limits
without regard for my own momentary preferences, I root myself in a
tradition that extends beyond my own life, my own desires. I anchor
myself in a community whose commitment can ground me and sustain me, even when I waver. I surrender myself to a practice that can
hold me, even when I falter.

Shabbos doesn't only work when I am feeling good or when I'm
feeling spiritual. When I was in rabbinical school, one of my teachers
promised: *Keep Shabbat long enough and one day, when you need it, Shabbat
will keep you.* Over the years, I've felt the truth of that counsel, the way
Shabbos peace has wrapped around me even when I wasn't ready,
when I had nothing to offer, nothing to give. The Friday night I wel-
comed Shabbos in the midst of grief. The Friday night when I was
furious, when I couldn't clear my head. The times I've lit my candles
with a shaking hand. The times I didn't want and didn't care and
couldn't trust.

The act itself has steadied me. To light, to say the words, to let
the day sustain me. Had you asked me years ago, I would have said
that our intention is what matters, that we get from practice only what
we give. But I no longer believe that's the full story. When we keep a
practice regularly, when we let it work its way into our body and our
bones, the physicality itself can be a door. Sometimes my hands can

lead me when my heart is closed. Sometimes the gesture is enough to
guide me home.

Keeping Shabbat in a disabled key is a delicate balance, a balance
between the labors of love that make Shabbos special and a deep
respect for the limits of my own life. When I think back to that Friday night in Berlin, with that bountiful but modest spread? There's
something precious about that Shabbos memory, something true to
my own disability experience. I was alone in the city for several weeks
on a research trip. To travel solo means I think incessantly about logistics. Everything I bring must fit securely in a duffel bag, the one piece
of luggage I can sling on my wheelchair's sturdy back. When I move
through the city, my day pack is a cloth or canvas bag, hung behind
my wheelchair. Anything I want to carry gets dropped into the sack. It
must withstand the jostle of uneven pavement, the jut of cobblestone,
the uncertainty of curb cuts, the likelihood that some stranger may
well get deployed to boost me up a step.

   When I'm on the road, the usual customs of Shabbat give way
to practicality. Jewish tradition calls us to usher in Shabbat with a
blessing over wine and bread. But carrying wine across the city when
I'm alone on wheels? Too risky and too complicated. Add to that the
fact that kosher wine is likely halfway across town, or up a flight of
stairs, or tucked into a storefront too small for me to navigate. Idea
dismissed, on principle. In the same way, I set aside the expectation
for a lavish meal. When I shop for Shabbos, I look for hearty food
that's easy to procure and simple to prepare: bread and cheese, tomatoes and cucumbers. Sometimes I take a chance, tuck berries in
my bag like purloined gold. My evening plans are often solitary. On
Shabbos, I release myself from expectation. I don't schlep across an
unfamiliar city to a synagogue where access is uncertain. I've called
ahead to any number of synagogues in any number of towns only to
encounter some unexpected barrier. *Oh, yes, the synagogue has an elevator*,
a kindly Jew in another German city once told me. When I arrived, I

took that elevator up to the second floor, only to find the entrance to the women's section up several additional steps.

Even at home, I like to keep my circle small. I let myself be satisfied with simple things, with elemental pleasures. I practice what I've come to call *crip Shabbat*, a way of being where I tend the needs of my own body-mind. Sometimes that means letting go of expectation, letting go of *ought* and *should*. I recall with vivid clarity the Friday night when all I did was pop a frozen pizza in the oven, or the Shabbos days I've lain in bed. I recall the services I've skipped, when a week of work snapped back upon my bones, inexorable. When exhaustion swallowed me, when all those body needs I held at bay came home to roost, when rest was not a choice but a demand.

I'm only an occasional traveler in the land of deep fatigue, an intermittent visitor. There's a lot I do not know about weariness, about pain, about the need to always weigh my choices and always marshal strength. To learn the contours of this landscape, I turn to the wisdom of disabled people living with chronic illness, with chronic pain or fatigue. In a searing essay, "Six Ways of Looking at Crip Time," disabled writer Ellen Samuels writes about the way chronic illness "forces us to take breaks, even when we don't want to, even when we want to keep going, to move ahead."[5] Sitting with her words, I want to name the limits of Shabbat, the way it might not work for everyone's experience. Hold too tightly to the particulars and Shabbos rest becomes just one more imposition, one more forced pause, one more assumption about how bodies work, what they can do, and what they need.

Chronic illness refuses the assumptions most of us make about health and wellness, rest and recovery. American culture and work habits are built on the belief that people get sick only occasionally and briefly, that they "get better" on schedule. Young people or middle-aged folks are expected to get over illness quickly, to press on with productivity, to bounce back quickly like good, reliable workers. That expectation runs hand in hand with ageism, with the way American culture sidelines elders when they can no longer work at full speed, and dismisses them when their strength or health begins to decline. But people with chronic illness throw a wrench into the conventional chronology, the map of normative time. As disability theorist Susan Wendell observes, people with chronic illness "are considered too young to be ill for the rest of our lives, yet we are not expecting cure or recovery. We cannot be granted the time-out that is normally granted to the acutely ill, or we were given it at first and have now used it up, overused it."[6]

Here, too, I confess I fear that conventional Shabbos practice gives too little and assumes too much. Disabled folks with chronic illness or chronic fatigue are often sick for a long time, sick with no end in sight. What's a single day of rest stacked against that truth? Nothing but another stingy sick-day policy.

Shabbat can be a crucible for disability liberation. But to tap its power, we have to use it differently. We have to let it be a catalyst for our imaginations, a space for committing to the long, slow work of unlearning the ways that we've been taught to think and feel. Can we use the practice of Shabbat to help erode the workings of a world where pace gets weaponized, where worth and work are so tightly entwined? Can it give us the impetus to build a world that supports and affirms disabled folks who work and make, or think and create, in radically different ways, as well as those who cannot work at all? Otherwise, Shabbat is nothing but a private holiday, a personal oasis, a little breath of calm that only serves to charge us up so we can work again.

I'm not a stellar example of someone who's got this sorted out. For six days of the week, my life is pitched for productivity. I teach at an elite university, where stress is a competitive sport. Disability has only raised the stakes. To challenge the doubters and defang assumptions that disabled folk aren't good enough, I've doubled down on proving otherwise, stacking up accomplishment like armor. As a woman in a male-dominated field, as a wheelchair user in a world built for striders, the rules of the game are absolutely plain: *Never let them see your limits. Never falter. Never pull back.*

Changing this landscape isn't simply a matter of personal spiritual practice. To suggest we simply opt out of dominant culture's demands fails to reckon with the way expectations about production

and productivity are baked into the very structure of society. I live in
a country where 22 percent of the workforce has no access to paid
sick leave, where calling off can get you fired or keep you from making
rent.[7] I live in a country where many folks work two and three jobs to
make ends meet, where caregivers almost never earn a living wage. I
live in a country where access to good health insurance often depends
on a person's ability to secure and keep a job with benefits. I live in
a country where most parents of disabled folks get no respite unless
they can arrange and fund it themselves, where care is so privatized
that it almost always falls on family alone.

Who gets to rest? Who gets to live with ease? The transformation
we need isn't simply a transformation of the heart, a matter of spiritual
awakening. There's a risk here, a risk that we privatize these questions,
a risk that we fail to challenge the social structures and public policies
that make rest a luxury that only a few can afford.

Jewish tradition describes Shabbat as a foretaste of the world to
come, a little touch of paradise, a promise. But I am not content to wait.
I'm not content to put off gentleness and generosity. I'm not content
to leave intact a world whose pace pushes certain bodies and minds
to the margins, a world that runs roughshod over anyone who can't
perform to a high-pitched standard. That's part of what I keep, when
I keep Shabbos—a commitment to building and dreaming a different way of being. For those few hours, I feel it in my bones. I taste its
sweetness on my tongue. A world that offers each of us enough, that
gives us all the space to savor. A world that values us for who we are,
not just for all that we have done. A world that teaches us to sink into
the slow, to linger over twilight, to tune our hearts to a different kind
of time. A world that shelters us. A world that's made for us. A world
in which we know ourselves whole.

CHAPTER THIRTEEN

God on Wheels

Disability Theology

Let me begin with a story, a story of finding God in my own bones. As a woman who uses a wheelchair, the world throws me a thousand reflections of my own body as an aberration, as a defect. Strangers on the street stare at me or pray for me. They shush their children or turn their eyes away. My wheels get taken as a sign of tragedy, a mark of something broken. The process of being turned into a symbol strips my life of richness and particularity. It doesn't matter what I think or how I feel. It doesn't matter what I know or what I love: the feel of dirt beneath my tires or the pavement pulsing beneath my wheels, the play of the wind against my skin. The vivid, complex textures of my own embodied life get pressed into an icon of lament, a story of loss, a testament to other people's fears.

I tell you that so you know why it matters to feel God in and through this flesh. I tell you that so you know why it matters to claim this life as sacred.

Several years ago, I was sitting in synagogue one Shavuot morning, listening to the reader chant the first chapter of the book of Ezekiel. Shavuot is the Jewish holiday that celebrates the giving of the Torah, a holiday marked by the recitation of one of the most vivid visions of God in the Hebrew Bible. It's a vision that comes to the prophet Ezekiel, an intense young priest who lived through the destruction of

Jerusalem, when the Babylonian army poured into the holy city and set it ablaze. The conquering army set fire to the Jerusalem Temple. They desecrated the altar where Ezekiel and his fellow priests used to offer sacrifice. They destroyed the sacred places where the people had sung and chanted and gathered with their God. They turned the sanctuary to rubble, the stones into ruin.

Ezekiel was part of the ragged group of elites and aristocrats the Babylonian general forced into exile, a deliberate strategy designed to subjugate and dominate the conquered kingdom and crush resistance. I imagine Ezekiel walking beside the other captives, the memory of that smoke stinging his face like shame. Zeke is twenty-five years old, his world turned to ash. By the banks of the Kebar River, in the land now called Iraq, he opens up to prophecy.

Ezekiel sees his God. He sees God as a radiant fire, borne on a vast chariot, lifted up by four angelic creatures. The chariot itself is barely described, save for one extraordinary feature: its vast, vibrant wheels. The wheels are what grabbed me when I first heard this passage chanted; the wheels are what opened up my heart. Sitting in synagogue that Shavuot morning, I felt the recognition shiver down my bones.

God has wheels.

When I think of God on Wheels, I think of the delight I take in my own wheelchair, the satisfaction I find in my own disabled life. My wheels set me free and open up my spirit. I draw a powerful, sensual joy in tandem with my chair: the way her tires grip into asphalt or concrete, the way I lean into a curve and flow down a gentle grade, the way I feel the twinned vibration of earth and wheel through the soles of my shoes or the balls of my feet. My sense of Spirit is bound up with this bone-deep body knowledge: the way flesh flows into frame, into tire, into air. This is how the Holy moves through me, in the intricate interplay of muscle and spin, the exhilarating physicality of body and wheel.[1]

This recognition of God on Wheels is the ground of a powerful theological claim: that God knows disability experience from the inside out. It's an affirmation that God knows and shares the pleasures of

disability life and that God also knows the shape of its pain, its loneliness, its frustrations and loss. It's also an invitation, an invitation to
craft theology that speaks to the specificity of my own experience. As
a disabled theologian, the practice of turning my attention to a God
who wheels through the world has permitted me to let go of apology,
to stop trying to press my spiritual insights into a walking person's skin.
It has invited me to probe more deeply the depths of my own disabled
knowledge, to consider how disability has shaped my own perception
and awareness, and then to ask how those insights might shed light on
God's own relationship to the world.

To do this means to consider God's body, a practice that runs
counter to the ways many of us have been taught to think about the divine. Judaism is a powerfully aniconic tradition, a tradition that forbids
making tangible representations or physical images of God. Medieval
Jewish philosophers like Saadiya Gaon and Moses Maimonides laid
out a strong theological claim that God *has* no body, a tradition that
remains deeply influential to this day.[2] But the Bible treats God as a
thoroughly embodied subject, albeit one whose presence and form
can rarely be seen by mortals. In Genesis 3:8, God walks through
the Garden of Eden, a presence physical enough that Adam and Eve
hear the sound. In Exodus 33, Moses begs to see God's face and God
demurs but tells him instead to stand in the cleft of the rock so that
Moses can see a glimpse of God's back. Biblical verses evoke the sight
of God's eyes and the presence of God's hands. The Bible often evokes
the power of God's right arm, a phrase that's always left me wondering
about the silence that surrounds the left. Is it a place of weakness? A
site of disability? As someone who grew up with a recalcitrant left leg,
I know a thing or two about silence, about the unspoken.

For readers today, it can feel shocking or strange to consider God's
body as anything but a metaphor. I myself tend to think about God's
body in primarily poetic terms, as a way of evoking presence and feeling,
as a way of inviting kinship with my own flesh. In the deepest sense, the
Holy Presence I call God pulses in and through skin and sinew, through
the physical presence of this world, through trees and sidewalks and

stones. I would never want to bind God to the body or pin God to a single form. If God is body, God is also breath. If God is body, God is also wind and rain, being and becoming, infinite and unspeakable.

But another thing I know is this: Our spiritual lives are shaped and grounded by our own embodied experience, by the way we touch and sense and feel and know. Our spiritual lives and spiritual practices are affected by the way we think about bodies. And even when we say God doesn't have a body? Even when we dismiss the notion that God has a physical embodied form? Most of us hold on to the implicit assumption that if God *did* have a body, it would be powerful, beautiful, splendid, and strong. God's body would surely be physically adept. It would be lean and limber, flexible and capable. It would, in short, have the very attributes we value when it comes to human bodies. It would steer clear of disability. When God walks through the garden, God surely doesn't limp.

If we drop into the depths of Ezekiel's vision, we get a very different picture. The cosmos that Ezekiel sees is filled with unusual angel bodies, bodies whose physical form and modes of movement resonate deeply with disability experience. Let's look more closely at this text to probe some of what the prophet sees.

In the first chapter of Ezekiel, the prophet recounts how "a stormy wind came sweeping out of the north." As the vision opened up before him, Ezekiel sees "a huge cloud and flashing fire, surrounded by a radiance; and in the center of it, in the center of the fire, a gleam as of amber."[3] From within that fire, four angels appear. These are not angels as we've come to imagine them, not chubby-cheeked cherubs or serene, ethereal figures. They are strange and powerful creatures with uncanny bodies. Ezekiel 1:5–7 recounts:

> They had the form of human beings.
> But each had four faces, and each had four wings.
> Their legs were fused into a single rigid leg.

Their feet were like a single calf's hoof.
And they shimmered with the luster of burnished bronze.[4]

The images Ezekiel draws are resonant with disability: a single fused leg, held rigid, unable to bend. A strange foot, one that would clomp or stomp if it tried to walk, one that cannot curl against the ground. Of course, angels don't need their legs for mobility. Wings make walking obsolete. But there's something striking about the recognition that these angels *cannot* walk, something that evokes disability experience. Ezekiel's angels cannot stride through the world. They stand rigid, or they fly.

But *can* they fly? Not in the traditional sense. The next verses from Ezekiel's vision offer a vivid sense of these angels' bodies, describing their unusual wings, their uncanny faces, the strangeness of their forms. Ezekiel 1:8–12 reads:

They have human hands beneath their wings.
At each of their four sides, they have their faces and their wings.
Each one's wings touched those of the other.
They did not turn when they moved,
But each could move in the direction of any of their faces.

Each had a human face.
Each the face of a lion on the right.
On the left, the face of an ox.
And the face of an eagle behind.

Those were their faces.
Their wings were separated.
Above, each had two wings touching their neighbor.
The other two wings covered their bodies.

Each could move in the direction of any of their faces.
They went where the spirit sent them,
And they did not turn.[5]

Each angel has four faces, one on each of their sides. While one of those faces looks human, the others have distinctive animal characteristics: the thick broad muzzle of the ox, the chiseled face of the feline, the peaked hook of the avian beak, the hooded eyes. In the biblical tradition, the ascription of animal characteristics to the creatures of the chariot is often taken as a sign of the angels' strength, or an invitation to awe. But reading Ezekiel's words, I can't help but think about the long, sordid history of linking human difference to animality, the way racist and ableist caricatures alike have mocked certain bodies as being more animal than human.[6] Disabled writer Eli Clare tells the story of being surrounded by a taunting group of children on the playground, chanting *monkey, monkey, monkey.*[7] To be likened to an animal is to be different, despised, cast out of the privileged circle of the human.

It's not just the uncanny faces that make me think of disability; it's also the way the angels' bodies are described. They have a plethora of hands, at least four, but likely eight or maybe even sixteen—a hand for every wing. But we never see them grip or grasp. We never hear if they have arms. Are the hands small? Vestigial? Are they tucked close to the wing, close to the flesh? The wings, too, are unconventional. The lower wings serve as cover for the angel's body; they are for adornment, not for motion. But the upper wings likewise seem pinned in place, too close to the others to lift and fly. When Ezekiel describes how the angels move, he describes a striking blend of freedom and constraint. The angels can go anywhere, he tells us. They can move in the direction of any of their faces. Yet when he describes the angelic body, he returns again and again to evocations of rigidity, of fixedness. The angels do not veer from their position. They cannot turn. They do not even move under their own power.

Ezekiel's angels are propelled by spirit; they move according to its direction and desire. Most readers understand this spirit as the will of God, a kind of disembodied force. But the verse uses the Hebrew word *ruach*, a word that literally translates as breath. It's an image that calls to mind the way some disabled folks move, using a puff of breath to power an electric wheelchair.[8] In the Bible, ruach is God's creative force, the power of life unfolding itself. Consider the very beginning of Genesis, where "the breath of God rustles over the face of the waters," a prelude to creation, its first stirring. Ruach is spirit at its most elemental, the touch of air against water, the breath of possibility.

In Ezekiel's vision, the wheels of the chariot likewise move through spirit, through the ebb and flow of the divine breath. As the heavens open for Ezekiel, the wheels are a site of awe and wonder. In Ezekiel 1:16, the prophet recounts:

> The wheels gleamed like beryl.
> All four had the same form . . .
> A wheel within a wheel.[9]

Many commentators understand the phrase "a wheel within a wheel" to mean something like a gyroscope, an ancient sphere with one wheel mounted inside the other, allowing the device to rotate rapidly and move in any direction. The dynamism of the gyroscope was likely quite different than the motion of ancient war chariots, which were often difficult to steer with precision.[10] Ezekiel's "wheels within wheels" give God's chariot the capacity for fluid, flexible movement, one that mirrors my own experience on wheels. In a modern manual wheelchair, the big back wheels power the enterprise and cover the distance. It's the tiny front casters whose free rotation opens up a different kind of motion, the capacity to spin, to twirl.

Another thing I love about the way Ezekiel describes the chariot is the intricate connection between the creatures, the spirit, and the wheels. They move together, all three in tandem:

> When the creatures moved forward, the wheels moved with them.
> When the creatures rose above the earth, the wheels rose up.
>
> Where the spirit sent them, they went—
> Wherever the spirit sent them.

The wheels rose up with them,
For the living spirit was in the wheels.[11]

It is an intimate relationship, an interlocking harmony, one I know well in my own life. In my wheelchair, I flow together with my wheels—two intertwined bodies becoming one as we roll. The creatures of the chariot likewise move in tandem with their wheels. When the angels stir, the wheels stir. Where the angels go, the wheels go. There is no separation. Movement is a dance, a partnership.

Perhaps that seems a strange thing to celebrate in a world that values independence above all else. But it's one of the things I cherish about wheelchair life, this intimate connection between body and wheel. Folks often treat wheelchairs as nothing more than objects, if they don't flinch from them or disdain them outright. Yet from where I sit, wheelchairs feel vibrant and alive. When I got my first electric scooter, I made a conscious choice to turn toward her, to think of her not just as a clever piece of tech but as a friend, a companion. I have friends who share this closeness with their cars, who have settled into intimacy. Over the decades, I've built relationships with many different wheelchairs, getting to know their preferences and particulars, coming to understand how they move through the world and what that means for how we move together.

This intimacy with wheelchairs isn't simply a matter of whimsy. Linguists call this recognition of liveness a recognition of *animacy*. To grant animacy to another is to treat her as subject, to regard her as a being in her own right, not just an object or a thing. Different cultures fashion their own animacy hierarchies, ways of ordering and ranking the value of diverse beings and things based on the perceived liveliness of each being.[12] The white Euro-American culture I was raised in has long drawn these kinds of distinctions, lifting people over animals, animals over plants, plants over rocks. But I've always been a bit of a rebel in this regard. I was a kid who talked to trees, who felt stones as living presences. I still do.

Animacy shapes the way we understand our connection to the world. Potawatomi biologist Robin Wall Kimmerer argues that we need different pronouns for the natural world, a different way to speak of our relations with plants and animals, to mark our kinships with all the creatures who inhabit the earth. "We use a special grammar for humans," Kimmerer observes. "We distinguish them with the use of he or she." This special marker of personhood is a privilege we afford to humans, whether they are alive or dead. "Yet we say of the oriole warbling comfort to mourners from the treetops or the oak tree herself beneath whom we stand, '*It* lives in Oakwood Cemetery.'"[13] As Kimmerer makes plain, language is not destiny. Language doesn't compel us to treat the world around us as an object free for our own taking, nor does a more generous way of speaking guarantee that we will grant reverence and respect to the animals and lands with which we live.

But it matters still. It matters to me. Among friends, my wheelchairs have gender and animacy.[14] They are subjects and actors in our lives. "She bit me," my partner remarks, when one of my chairs gets unruly during disassembly, when she leaves her mark on shin and flesh. To be more than a casual acquaintance in my life, you've got to understand my relations with wheels. To know me is to know how I move through the world, to know my loves, to know the way these kinships flow.

When I speak of my wheelchair to outsiders, I am always biting my tongue. When I talk about her to doctors, when I give instructions to taxi drivers, I speak of her as *it*. It's a strategic choice, a choice to match the speech patterns of the nondisabled world, a choice to protect something precious from the eyes of outsiders. But it feels foreign on my tongue. It shears away the intimacy between us. It pulls me away from the truth of who I am. When I'm centered in my deepest self, I am part of an intricate web of relations. I'm in touch with the pulse of ruach, the living presence that flows through body, world, and wheels.

One of the things I relish about the invitation to see God on Wheels? It calls me to place my own disability experience at the very center of my spiritual imagination. It calls me to investigate the particularity of my own life experience, to treat my distinctiveness as the ground of spiritual insight. Instead of searching for universal truths, I've chosen to lift up the rare, the unusual, the decidedly personal. Rather than seeking out God's presence in the qualities that all humans share, I aim to turn and turn the mirror so it catches a thousand reflections of all our brilliant differences.

God on Wheels puts a striking twist on a familiar religious claim, the claim that humans are all created in the image of God, *b'tselem Elohim*. As the Bible narrates God's creation of the world, Genesis 1:26 has God say, "Let us make the human in our image, in our likeness."[15] That idea, that humans are made b'tselem Elohim, in the image of God, has a powerful place in Jewish and Christian theology. In many communities today, the principle of b'tselem Elohim is used to ground a deep affirmation of human rights and dignity, an affirmation of the fundamental equality of all persons. Jewish and Christian disability theologians often use this verse as a powerful affirmation of disabled people's belonging. It's a powerful bedrock claim in a world that has pushed so many of us to the margins, that has refused to recognize the fullness of our humanity.

I value that work, and I affirm those commitments. But I'm also troubled by the way we use this verse, by its implications. I'm not convinced that, on its own, b'tselem Elohim gives us the theological tools we need to affirm the vivid particularity of different disability experiences. I worry that it dismisses difference in the interest of affirming the universal. But perhaps most of all, I'm uneasy with its intellectual history, with the way this very principle of universal belonging has been used to buttress a notion of "the human" that profoundly devalues disability.

Let me explain what I mean. In Jewish tradition, the idea that humans are created in the image of God has often been used to distinguish human beings from other animals, setting up a hierarchy of higher and lesser creatures. It's deeply bound up with a claim to human exceptionalism, an assertion that humans are more holy than other animals, that we are God's final and favorite creation, the pinnacle of God's making.[16]

I reject that notion on ethical and ecological grounds. I simply can't countenance the idea that humans have a lock on God's love, that our story is the only way to speak of the sacred. When I consider the intricacy of earth's creatures, when I sink my awareness into the vast splendor of creation, I see a world that mirrors back divine presence in a thousand different ways. I think of what wolves know about kinship and the primal pull of the pack, how they move in tune with a holiness that whispers through the trees. I think of how elephants honor the history of their families and their lineage, how the ravens recount God on the wing. I wonder how cephalopods evoke creation in their own language, how the bees imagine the first Queen.

It seems like hubris of the highest order to imagine we're the only ones who know the sacred, that we're the only ones who share God's image, that we're the only ones who really count. While my interest in the spiritual lives of other animals is rooted in an ecological commitment, it's also an insight I learned through working in disability communities. So many of our assumptions about human superiority are grounded in the choice to privilege specific norms of communication, language, and rationality. While I value deeply my own ability to speak and hear and think as I do, I no longer believe they're the only way to engage in meaningful communication, the only route to value or belonging. Speech isn't inherently superior to signed language. An ability to quickly calculate numbers is a useful skill in the world in which I live, as is the capacity to transform letters into words and to store them in memory in verbal form. But I no longer assume those are the only ways of thinking that matter, the only modes of knowledge worth considering.

My own instincts run counter to a long tradition of privileging the human—and doing so explicitly on the basis of speech and intellect. In his landmark work *The Guide for the Perplexed*, the medieval Jewish philosopher Moses Maimonides asserts that humans are described as made in the image of God because of our intellectual capacity. "The

human being," he says, "is made unique by a very wondrous thing
that is in him, as it is not to be found in anything else that exists under
the sphere of the moon."[17] That quality is our capacity to know and
to reason, a quality that Maimonides attributes to "the divine intellect" that is "conjoined" within us. According to Maimonides, it is our
smarts that make us human.

It's no far cry from this formulation to derive a much more chilling
principle: that those who aren't smart are not really human at all. It
isn't just Maimonides who has acted on such claims. The assumption
that a certain degree of intelligence is a threshold requirement for
human belonging runs like a terrible, bitter thread throughout modern American history. It's the story of Carrie Buck, forcibly sterilized
in 1924 as an inmate of the Virginia State Colony for Epileptics and
the Feebleminded. It's Supreme Court justice Oliver Wendell Holmes
rationalizing her treatment and laying a legal foundation for eugenic
practice on the basis that "three generations of imbeciles are enough."[18]
It's the story of Junius Wilson, a Black Deaf man from North Carolina, castrated and confined to an institution for decades after a false
accusation of sexual assault. It's the state's decision to keep him under
lock and key, even after his conviction was overturned, because they
said he'd become accustomed to the place, to the prison, because they
said it wouldn't be a kindness to set him free.[19]

It's these stories and a thousand more, the stories of people whose
names we'll never know. And it isn't just history. It's the sheltered workshops that still operate today, where people with intellectual disabilities
labor for pennies an hour.[20] It's electric shock treatment, used to force
Autistic people to comply with conventional behavior patterns.[21] It's the
institutions where people still get warehoused; the group homes where
the bedbugs run like kings.[22] It's the R word, the ubiquitous insult.[23]
It's the taunting and the turning away and the too-saccharine praise.
It's the denial of people's sexuality. It's the denial of people's right to
autonomy, the capacity to manage their own time, to pursue their own
desires.[24] Those without intellectual disabilities routinely exercise power
and control over the folks we define as cognitively deficient. Sometimes

that power rears up with utter brutality. Sometimes it's wrapped in the mantle of paternalism and benevolence.

Intellect isn't the only exclusionary way we've tried to define the human. Classical Jewish traditions assert that humans are distinguished from other creatures by our capacity for speech, as well as by other distinctive physical attributes that are said to confirm our unique place before God. In a well-known midrash on Genesis, the rabbis teach that humans are a mixture of higher and lower elements, that some of our qualities make us like the angels, while others make us like the beasts. We eat and drink as animals do; we copulate like animals, we excrete like animals, and we die like animals. What makes us like the angels? We speak like angels, we see like angels, we understand like angels, and we stand like angels.[25]

The implications for disabled folks are brutal. If it's speech that justifies our specialness, do nonspeaking people forfeit their status as human? Is a certain kind of sight a prerequisite for being made in God's image? Does a person have to be able to stand in order to belong?

From where I sit, it isn't a rhetorical question. These notions have been weaponized against disabled folks, sometimes explicitly so. In his masterful study of the concept of b'tselem Elohim in Jewish tradition, Rabbi David Seidenberg examines the idea of "proper human stature" in the writings of the illustrious sixteenth-century thinker, the Maharal of Prague. For the Maharal, walking upright is a sign that humans have the bearing of a king. Our kingship reveals not just human closeness to God but our right to dominion over other creatures. The proof of that kingship is stamped within the very nature of our muscles and limbs. It's part and parcel of a man in his prime. But when a person begins to age? "He begins to walk hobbling," the Maharal concludes, "as if he were no longer a complete human." The logic flows with terrible precision. "Since the superiority of the human is uprightness," the Maharal asserts, a person who can no longer walk "no longer has God's image."[26]

It's a shocking claim, one that flies in the face of the cornerstone Jewish obligation to honor elders, to treat all people with dignity and respect. It's an affront to the Jewish values I hold dear, a violation of my deepest understandings of Jewish ethics. But even as I recoil from that teaching, I confess I'm not entirely surprised. The most astonishing thing about the Maharal's teaching, as far as I can tell, is that he has stated outright what so many of us implicitly believe. It's our abilities that make us worthy of distinction, our strength that defines us, our capacities that make us special.

When most Jews and Christians today lift up the affirmation that humans are made in the image of God, we're not thinking of this brutal history. We don't intend to make divisions between the worthy and the unworthy, between the holy and the less than holy. Quite the contrary. We mean to cherish, to celebrate, to honor human dignity.

But to make b'tselem Elohim work as a tool for spiritual liberation, we must let go of attachment to hierarchy, to our investment in defending humans as the best and most beloved before God. Every time we set ourselves the task of defining what makes humans worthy of a privileged place in God's eyes, we end up with a set of characteristics that only *some of us* fulfill. When we double down on the notion of human superiority, we can't help but fashion distinctions that elevate certain humans over the rest.

To make b'tselem Elohim work as a tool for spiritual liberation, we must let go of our investment in norms and universals. We must cultivate a spiritual imagination that turns toward difference and diversity. When I lift up the notion that humans are all b'tselem Elohim, this is what it means to me: that God reflects each one of us. Human beings, in all our radical particularity, offer a hundred thousand windows into holy possibility. God's gender is nonbinary, stone butch, faerie, and a thousand words we haven't named. God knows wheels and blindness from the inside. God has felt a runner's high and the exhilaration of the climb. God is Deaf. God is Black. God is Brown. God is queer. And it isn't only humankind. The dolphin's God has a dorsal fin. God is kin to us, to each of us, with all the paradox that this implies.

When I first glimpsed God on Wheels, I was drawn to the fact of representation. I was drawn to the subversive power of recognizing my own wheelchair as a reflection of God's chariot, to imagining my own bones as a witness to God's being. For those of us whose bodies are persistently devalued, for those of us who have been told in a thousand subtle and not so subtle ways that we fail to measure up, finding God in the mirror of our flesh is a powerful reorientation.

Representation matters. Theologians of color have written powerfully about why it matters for religious communities to refuse a theology that's rooted in whiteness, to move beyond Euro-American norms and notions as the only proper way to name and know the sacred. As Asian American feminist theologian Grace Ji-Sun Kim observes, it is "long overdue to open theology's door," to call "the rich beauty of global voices to enter the theological house."[27] Queer and feminist theologians have called religious communities to cultivate a gender-expansive vision of God, to offer metaphors and modes of imagining God that center femme and queer experience. Jewish feminist theologian Judith Plaskow reminds us: "The God-language of a religious community is drawn from the qualities and roles the community most values, and exclusively male imagery exalts and upholds maleness as the human standard."[28]

Plaskow's insight, that our images of God buttress and affect the way we understand "the human standard," feels strikingly resonant when it comes to disability. Conventional theology has a strong investment in God's power, God's strength, God's physical capacity. The metaphors we use for God consistently valorize nondisabled experience. Jewish liturgy calls on God to hear our voice, to *not be deaf to our plea.* We ask God to see us. We want God to hold us, to rescue us with that mighty right arm. God walks unbowed through the Garden of Eden. God does not crawl. Even when we only mean it as a metaphor, the embodied language we use for God helps build a conceptual world that lifts up sight and hearing, that honors physical dexterity and strength. It reinforces the rightness of the nondisabled norm.

When folks protest that God *can't* be disabled? That it's blasphemous to think of God this way, or theologically impossible? Their hesitation is often rooted in the assumption that disability is a defect, that disability is a diminishment. To imagine God as disabled is to diminish God, to associate God with limits and flaws. But it need not be so.

In her pioneering book *The Disabled God*, disability theologian Nancy Eiesland tells a story about her own moment of revelation, a moment of encountering God in and through disability experience. Eiesland writes:

> I had waited for a mighty revelation of God. But my epiphany bore little resemblance to the God I was expecting. I saw God in a sip-puff wheelchair, that is, the chair used mostly by quadriplegics enabling them to maneuver by blowing and sucking on a straw-like device. Not an omnipotent, self-sufficient God, but neither a pitiable suffering servant. In this moment, I beheld God as a survivor. I recognized the incarnate Christ in the image of those judged "not feasible," "unemployable," "with questionable quality of life."[29]

Eiesland's epiphany unsettles conventional assumptions about God's nature. Eiesland's God is not all powerful. But perhaps even more significantly, Eiesland's God isn't positioned over and above disabled folks. Her God isn't the caseworker who double-checks our benefits paperwork or the administrator who evaluates our claim. Her God isn't the doctor or the judge, or even the kindly soul who stops by on occasion to visit the shut-ins. Eiesland's God is one of us. The Disabled God knows disability from the inside.

Eiesland's God knows stigma and judgment. To see God in a sip-puff wheelchair is to see a God who has been scorned, a God who's been disdained and overlooked, a God who's been judged worthless or better off dead. To see God this way doesn't just ask us to rethink our theology. It asks us to confront our ableism. It shakes up the assumptions we make about where holiness lives, about where dignity dwells. It upends the conventional hierarchy we use to order social worth, the snap judgments we make about who matters and who doesn't. It forces us to reevaluate the bodies that our world treats like trash.

Eiesland roots her theology of the Disabled God in the very center of the Christian story: in the crucifixion and resurrection of Jesus. Eiesland calls Christians to recognize the brutality that Jesus faced at Roman hands, the violence that wounded and scarred his flesh. But that violence is not the end of the story. "In the resurrected Jesus Christ," Eiesland writes, "they saw not the suffering servant for whom the last and most important word was tragedy and sin, but the disabled God who embodied both impaired hands and feet and pierced side and the *imago Dei*."[30] For Eiesland, one of the signature moments of Christian truth is that Christ's physical wounds remain a part of his resurrected body, an integral witness to the story of his own human life. "Jesus," she writes, "the resurrected Savior, calls for his frightened companions to recognize in the marks of impairment their own connection with God, their own salvation."[31]

It's an extraordinary theological insight, one that resonates with me even though I am not a Christian. It's a story that recognizes and claims Jesus's human experience, his experience of terror and pain. It's an insight about violence transformed, about meaning made new, about disability recognized and reconfigured as a central part of personhood.

But I want to tell a different kind of story, a story where disability is not always and only a story of violence. Alongside Eiesland's image of the Disabled Christ, I want to envision disability as part and parcel of God's intricate design. I want to tell a story where disability is part of God's own brilliant beauty, a story where disability pulses through the very fabric of God's making. I want to look anew at the biblical account of creation, to imagine the mythic pulse of Genesis through the prism of disability culture, to see it as the artistry of God on Wheels.

Imagine the beginning, told differently.

The stage is dark. When the lights rise, the backdrop is a luminous blue. A dancer in a wheelchair hangs high above a bare set, tethered to a point beyond our gaze. A strap encircles his legs and the seat of his chair, and a thick rope extends upward. He spins, a slow motion, lazy and languid, a light bit of leftover momentum from the ascent. The wheels of his chair are still. How do you roll without surface? How do you roll in the air?

The dancer is Rodney Bell, a Maori artist and wheelchair user whose solo work is part of a 2008 performance by Sins Invalid, the San Francisco-based disability justice performance collective that centers and celebrates the work of queer and trans disabled artists of color.[32] Bell is seated in his wheelchair. He wears black pants and shoes; his upper body is muscled and bare. Half of his face is painted with strong black lines and curves. His back is adorned with an intricate symbol traced in black, showcasing copper skin beneath.

Bell pivots in the air, one hand on the rope, then the other. He arches backward, rolling over, wheels toward the heavens and head toward the earth. Arms outstretched, he draws his body and chair into a smooth rotation. He spins upside down, hands slapping at his bare chest, then extending outward, fingers fluttering like little wings. Verticality is a dance, an unexpected axis of motion.

Bell descends, the tether lowering him slowly toward the floor. He pulls at the tether, curling his body upward until he spins upright. Then he leans over the edge, his arms and his torso spilling over the side of the chair, sweeping backward. The motion has a vital athleticism, grace punctuated by the pulses of drum, and the call of a chant in a language I do not know. Upside down again, he thrusts his arms toward the ground. Then he spins, his body whirling like an inverted dervish. When he pulls himself upright once more, his eyes are drawn to the stage, to the surface he is meeting. Wheels land lightly. The tether makes the touch unexpectedly tender. The image closes on his face, so I do not see the moment of contact. Do I imagine an almost imperceptible rocking? How does it feel to find ground beneath wheel?

When I read the opening words of Genesis, when I imagine creation as the artistry of a disabled God, I lay the image of Rodney Bell's luminous descent over these ancient words. I imagine Jewish story made new. In the beginning, God is rolling through what isn't yet the world. She spins on the axis of eternity, tethered to the heart of the heavens. Her wheels turn in slow, shimmering revolutions. This is the movement of being and becoming, the primal rotation. To give life to the world is to set it in motion.

That isn't just a poet's flourish. Scientists recognize spin as the very beginning of our galaxy. Astronomers speculate that when our solar system was still a floating cloud of unformed gas and dust, a nearby star exploded and caused the cloud to collapse. Gravity pulled that collapsing mass into a flat, whirling disk. The kinetic force and heat of that revolution kindled our sun. But it didn't stop the spin. The disk kept whirling, birthing the planets and the world we know. Their bodies began as grains of dust and elemental matter, drawn together by gravity. As those particles whirled around the sun star, they clustered together. They collided and contracted into spheres, still spinning with the imprint of their own beginnings.

And here on Earth? Spin structures the rhythm of our days. Daytime and night, sunrise and sunset are the product of our planet's rotation, Earth's slightly tilted spin on her own axis, while the seasons result from Earth's revolution around the sun. Even the sun spins. The equator rotates the fastest, while the poles move more slowly; the core of the sun spins more rapidly than the outside, giving the gaseous body a powerful flux and flow.

Our universe is a universe in motion. From the smallest of asteroids to the greatest of galaxies, everything spins—a movement that can be traced back to the very beginning of time. Stars spin in the heavens, orbited by rotating planets with their moons. The cosmos itself is aswirl. Our own Milky Way moves at a speed of 1.3 million miles per hour, its luminous arms of light trailing in the direction of its own rotation.

To give life to the world is to give it spin.

This is a joy that wheelers know, this glorious abandon. Children know it too, arms outstretched on the playground merry-go-round, and so do Sufi dancers. We know how it feels to surrender into bliss, to twirl around a central axis, to give over the body to the push and pull of a force more powerful than our own.

I still remember the first time I felt the incandescence of spin. It was years ago at a wedding, I can't remember whose. It was one of those stilted, stylish venues that crimp my style and make me want to tuck my elbows in. I was at one end of the room and my partner was at the other, laughing with a group of friends.

For no reason I can recall, we caught each other's eyes. There were no words that I remember, just a look that passed between us. A look, an invitation. I set down my plate of hors d'oeuvres. I put my hands to the rims, and I stroked hard and fast. The floor was set up for dancing, smooth parquet and firm beneath my wheels. When I got close, I caught my partner's outstretched hand and pushed.

I let go into a brilliant, unexpected spin.

The unabashed daring of that moment was like nothing I'd ever felt before. The whole room stopped and stared. It was physics. It was magic. I knew in my bones that it was beautiful and right. I knew in my bones that it was good.

But to move through the world on wheels isn't always a pleasure. If God rolls along the sidewalks of my city or yours, then God knows the sharp frustration of wheelchair life: the building with no elevator, the bus with the perpetually broken lift, the curb without a cut, the set of steps in front of the closest grocer, the church with no accessible place to pee. God knows the slow burn of exclusion, the anger and the weariness.

God has an access problem.

Spiritual seekers often lament how hard it is to find God in this world. Our teachers try to help us open our hearts to holiness, to find the sacred everywhere we turn. Divine presence often feels elusive. "Where is God?" we ask. "How can we get close?"

To think of God on Wheels flips that problem on its head. It asks us to orient our attention to the architecture, to the built environment, to all the norms and habits we've allowed to shape our days. It asks us to investigate the structures we have fashioned, to pull down the barriers, to root out the impediments to God's full, flush presence in this world we've made.

When I think of God on Wheels, I think: God knows what it is like to make a long and lonely trace of the perimeter, to go round and round a building, searching for the one accessible route inside. God knows what it's like to get stopped by a curb, to have the access routes buried by the snow plow or blocked by the construction crew. God knows the frustration of seeing the paved path stop just before the vista. God knows the locked lift, when the key cannot be found. God knows the haggling, the negotiations at the door, the phone call to the manager, the apologies for yet another misunderstanding. God knows the shut-out. God knows the longing. God knows the giving up, the slow trudge home.

I mean this as a metaphor. But metaphor is tactile; metaphor is true.

Some access barriers are the result of deliberate social choices, large-scale city planning and building campaigns that didn't account for disabled people's presence. But many of the frustrations in my life on wheels are smaller, more intimate. There are a thousand ways I get stopped in my tracks. By casual thoughtlessness, by people in a hurry, by someone who dropped their bag in the aisle. By chairs set too close together. By a room that's too small for the people crammed inside.

When I think of God on Wheels, I think of all the ways I shut God out. Most days, it's not a conscious choice. It's a forgetting, a different kind of failure. It's a wall built out of a thousand rushed decisions, the weight of other pressing obligations. It's going too fast. It's stacking too high. It's a slipshod shortcut, a locked door I didn't even notice. Access refused. Access denied.

Recognizing God on Wheels puts access at the very center of our spiritual work, at the heart of our efforts to build spiritual community. How do we leave space for the wild, free-wheeling movement of the chariot? How do we open the inaccessible spaces of our hearts? How can we break down barriers within ourselves and our communities?

How can we refashion the crusted architecture of our minds that keeps the Holy at bay?

As I lift up this image of God on Wheels, I also want to call out a danger. Because wheelchairs are a ubiquitous symbol for disability in this culture, there's a very real risk that wheelchair accessibility is the only type of access people imagine. But it isn't just wheels we need to plan for. Access needs vary profoundly across the disability community, and what ensures welcome for one person doesn't guarantee access for another. Access isn't one-size-fits-all.

So let's widen the frame. Let's plan for sensory access. For access to quiet space and access to refuge, for stim-toys and sensory-friendly gatherings that are built from the ground up for Autistic people's pleasure. Let's plan for spaces that celebrate and cultivate neurodiverse joy.

Let's insist on cognitive access. Let's recognize that people with intellectual disabilities deserve meaningful access to information so they can be a part of conversations that matter. Let's come together in ways that allow all of us to flourish, in ways that don't always privilege a certain kind knowing. Let's build community through music and movement, through art and sport and laughter.

Let's think about multiple modes of access, multiple doorways. One single way will never be enough for us. Let's think about sign language and alternative communication tech. Let's think about Braille and large print, about the time and care it takes to offer multiple formats, to make materials available in advance. Let's think about social media in a deeply visual world, about default norms and expectations. About digital access and image descriptions. About automatic captions that don't know a mitzvah from a matzo ball, that reduce Jewish culture to garble and gaffs.

Let's think about all the habits we need to change.

When I think of God on Wheels, I think about a Deaf God, about a God with Down syndrome. I ask myself what a Blind God knows, how an Autistic God perceives this world, what She unfolds about the nature of the sacred, how She invites us to encounter the infinite. I want to know the sacred through a thousand disabled languages, and I want to revel in the holy silence of a nonspeaking God's heart. I want to glimpse God through each way disability unfolds in this world, through your flesh and mine.

I don't know how to write those stories from the inside. So when I turn to theology, I turn to the one life I know, to the way God lives in and through this wheeler's body, to the pulse and flow of spirit in and through these bones.

To wheel through the world is to live a life of intimate relationship with ground. I feel every ridge and rut, every crack in the pavement. I feel smooth surface like an invitation, a warm welcome. The land over which I roll flows back into my body, a pulse I feel through the frame of my chair, the tremble of my front caster wheels.

I know the contours of every place I've ever lived on wheels. I know the slant and pitch of Berkeley sidewalks as they slope lazily toward the Bay. I hold within the compass of my memory a thousand small gradations in terrain, the flow of slope and surface, where the ground swells and how it rises, how the pavement cracks, and where the water pools after a hard rain. I know the loose three bricks that play like a xylophone just outside the threshold of my Georgetown office, the ripple and the shiver, the feel of coming home.

Wheels deepen my relationship with the material world. When I imagine God on Wheels, I think of the way wheels make connection. When a walker takes a step, her stride pushes her up and away from the ground. Wheels offer a different kind of contact, an intimate relationship. With every revolution, I sense the ground beneath my wheels, its texture trembling through the frame of my chair, into my sit bones, along my spine. When I roll, I feel earth roll its way through me: asphalt, sidewalk, hard-packed dirt, the bulbous ripple of tree roots, the sudden jut of an unexpected stone. Is this how God feels the world? This tangle of earth and flesh and wind and breath all flowing into each other in one interconnected chain?

God on Wheels doesn't sit high in the sky. God on Wheels is intimate with earth, with the grit of the city, with smell and scent. Wheeling home through Washington, DC, I come into intimate contact with
mud and dirt, with litter and all kinds of human leavings. To wheel
through this world is to know the feel of stale urine as it seeps into the
wheels from the subway elevator floor, one of the few private spaces
in American cities where a person can pee for free. To wheel through
this world is to know the way it feels on your hands. How it sticks to
your gloves, how it lingers long after first contact.

To wheel through this world is to always watch the ground. While
walkers are free to let their attention wander, wheelers keep our focus
on the path. There's an intimacy here, an attention to the specificity
of place. I can skip my wheels a little to hop over an ungainly join in
the sidewalk, or curve to evade a rock. When I'm distracted, I slam a
caster against an uneven curb cut or stub a wheel against an uneven
patch of pavement. The jostle grounds me, shocks me back into my
bones. Rolling is a reminder: Pay attention. Eyes on the earth.

This is the world I live in, the world I want to dream with you. A
world where your skin is bound up with my own. A world that knows
God thrums like a bass line in the ache of every body, in the tenderness.
In the curl of every hand, in the burn scars, in the marrow of the bone.
A world that feels God breathe in all our bodies, in our weariness and
wanting, in our tremble and our loving. In the bitter and the beautiful.
In the rage and in the grief. A world that hums in satisfaction when
the egret and the pelican slide their low-slung languid wings across the
sky. A world that turns to welcome us, a world whose every shattered
glass becomes a mirror and a prism, a world that's tuned to catch
the beauty of our making, where each of us throws back a thousand
brilliant sparks.

GLOSSARY OF
JEWISH TERMS

Need an orientation to some of the Jewish terms used in this book? While I explain Jewish vocabulary when I first use it, I've also put together this quick guide to some key words.

AMIDAH: A central set of Jewish prayers, known as "the standing prayer," usually first recited individually in silence and then repeated aloud by the prayer leader. The traditional custom is that Jews rise before reciting these prayers.

BAVLI: A colloquial term used to describe the Babylonian Talmud, one of the major works of rabbinic Judaism.

BENCH GOMEL: To make a public affirmation of gratitude, traditionally recited after recovering from a serious injury or illness.

B'TSELEM ELOHIM: A biblical phrase that means "in the image of God."

BIMAH: The place in a synagogue from which the Torah is read and from which the service leader usually leads prayer. The bimah is often a raised platform.

HALAKHAH: Jewish law; the term "halakhah" arises from the verb "to walk/to go" and it offers guidance for all aspects of life—from ritual expectations and sacred practices to appropriate conduct in business.

HEBREW BIBLE: A name that scholars often use to describe the Jewish Bible (Tanakh); the Hebrew Bible refers to the same body of texts that Christians commonly call the Old Testament, though the order of books in the Hebrew Bible is somewhat different.

KOHANIM: A biblical term, referring to priests of an elite lineage.

MAIMONIDES: Moses ben Maimon (1128–1204), one of the foremost scholars of medieval Judaism, especially well known for his influential philosophical works.

MI SHEBEIRACH: A traditional prayer for healing. In many synagogues, when the Mi Shebeirach is recited, it is customary for community members to speak aloud the names of loved ones for whom they wish healing.

MIDRASH: A deeply influential genre of traditional Jewish biblical interpretation that expands upon and embellishes verses from the Hebrew Bible.

MIKVEH: A pool for ritual immersion. Ritual immersion is used to mark many life-cycle events like marriage and conversion, or other moments of spiritual significance. In traditional practice, it is customary to immerse in the mikveh after every menstrual cycle.

MISHKAN: The portable wilderness sanctuary described in the Hebrew Bible. The mishkan is a sacred space that predates the Temple.

MUM: A biblical word meaning "blemish."

RASHBAM: Rabbi Shmuel, son of Meir, lived in northern France in the twelfth century and was Rashi's grandson. Rashbam was one of the scholars known as the "Tosafists," whose commentaries were influential in shaping medieval Jewish law.

RASHI: Rabbi Shlomo ben Itzhak (1040–1105), a towering figure in traditional Jewish thought. Rashi's line-by-line commentaries on the Torah and Talmud have had a profound influence on Jewish biblical interpretation.

RUACH: A biblical word that refers to wind, breath, or spirit.

SHABBAT: The Jewish Sabbath. Shabbat is a day of rest, and in traditional Jewish practice, it is associated with significant prohibitions on labor and activity. Shabbat begins on Friday night, eighteen minutes before sundown, and it lasts until the first stars appear on Saturday night. In Yiddish, the traditional language of Eastern European Ashkenazi Jews, Shabbat is often lovingly known as "Shabbos."

SHAVUOT: A Jewish holiday in early summer that celebrates the giving of the Torah on Mount Sinai; it also honors the conclusion of the Israelite wheat harvest.

TALMUD: One of the foundational texts of rabbinic Judaism, a massive set of texts that recount deliberations and debates over rabbinic Jewish law and include an extensive collection of legends, stories, and other teachings. There are actually two different versions of the Talmud: one that was canonized in Babylonia (modern-day Iraq and Iran) and the other that was completed in Israel-Palestine.

TEMPLE: A central sacred site for ancient Jewish worship in Jerusalem, and the sole acceptable site for sacrifice for most of early Jewish history. The Temple was destroyed twice—once in 586 BC by Nebuchadnezzar, the King of Babylon, and then a second time in 70 CE by the Romans. After the second destruction, the Temple was never rebuilt. The remnant of one of the Temple's outer walls, known as the "Western Wall," remains a site of pilgrimage and prayer for many Jews today.

TORAH: The first five books of the Hebrew Bible, beginning with Genesis and ending with Deuteronomy. According to Jewish tradition, the Torah was revealed to Moses by God at Mount Sinai. Torah literally means "teaching," so the term can also be used to encompass a wide range of Jewish sacred texts and Jewish wisdom.

TSARAAT: A biblical term that describes a skin disease or discoloration of the skin, causing the skin to turn white and scaly. The biblical book of Leviticus requires people with tsaraat to remain outside the camp for a certain period of time and to undergo rituals of purification before their return. Tsaraat has sometimes been translated as leprosy, but the biblical description of the condition does not align with the modern understanding of Hansen's disease.

ACKNOWLEDGMENTS

So many hands and hearts have touched this book to help bring it into the world. Devorah Greenstein read the manuscript, page by page, chapter by chapter, with profound care and wisdom. Judith Plaskow has been a champion of this project since its earliest days, and her incisive insights have been both an encouragement and a gift. Deep thanks go to Ariana Katz for friendship that has sustained me at every turn. To Claire Cunningham, for creative collaborations that have lit my life with joy and for deep disability kinship. To Sofia Betancourt, for companionship in the writing and decades of spiritual community. To Eli Andrew Ramer, for lighting the fire. To Mara Benjamin, for rich conversation. To Sara Nesson, for creative visioning.

I'm honored to be in the company of beloved friends, rabbis, and spiritual teachers who are ushering in a bold new world of disability-informed Torah, especially Jess Belasco, Elliot Rose Kukla, Ruti Regan, and Lauren Tuchman. I'm grateful to disability artists, activists, and cultural workers who are forging bold new paths, especially to Naomi Ortiz, Alice Sheppard, Riva Lehrer, and Eli Clare for their friendship.

My agent, Sharon Pelletier, has been an unfailing source of wisdom and guidance, and it has been an extraordinary gift to work with someone who knows my heart and shares my vision. Thank you for saying yes. Many thanks to the entire team at Dystel, Goderich & Bourret, especially Lauren Abramo, and to Anna Carmichael at Abner Stein for making the UK publication possible.

It's been an absolute joy to work with the team at Beacon Press. Amy Caldwell, my editor, has been a wise and sensitive reader, as well as an extraordinary champion of this project. Louis Roe created a cover that speaks profoundly to my spirit. Many thanks to Rebekah Cotton and Susan Lumenello for exquisite copyediting, to Nancy Zibman for a beautiful index, and to Beth Collins for shepherding the book through production. It has been a pleasure to work with Jessica Lacey and colleagues at Hodder Faith on the UK edition. Thank you all, for everything you have done to bring this book so beautifully into being.

Georgetown has been an extraordinary place to write and teach at the intersections of disability culture and religion. Students in my classes "Religion and Disability Studies," "Disability and the Jewish Bible," and "Disability Ethics and EcoJustice" have asked important questions and offered keen insights. During the writing of this book, I've been honored to work with a fabulous group of graduate students in disability studies and religion: Halla Attallah, Danielle Clausnitzer, Sherie Gayle, Kirsty Jones, and Georgia Kashnig. Our conversations have deepened my thinking in so many ways.

Wonderful colleagues in the department of Theology and Religious Studies have helped make this book possible, especially Ariel Glucklich, who has offered tremendous support as chair. My writing has been immeasurably enriched by Georgetown's vibrant Disability Studies Program. Special thanks are due Jennifer Natalya Fink for profound support and encouragement to pursue this project and to write for a broad audience, to Libbie Rifkin for her tremendous support as I navigate access needs, and to Lydia XZ Brown, Quill Kukla, Toby Long, Sylvia Önder, and Joel Michael Reynolds for collaboration and friendship. Amy Kenny at the Disability Cultural Initiative has been a wonderful conversation partner. Maggie Little, Jonathan Healey, and Sydney Luken at Georgetown's Ethics Lab have been brilliant creative partners. And Carole Sargent, director of Georgetown's Office of Scholarly Publications, has once again offered invaluable guidance and generous insights.

I've had the pleasure of sharing ideas from this book with students and faculty at many different communities, including Harvard Divinity School, Hebrew College, the Methodist Theological Seminary of Ohio, the Protestant Kirchentag in Germany, the Reconstructionist Rabbinical College, Yale Divinity School, and Yeshivat Chovevei Torah. The Institute for Theology and Disability, where I serve as core faculty, brings together a powerful group of disability advocates, scholars, and religious leaders to dive deep into disability and spirituality. Many thanks to Bill Gaventa, Ben Conner, Kathy Dickson, and John Swinton for their ongoing support and encouragement. My thinking has also been shaped by wonderful conversations with synagogue communities at Adas Israel, Etz Chayim, Kehila Chadasha, Kol Tsedek, Shaare Torah, Temple Israel Long Beach, and many more. And I'm grateful for opportunities to teach among so many spiritual justice communities, including Allies for Change, Bend the Arc, JOIN for Justice, the Leaven Center, and Svara. My thanks especially to Lia Bass, Allegra Heath-Stout, Marie Hecke, Melanie Morrison, and Elsie Stern.

The Association for Jewish Studies hosted a summer intensive on Writing beyond the Academy, led by Samuel Freedman, who offered generous commentary and encouragement on early portions of this book. Gratitude also goes to academic friends and coconspirators in the American Academy of Religion's Religion and Disability Studies Group, especially to Mary Jo Iozzio, Heike Peckruhn, and Darla Schumm. Steven Kepnes extended a warm invitation to share portions of my work at the Colgate Jewish Theology conference, and Jay Michaelson and Danya Ruttenberg offered generous help with publishing questions. Thanks also to Rebecca Parker for a long-ago call to write this book.

To beloved queer, Jewish, and disabled ancestors, may their memories be a blessing and their brilliance ripple between worlds: Ibrahim Baba, mel baggs, Steve Bloomquist, Rachel Brodie, Sheryl Grossman, and Stacey Park Milbern.

To my parents, for abundant love and support that has sustained me through the years. To my partner, in love and in life. To the stones and the trees and the first toad I ever cradled in the palm of my hand.

A NOTE ON TRANSLATION

Translation is a matter that lies close to my heart. My general practice in this book is to follow the Jewish Publication Society 1985 translation when I quote from the Hebrew Bible. In some cases, I've chosen to offer my own translations instead, sometimes to capture a nuance that isn't available in a published translation or to share my own sense of the poetry of the Hebrew. If the translation is my own, I have indicated that in the notes and share further information about the choices I've made. When translation questions have particular significance for disability, I call attention to those matters in the body of the book.

Quotations from the New Testament follow the New Revised Standard Version translation. There are sometimes small variations in the numbering of verses between Jewish and Christian bibles. I cite texts from the Hebrew Bible according to the numbering adopted by the Jewish Publication Society. I cite texts from the New Testament according to the New Revised Standard Version.

Translations from rabbinic texts are my own, unless otherwise noted. For ease of reference, I cite midrash collections according to the versions available online at Sefaria.org.

NOTES

CHAPTER ONE: CLAIMING DISABILITY

1. Deuteronomy 16:20. Quotations from the Hebrew Bible generally follow the Jewish Publication Society's 1985 translation, though I occasionally make minor stylistic edits for readability or flow. When I make changes to the translation, I will call attention to those shifts for the reader. If I use my own translation instead, I will indicate that in the notes.

2. Adrienne Rich, "If Not With Others, How?" in *Blood, Bread, and Poetry: Selected Prose 1979–1985* (New York: W. W. Norton, 1986), 204–5.

3. Ezekiel 1:1; Ezekiel 1:16; Ezekiel 1:20.

4. I've written about this experience in Julia Watts Belser, "God on Wheels: Disability and Jewish Feminist Theology," *Tikkun Magazine* (Fall 2014). Some other elements of this chapter are likewise drawn from that piece, but I will explore the implications of God on Wheels in more detail in the final chapter of the book.

5. Psalm 85:11. Translation is my own. The Jewish Publication Society (JPS) translates this verse as "justice and well-being kiss," and while "well-being" conveys the broad sense of the Hebrew word shalom, I find "peace" to be both more straightforward and evocative. Meanwhile, a note on verse citations: There are sometimes small variations in the numbering of texts between Jewish and Christian bibles, and this verse is one example. In this book, I will cite texts from the Hebrew Bible according to the numbering adopted by the Jewish Publication Society (1985 version). I will cite texts from the Christian New Testament according to the New Revised Standard Version.

CHAPTER TWO: GRAPPLING WITH THE BIBLE

1. Isaiah 35:5–6. Translation is my own. JPS translates the final phrase as "the tongue of the dumb shall shout aloud." But *'ilem* means "mute." To translate it as "dumb" reinforces a long and incorrect association between "non-speaking" and "unintelligent."

2. Isaiah 35:1. JPS translates the verb as "shall," but I find "will" more straightforward for the contemporary reader.

3. Isaiah 35:6.

4. Margaret Moers Wening, "A Covenant Made with All of Us" (printed, without its title, as part of a Roundtable, "Women with Disabilities: A Challenge to Feminist Theology"), *Journal of Feminist Studies in Religion* 10, no. 2 (Fall 1994).

5. Jeremiah 31:8–9. Translation is my own.

6. Charles Taylor, *A Secular Age* (Cambridge, MA: Harvard University Press, 2009), 25.

7. I've written about this story in greater detail in Julia Watts Belser, "Making Room for the Divine She," *Zeek: A Jewish Journal of Thought and Culture* (August 2007).

8. Rabbi Harold Kushner, *When Children Ask About God: A Guide for Parents Who Don't Always Have All the Answers* (New York: Schocken Books, 1971, rep. 1989), 26, following C. G. Montefiore and H. M. J. Loewe, eds. *A Rabbinic Anthology* (London: Macmillan, 1938), 6. The midrash Kushner references is found in Pesikta de-Rav Kahana 12:25 and in Midrash Tanhuma Buber, Yitro 17. (For ease of reference, I will cite midrash collections according to the versions available online at Sefaria.org, unless otherwise noted.) Interestingly, the original sense of the midrash seems to be less that God's visage mirrors the faces of everyone who looks, but that God is like an icon or image (*ikonin*) with many faces, able to gaze directly upon each and every person who looks toward the divine. Kushner's mirror version, however, has become a widely cited and shared version of this teaching, one that has resonated with contemporary audiences.

9. The name for God, sometimes translated, "I will be who I will be," appears in Exodus 3:14. It is God's answer to Moses's question, when Moses asks for the divine name.

10. Deuteronomy 16:20.

11. The topic of Christian and Jewish responses to same-sex love and to LGBTQ lives is rich and varied. Readers interested in diving further into these topics might consult Jay Michaelson, *God vs. Gay: A Religious Case for Equality* (Boston: Beacon Press, 2012), and Steven Greenberg, *Wrestling with God and Men: Homosexuality in the Jewish Tradition* (Madison: University of Wisconsin Press, 2004). For a rich historical account of women loving women in early Christian contexts, see Bernadette Brooten, *Love Between Women: Early Christian Responses to Female Homoeroticism* (Chicago: University of Chicago Press, 1996).

12. Babylonian Talmud, Ketubot 16b–17a. Translations from rabbinic texts are my own, unless otherwise noted. I've discussed this story in more detail in Julia Watts Belser, "Drawing Torah from Troubling Texts: Gender, Disability, and Jewish Feminist Ethics," *Journal of Jewish Ethics* 6, no. 2 (2021): 140–52.

13. Babylonian Talmud, Ketubot 17a. The biblical verse cited by the House of Shammai is Exodus 23:7.

14. The discussion in Ketubot 17a is widely referenced in both popular and scholarly discourse of Jewish ethics on the subject of a permissible lie. Telushkin uses it to frame his argument that untruths for the sake of sparing another's feelings are permissible according to Jewish law. Joseph Telushkin, *The Book of Jewish Values: A Day-By-Day Guide to Ethical Living* (New York: Random House, 2000), 102–4.

15. Pirke Avot 5:22. Passage numbering follows the version available online at Sefaria.org.

16. Rabbi Ruti Regan, remarks delivered at the White House summit meeting on Jewish Disability Awareness and Inclusion, February 18, 2016.

17. Thelathia Nikki Young, *Black Queer Ethics, Family, and Philosophical Imagina-tion* (New York: Palgrave Macmillan, 2016), 58.

18. Toni Morrison, "Unspeakable Things Unspoken: The Afro-American Presence in American Literature," in *The Tanner Lectures on Human Values*, ed. R. Dworkin et al. (Salt Lake City: University of Utah Press), 132.

CHAPTER THREE: HIDDENNESS AND VISIBILITY

1. On the experience of ambulatory wheelchair users and the accusations many of us face, see Marisa Zeppiri, "Taking a Stand: Fighting Ambulatory Wheelchair User Discrimination Through Education," *Lupus Chick: Autoimmune Life*, July 11, 2019, https://lupuschick.com/taking-a-stand-fighting-ambulatory-wheelchair-user-discrimination-awareness-education/.

2. For an astute analysis of public surveillance of disability and the extraordinary interest among strangers about whether a person "deserves" a disability parking placard, see Ellen Samuels, *Fantasies of Identification: Disability, Gender, Race* (New York: New York University Press, 2014), 121–40.

3. See Doron Dorfman, *Fear of the Disability Con: Public Perceptions of Abuse of Disability Rights* (Stanford, CA: Stanford University Press, 2019); Samuels, *Fantasies of Identification*, 66–79.

4. Recent implementation of "straw bans" offers a striking case in point about the way that policies requiring disclosure of disability put additional burdens on disabled people. See Alice Wong, "The Last Straw," *Eater*, July 19, 2018, https://www.eater.com/2018/7/19/17586742/plastic-straw-ban-disabilities.

5. On austerity politics in the UK and elsewhere, see Robert McRuer, *Crip Times: Disability, Globalization, and Resistance* (New York: New York University Press, 2018).

6. Francis Ryan, *Crippled: Austerity and the Demonization of Disabled People* (London: Verso, 2019).

7. According to the Kaiser Family Foundation, the median annual cost for nursing facility care was $91,250 in 2015, while the median cost for one year of home health aide services (at twenty dollars an hour and forty-four hours per week) was $45,800. Erica L. Reaves and MaryBeth Musumeci, "Medicaid and Long-Term Services and Supports: A Primer," KFF, December 15, 2015, https://www.kff.org/medicaid/report/medicaid-and-long-term-services-and-supports-a-primer. Perhaps even more significantly, a 2018 survey of older adults found that 77 percent wished to receive home health care in order to age in place, but only 46 percent believed they would be able to do so. Joanne Binette, Kerri Vasold, and AARP Research, *2018 Home and Community Preferences: A National Survey of Adults Ages 18-Plus*, AARP, revised July 2019, https://www.aarp.org/research/topics/community/info-2018/2018-home-community-preference.html. That discrepancy is due to institutional bias in US health care policy, which makes it much more likely for Medicaid funds to support nursing home care than nursing facility care. See the Autistic Self Advocacy Network, "The Institutional Bias: What It Is, Why It Is Bad, and the Laws, Programs, and Policies Which Would Change It," https://autisticadvocacy.org/actioncenter/issues/community/bias, accessed October 19, 2022.

8. Disability activists and artists have been documenting the toll of these policies in powerful ways. In 2012, in advance of the Paralympic Games in London, more than 150 disability activists protested the sponsorship of the British IT firm Atos, which performs "fit for work" assessments. "Atos Protest: Disability Rights Groups Target Firm," BBC News, August 31, 2012, https://www.bbc.com/news /uk-england-london-19437785. In the 2015 exhibition *Figures* in London, disabled artist Liz Crow showcased 650 small human sculptures, which aimed to "make visible the stark human cost of austerity." "#WeAreFigures," http:// wearefigures.co.uk, accessed October 19, 2022.

9. Kenji Yoshino, *Covering: The Hidden Assault on Our Civil Rights* (New York: Random House, 2006).

10. Active efforts to disclose disability also deserve our attention. Heather Dawn Evans has drawn attention to a practice that she calls "un/covering," in which people living with non-apparent or intermittent disabilities often use disability disclosure and other repeated reminders of impairment in order to assert difference and negotiate accommodation, a set of practices that often create "a form of visibility that can be read by the nondisabled and disabled alike." Heather Dawn Evans, "Un/covering: Making Disability Visible," *Disability Studies Quarterly* 37, no. 1 (2017).

11. Yoshino's discussion of covering offers a powerful account of its impetus. In our contemporary moment, he argues, discrimination rarely presents itself explicitly as targeting an entire group. Instead, it targets "the subset of the group that fails to assimilate to mainstream norms." Yoshino, *Covering*, 22.

12. Hugh Gallagher, *FDR's Splendid Deception: The Moving Story of Roosevelt's Massive Disability—and the Intense Efforts to Conceal It from the Public* (New York: Dodd, Mead, 1995). For an insightful account of FDR in light of contemporary disability studies theory, see Daniel Wilson, "Passing in the Shadow of FDR: Polio Survivors, Passing, and the Negotiation of Disability," in *Disability and Passing: Blurring the Lines of Identity*, ed. Jeffrey A. Brune and Daniel J. Wilson (Philadelphia: Temple University Press, 2013), 13–35.

13. Wilson, "Passing in the Shadow of FDR," 17.

14. Gallagher, *FDR's Splendid Deception*, 96.

15. Monica Coleman speaks powerfully to the cost of passing, of concealing her experiences with depression. "I received such affirmation for my professional successes and my effervescent personality," she writes, "that I came to believe that this was the part of me that people loved—the only part of me that people loved. If people knew who I really was, how sad I really was, they would not love me." Monica A. Coleman, *Not Alone: Reflections on Faith and Depression* (Culver City, CA: Inner Prizes, 2012), 4.

16. Babylonian Talmud, Shabbat 53b.

17. Babylonian Talmud, Shabbat 53b.

18. Rosemarie Garland-Thomson, "The Case for Conserving Disability," *Bioethical Inquiry* 9 (2012): 339–55, 342.

19. Laura Hershey, "You Get Proud by Practicing," *In the Way: ADAPT Poems* (Denver: Dragonfly Press, 1992). Go to www.laurahershey.com to read more of Laura Hershey's work.

CHAPTER FOUR: ABLEISM

1. On the history and significance of the Americans with Disabilities Act, see Lennard J. Davis, *Enabling Acts: The Hidden Story of How the Americans with Disabilities Act Gave the Largest US Minority Its Rights* (Boston: Beacon Press, 2015).

2. Carly Findlay, *Say Hello* (Sydney: Harper Collins Australia, 2019), chapter 1.

3. In recent years, the social model has faced some critiques by other disabled activists, especially people with chronic illness and chronic pain, who have pushed for a more supple recognition of the way disability is both about social barriers and a matter of impairment. These activists have reminded us not to overlook the complicated, sometimes painful elements of disability in terms of our bodies and minds. For an excellent orientation to these questions, see Alison Kafer, "Imagined Futures," *Feminist, Queer, Crip* (Bloomington: Indiana University Press, 2013), 1–24. Throughout this book, I aim to use social model thinking in ways that also recognize and attend to the full complexity of disabled bodies and minds.

4. For a compelling poetic account of ableism in action, see Maria Palacios, "Naming Ableism," *Crip Story*, 2017, https://cripstory.wordpress.com/2017/04/01/naming-ableism. Paul Longmore gives a brutal account of structural disincentives that cause many people with disabilities to lose their medical benefits if they earn income. See Paul Longmore, *Why I Burned My Book and Other Essays on Disability* (Philadelphia: Temple University Press, 2003), 230–59. For introductions to ableism as a form of structural violence against people with disabilities, see Benjamin Ostiguy, Madeline Peters, and Davey Shlasko, "Ableism [excerpts]," in *Teaching for Diversity and Social Justice*, 3rd. ed., ed. Maurianne Adams and Lee Anne Bell (New York: Routledge, 2016); and Michelle R. Nario-Redmond, *Ableism: The Causes and Consequences of Disability Prejudice* (Hoboken, NJ: Wiley Blackwell, 2020).

5. Rosemarie Garland-Thomson, *Extraordinary Bodies: Figuring Physical Disability in American Culture and Literature* (New York: Columbia University Press, 1997), 8.

6. Erving Goffman, *Stigma: Notes on the Management of Spoiled Identity* (Englewood Cliffs, NJ: Prentice Hall, 1963), 128.

7. In the Middle Ages, Christian writers and some Jewish ones began to fashion this story as a story about sexual sin, as a condemnation of male-male sexuality. It's a choice that runs quite counter to the ethical sense of the text. For a discussion of the history of interpretation around these passages, see Mark D. Jordan, *The Invention of Sodomy in Christian Theology* (Chicago: University of Chicago Press, 1997).

8. Michaelson, *God vs. Gay*, 69.

9. Babylonian Talmud, Sanhedrin 109a.

10. Eli Clare, *Exile and Pride: Disability, Queerness and Liberation* (Cambridge, MA: South End Press, 1999), 6.

11. For an account of Alexander Graham Bell's campaign against Deaf people, see Katie Booth, *The Invention of Miracles: Language, Power, and Alexander Graham Bell's Quest to End Deafness* (New York: Simon & Schuster, 2021). For a discussion of oralism and the campaign against sign language, see Douglas C. Baynton, *Forbidden Signs: American Culture and the Campaign Against Sign Language* (Chicago: University of Chicago Press, 1996).

12. On the Nazi killing of disabled people, see Kenny Fries, "The Nazi's First Victims Were Disabled," *New York Times*, September 13, 2017; Sharon Snyder and David Mitchell, *A World Without Bodies*, film, 2001 (35 mins.); and Sharon L. Snyder and David T. Mitchell, "The Eugenic Atlantic: Disability and the Making of an International Science," in *Cultural Locations of Disability*, ed. Snyder and Mitchell (Chicago: University of Chicago Press, 2006).

13. Monica A. Coleman, *Not Alone: Reflections on Faith and Depression* (Culver City, CA: Inner Prizes, 2012), 81.

14. Patty Berne, "Disability Justice: A Working Draft," Sins Invalid, June 10, 2015, https://www.sinsinvalid.org/blog/disability-justice-a-working-draft-by-patty-berne.

15. TL Lewis, "January 2021 Working Definition of Ableism," *Talila A. Lewis*, January 1, 2021, https://www.talilalewis.com/blog/january-2021-working-definition-of-ableism. Lewis notes that the definition has been "developed in community with Disabled Black and other negatively racialized people, especially Dustin Gibson."

16. Moore's documentary demonstrates the way disability is often overlooked or undocumented in cases of police violence; he estimates that over 50 percent of the victims of police brutality have a disability that contributed to the incident. Leroy F. Moore, *Where Is Hope? Police Brutality Against People with Disabilities*, film, Wabi Sabi Productions, 2015. On the critical interconnections between disability, the criminalization of poverty, and police violence, see Leroy F. Moore Jr., Tiny (aka Lisa Gray-Garcia), and Emmitt H. Thrower, "Black and Blue: Policing Disability & Poverty Beyond Occupy," in *Occupying Disability: Critical Approaches to Community, Justice, and Decolonizing Disability*, ed. Pamela Block et al. (New York: Springer, 2016). The Harriet Tubman Collective also issued a powerful statement on violence against Black disabled people. Harriet Tubman Collective, "Disability Solidarity: Completing the 'Vision for Black Lives,'" September 7, 2016.

17. A 2020 report from the National Center for Learning Disabilities documents the prevalence of racial disparities both in the identification of students as intellectually disabled, their placement in more restrictive environments, and their likelihood of receiving harsher discipline. National Center for Learning Disabilities, *Significant Disproportionality in Special Education: Current Trends and Actions for Impact* (Washington, DC: NCLD, October 2020). For further discussion, see David J. Connor, Beth A. Ferri, and Subini A. Annamma, eds., *DisCrit: Disability Studies and Critical Race Theory in Education* (New York: Teachers College Press, 2016).

18. Douglas C. Baynton, "Disability and the Justification of Inequality in American History," in *The New Disability History: American Perspectives*, ed. Paul K. Longmore and Lauri Umansky (New York: New York University Press, 2001), 33–57.

19. I want to acknowledge with profound gratitude two disability activists whose work has been crucial to my own practice of unlearning the violence of cognitive ableism: Cal Montgomery, who blogs at https://montgomerycal.wordpress.com, and mel baggs, whose writings can be found at https://ballastexistenz.wordpress.com.

20. Margaret Price, "The Bodymind Problem and the Possibilities of Pain," *Hypatia: A Journal of Feminist Philosophy* 30, no. 1 (2015): 268–84.

21. TL Lewis, "January 2021 Working Definition of Ableism."

CHAPTER FIVE: PRIESTLY BLEMISHES

1. A version of this chapter was published as Julia Watts Belser, "Priestly Aesthetics: Disability and Bodily Difference in Leviticus 21," *Interpretation: A Journal of Bible and Theology* 73, no. 4 (2019): 355–66.

2. Leviticus 22:19.

3. Eli Clare, *Brilliant Imperfection: Grappling with Cure* (Durham, NC: Duke University Press, 2017), 6.

4. On the biblical priesthood and disability, see Judith Abrams, *Judaism and Disability: Portrayals in Ancient Texts from the Tanach Through the Bavli* (Washington, DC: Gallaudet University Press, 1998), 16–70. On the construction of priestly norms, see Rebecca Raphael, *Biblical Corpora: Representations of Disability in Hebrew Biblical Literature* (London: T&T Clark, 2008), 31–39.

5. Elliot Dorff, "Judaism and the Disabled: The Need for a Copernican Revolution," in *Healing and the Jewish Imagination: Spiritual and Practical Perspectives on Judaism and Health*, ed. William Cutter (Woodstock, VT: Jewish Lights, 2007), 109.

6. Tamara M. Green, "Misheberach and the ADA: A Response to Elliot Dorff," in Cutter, *Healing and the Jewish Imagination*, 125.

7. Jacob Milgrom, *Leviticus 17–22: A New Translation with Introduction and Commentary*, Anchor Bible (New York: Doubleday, 2000); Saul Olyan, *Disability in the Hebrew Bible: Interpreting Mental and Physical Differences* (Cambridge: Cambridge University Press, 2008), 26–31.

8. Abrams, *Judaism and Disability*, 23–27.

9. Raphael, *Biblical Corpora*, 39.

10. Olyan, *Disability in the Hebrew Bible*, 30.

11. Jeremy Schipper and Jeffrey Stackert, "Blemishes, Camouflage, and Sanctuary Service: The Priestly Deity and His Attendants," *Hebrew Bible and Ancient Israel* 4, no. 2 (2013): 469.

12. Rashi on Leviticus 21:18; Malachi 1:6. The translation of Rashi's comment is my own; the verses follow JPS.

13. Moses Maimonides, *Guide for the Perplexed* 3:45. Translation is mine, in consultation with the English translation by Friedlander (1903), based on the Hebrew translation by Ibn Tibbon (1204). Maimonides originally wrote the *Guide* in Arabic.

14. In many contemporary Jewish congregations today, the priestly blessing, Numbers 6:2–7, is recited by the prayer leader without regard to priestly lineage. But some congregations continue to follow a more traditional practice, often known by its Yiddish name, *dukhenen*, where priests in the congregation are invited to come forward and recite the priestly blessing over the congregation. As part of the ritual, priests remove their shoes, raise their prayer shawls over their heads, make a specific gesture of raised hands with spread fingers, and recite the words of the blessing.

15. Pesikta de-Rav Kahana, Parshat ha-Hodesh, 8 (Mandelbaum edition, 91).

16. Rashi to Babylonian Talmud Ḥagigah 16a.

17. See Jacob Spiegel, "Why Do We Not Look at the Priests?" Parashat Naso 5760/10 (June 2000), Bar Ilan University, http://www2.biu.ac.il/JH/Parasha /eng/naso/spi.html.

18. Rosemarie Garland-Thomson, "The Politics of Staring: Visual Rhetorics of Disability in Popular Photography," *Disability Studies: Enabling the Humanities* (New York: Modern Language Association of America, 2002), 56–75.

19. Julia Watts Belser, "Reading Talmudic Bodies: Disability, Narrative, and the Gaze in Rabbinic Judaism," in *Disability in Judaism, Christianity and Islam: Sacred Texts, Historical Traditions and Social Analysis*, ed. Darla Schumm and Michael Stolzfus (New York: Palgrave Macmillan, 2011), 12.

20. Shulhan Aruch, Orach Chayyim, 128:30; Abrams, *Judaism and Disability*, 201.

21. Stimming refers to a range of practices that Autistic people enjoy and use to help regulate their senses or manage otherwise overwhelming sensory input. Stimming practices are often repetitive movements; the Autistic Self-Advocacy Network gives examples, explaining that "we might rock back and forth, play with our hands, or hum." "About Autism," ASAN, https://autisticadvocacy.org/about-asan/about-autism, accessed October 19, 2022.

CHAPTER SIX: MOSES

1. Exodus 4:10.

2. Marc Shell offers a powerful and evocative reading of the Moses story in light of his own experience as a stutterer, and his essay documents the ways that hostility toward stuttering and toward the stutterer ran through his formative Jewish education. Marc Shell, "Moses' Tongue," *Common Knowledge* 12, no. 1 (2006): 150–76.

3. Muslim tradition likewise holds that the Prophet Moses had a speech disability. In the Qur'an, Moses asks God to cure his disability before he approaches Pharaoh. See Mohammed Ghaly, *Islam and Disability: Perspectives in Theology and Jurisprudence* (London: Routledge, 2009), 47. Shell also observes that many biblical scholars translate this verse in ways that assume Moses expected his disability to be cured by God, though that claim is not present in the biblical text. Shell, "Moses' Tongue," 153.

4. Translation is my own. JPS translates this question as "Who gives man speech?" I prefer to translate the Hebrew less idiomatically, as I will discuss. The language of the verse refers to *peh*, the actual physical mouth. JPS also translates *'ilem* (mute) as "dumb," a translation that reinforces a long and incorrect association between "nonspeaking" and "unintelligent."

5. Noah Buchholtz and Darby Jared Leigh, "Religion and Deaf Identity," in *Deaf Identities: Exploring New Frontiers*, ed. Irene W. Leigh and Catherine A. O'Brien (New York: Oxford University Press, 2020), 72.

6. Bonnie Gracer, "What the Rabbis Heard: Deafness in the Mishnah," *Disability Studies Quarterly* 23, no. 2 (2003), http://dx.doi.org/10.18061/dsq.v23i2.423.

7. Hector Avalos has called attention to the importance of examining the way different biblical texts regard the senses; certain biblical materials have a

strong preference for the revelatory power of word and distrust the testimony of the eyes, while others recognize the power of the visual in communicating revelation. As Kirsty Jones has shown, the Priestly source within the Hebrew Bible often draws strongly upon the visual when conveying prophecy, a move that aligns powerfully with these divine signs. Hector Avalos, "Introducing Sensory Criticism in Biblical Studies: Audiocentricity and Visiocentricity," in *This Abled Body: Rethinking Disabilities in Biblical Studies*, ed. Hector Avalos, Sarah J. Melcher, and Jeremy Schipper (Atlanta: Society of Biblical Literature, 2007), 47–59. Kirsty Jones, "The Stammering Seer: Moses, Patriarchs, and the Priestly Source," paper delivered to the Society for Biblical Literature, November 11, 2018.

8. Exodus 4:3.

9. Pirke de-Rabbi Eliezer 40:2–3. Shell gives a powerful reading of Moses as also physically disabled and traces the way that cultural references to stuttering are frequently intertwined with imagery of physical disability. Shell, "Moses' Tongue," 158.

10. Exodus 4:6–7. On the difference between tsaraat and the medical condition often called leprosy, see Ephraim Shoham-Steiner, "Leprosy as a Concept," *On the Margins of a Minority: Leprosy, Madness, and Disability Among the Jews of Medieval Europe* (Detroit: Wayne State University Press, 2014).

11. The biblical rules for the diagnosis of tsaraat, the isolation of those affected, and the ritual requirements for their return are laid out in Leviticus 13 and 14. For a powerful account of the dynamics of fear, stigma, and isolation that surround a person with tsaraat in relation to contemporary stigma experienced by people with disabilities and people with dementia, see Rachel Adler, "Those Who Turn Away Their Faces: Tzara'at and Stigma," in *Healing and the Jewish Imagination: Spiritual and Practical Perspectives on Judaism and Health*, ed. William Cutter (Woodstock, VT: Jewish Lights, 2007), 142–59.

12. Exodus 4:9.

13. Amanda Mbuvi, "Multicultural Moses: Reexamining an Icon," *Biblical Archeology Review* 45 (2019): 16–18.

14. Acts 7:22.

15. Mbuvi, "Multicultural Moses," 16.

16. Rashbam, Commentary to Exodus 4:10. The translation follows Eliyahu Munk.

17. Herbert Marks, "On Prophetic Stammering," in *Literature, Speech Disorders, and Disability: Talking Normal*, ed. Christopher Eagle (New York: Routledge, 2013).

18. Ezekiel's muteness is described in Ezekiel 3:26–27; the restoration of his speech is described in Ezekiel 24:27 and Ezekiel 33:22. See Rhiannon Graybill, *Are We Not Men? Unstable Masculinity in the Hebrew Prophets* (New York: Oxford University Press, 2016), 97.

19. See, for example, a famous episode in the Babylonian Talmud's account of Elisha ben Abuya in the Babylonian Talmud, Hagigah 15a. On the role of the "prophetic" verses recited by a stuttering child, see Jeffrey Rubenstein, *Talmudic Stories: Narrative Art, Composition, and Culture* (Baltimore: Johns Hopkins University Press, 1999), 76.

20. Shell, "Moses' Tongue," 151.

21. Midrash Tanhuma, Devarim 2:1. The biblical allusion in the midrash comes from Exodus 4:10, when God instructs Moses to speak to Pharaoh, and Moses protests, "I have never been a man of words."

CHAPTER SEVEN: THE LAND YOU CANNOT ENTER

1. Numbers 20:5.

2. Numbers 20:10.

3. Numbers 20:12.

4. The Torah offers two different accounts of the mission; in Numbers 13:2, Moses sends the scouts at God's command, while in Deuteronomy 1:22, he sends them at the Israelites' request.

5. Deuteronomy 1:37. JPS uses the masculine pronoun to refer to God, following the original Hebrew text. I have substituted "God" in the interest of gender-expansive translation.

6. Deuteronomy 3:23-27. I have followed the JPS translation, with one exception. JPS translates this phrase, "the Lord was wrathful." But I prefer "angry." In my experience, the word "wrath" risks triggering an anti-Jewish trope that associates "the God of the Old Testament" with rage, while portraying Jesus and "the God of the New Testament" as a God of love. In the Hebrew Bible, God is depicted as experiencing a wide range of emotions, including delight, regret, grief, compassion, and anger.

7. Deuteronomy Rabbah 11:10.

8. The translation follows JPS, with one change. In Deuteronomy 4:22, JPS translates "For I must die in this land; I shall not cross…but you will cross," varying the intensity of the verbs. The Hebrew does not make these distinctions. Moses's words are simple and direct: you will cross, and I will not.

9. Deuteronomy Rabbah 3:11. The translation follows Aviva Gottleib Zornberg, *Bewilderments: Reflections on the Book of Numbers* (New York: Schocken Books, 2015), 295. I have added line breaks in the text for clarity and ease of reading.

10. Aviva Gottleib Zornberg, *Bewilderments: Reflections on the Book of Numbers* (New York: Schocken Books, 2015), 296.

11. The translation is from Robert Alter, *The Five Books of Moses: A Translation with Commentary* (New York: W. W. Norton, 2004), 1057. Alter translates the divine name as "The Lord," but in keeping with my practice throughout the book, I have substituted "God."

12. Rhiannon Graybill, *Are We Not Men? Unstable Masculinity in the Hebrew Prophets* (New York: Oxford University Press, 2016), 30.

13. Rebecca Solnit, *A Field Guide to Getting Lost* (New York: Penguin, 2006), 29.

14. Solnit, *A Field Guide to Getting Lost*, 30.

15. Rafael Rachel Neis, *The Sense of Sight in Rabbinic Culture: Jewish Ways of Seeing in Late Antiquity* (Cambridge: Cambridge University Press, 2013), 27–31.

CHAPTER EIGHT: THE PERILS OF HEALING

1. Luke 13:10–17. Passages from the New Testament follow the New Revised Standard Version translation. Luke 13:10 begins with the pronoun "he"; I have taken the liberty of changing that to "Jesus" for clarity.

2. John 5:5–9.

3. Gwendolyn Wallace and Roberto Sirvent, "Health Justice and Black Liberation: Dr. Angel Love Miles," *Black Agenda Report*, October 21, 2020, https://www
.blackagendareport.com/health-justice-and-black-liberation-dr-angel-love-miles.

4. Eunjung Kim, *Curative Violence: Rehabilitating Disability, Gender, and Sexuality in
Modern Korea* (Durham, NC: Duke University Press, 2017).

5. Eli Clare, *Brilliant Imperfection: Grappling with Cure* (Durham, NC: Duke University Press, 2017), 23.

6. s. e. smith, "Disabled Activists Should Not Have to Die to Have Our
Voices Heard," *Vice*, March 7, 2019, https://www.vice.com/en_us/article
/mbzkyn/disability-rights-activism-carrie-ann-lucas-death.

7. Heidi Ledford, "Medical Research: If Depression Were Cancer," *Nature:
International Weekly Journal of Science* 515, no. 7526 (November 12, 2014), https://
www.nature.com/news/medical-research-if-depression-were-cancer-1.16307.

8. Coleman has authored a powerful account of her experiences living with
depression amid an endemic of racial and gender violence and illustrated how
these realities have shaped her own identity as a Christian. See Monica Coleman,
Bipolar Faith: A Black Woman's Journey with Depression and Faith (Minneapolis: Fortress
Press, 2016).

9. Claire Cunningham, *Thank You Very Much*, theatrical performance commis-
sioned by the Manchester International Festival, 2019.

10. Riva Lehrer, *Golem Girl: A Memoir* (New York: One World, 2020), 87.

11. John 5:14.

12. John 9:2–3.

13. Noor Pervez, "I'm Disabled, I'm Muslim, and I Am Not Your Burden,"
Disability Visibility Project, May 5, 2019, https://disabilityvisibilityproject.com
/2019/05/05/im-disabled-im-muslim-and-i-am-not-your-burden.

14. Amy Kenny, *My Body Is Not a Prayer Request: Disability Justice in the Church*
(Grand Rapids, MI: Brazos Press, 2022), 148.

15. Daniel Boyarin, *Dying for God: Martyrdom and the Making of Christianity and
Judaism* (Stanford, CA: Stanford University Press, 1999), 12.

16. Luke 13:14-16.

17. John 9:8-11.

18. Levine has written a number of books that encourage Christians to better understand Jesus and the New Testament in light of early Jewish culture. For a
helpful introduction, see Amy-Jill Levine, *The Misunderstood Jew: The Church and the
Scandal of the Jewish Jesus* (New York: Harper Collins, 2009).

19. Amy-Jill Levine, "Quit Picking on the Pharisees!" *Sojourners Magazine* 44,
no. 3 (March 2015): 26–29.

20. Darla Schumm, "Holy Access," *Tikkun Magazine* 29, no. 4 (Fall 2014):
24–27. For further discussion of the significance of blindness and the spiritual
imagery of light in the Gospel of John, see Jennifer Koosed and Darla Schumm,
"Out of the Darkness: Examining the Rhetoric of Blindness in the Gospel of
John," *Disability Studies Quarterly* 25, no. 1 (2005), http://dx.doi.org/10.18061
/dsq.v25i1.528.

21. Kathy Black, *A Healing Homiletic: Preaching and Disability* (Nashville: Abingdon Press, 1996), chapter 2.

22. Levine, *The Misunderstood Jew*, 9.

23. John M. Hull, *The Tactile Heart: Blindness and Faith* (London: SCM Press, 2013), 31.

24. Hull, *The Tactile Heart*, 31.

CHAPTER NINE: ISAAC'S BLINDNESS

1. Genesis 27:11.

2. Genesis 27:34.

3. Blind theorist Georgina Kleege has written powerfully about the way that many depictions of blindness in film and popular culture reflect sighted people's fears of blindness. Georgina Kleege, *Sight Unseen* (New Haven, CT: Yale University Press, 1999), 43–66.

4. Midrash Tanhuma, Toldot 7:2.

5. Genesis 35:29 narrates Isaac's death, giving his age as 180. While we don't know the precise timing of the scene depicted in Genesis 27, we do know that at least twenty years have passed. Genesis 31:38 recounts how Jacob spent twenty years in Laban's service. Isaac is still alive during that time, because Jacob returns home and reconciles with his brother *before* Isaac's death.

6. Genesis 26:4.

7. Narrated in Genesis 22, this story is known as the Akedah ("the binding of Isaac") in Jewish tradition.

8. Søren Kierkegaard's *Fear and Trembling* was first published in Danish in 1843, under the pseudonym Johannes de Silentio.

9. For a powerful reading of this biblical narrative in light of contemporary feminist ethical concerns, see Tikva Frymer-Kensky, "Akeda: The View from the Bible," in *Beginning Anew: A Woman's Companion to the High Holy Days*, ed. Gail Twersky Reimer and Judith Kates (New York: Simon & Schuster, 1997).

10. The image of Isaac in the field at twilight is drawn from Genesis 24:63.

11. Genesis Rabbah 65:10. The midrash includes an additional prooftext from Isaiah 33:7 to ground the idea that the angels wept: "Behold, the valiant ones cry out; the angels of peace weep bitterly."

12. Leah Lakshmi Piepzna-Samarasinha, "Dirty River Girl," *Bodymap: Poems* (Toronto: Mawenzi House, 2015).

13. Piepzna-Samarasinha, "Dirty River Girl."

14. Rebecca Raphael, *Biblical Corpora: Representations of Disability in Hebrew Biblical Literature* (London: T&T Clark, 2008), 65–70.

15. Genesis 24:64. While most translations say that she "dismounts" or "alights" from her camel, the Hebrew word here is *nafal*—simply, "to fall." I first heard this wonderful reading from Reba Connell in a d'var Torah at Congregation Netivot Shalom in the 2000s and I've loved it ever since.

16. Georgina Kleege, "Flying While Blind," in *About Us: Essays from the Disability Series of the New York Times*, ed. Peter Catapano and Rosemarie Garland-Thomson (New York: Liveright, 2019), 149–52.

17. Georgina Kleege, "Look into My Eyes: Equating Blindness with Ignorance Discredits the Visually Impaired," Phi Kappa Phi Forum, Summer 2020, https://www.phikappaphiforum-digital.org/phikappaphiforum/summer_2020/MobilePagedArticle.action?articleId=1591776#articleId1591776.

18. Genesis 27:11–12.

19. Genesis 27:13.

20. The dialogue in this section is drawn from Genesis 27:18-24. I follow the JPS translation, save for the final portion of Genesis 27:24. JPS translates Jacob's response more idiomatically, having him answer "I am." But in Hebrew, his response is simply the word "I."

21. Genesis 27:28.

22. Genesis 27:38.

23. There's a debate among commentators about whether the first portion of Esau's blessing is the same as Jacob's. Some translations read Esau's blessing as a curse, meaning that he will be kept "away from the fat/goodness of the land." But the grammatical construction of this phrase is the same in both blessings, as Robert Alter explains in his commentary on the 1997 Genesis translation.

24. Rabbi Lauren Tuchman, "On Deception and Its Consequences: Parashat Toldot 5777," November 8, 2018, https://rabbituchman.com/on-deception-and-its-consequences-parashat-toldot-5777.

25. Tuchman, "On Deception and Its Consequences."

CHAPTER TEN: JACOB AND THE ANGEL

1. Translation is my own. JPS translates, "He wrenched Jacob's hip," instead of "touched." As I will discuss later in the chapter, this Hebrew word, which stems from the root nag'a, has a wide range of potential meanings.

2. I've written about some of the material in this chapter in a more academic context in Julia Watts Belser, "Improv and the Angel: Disability Dance, Embodied Ethics, and Jewish Biblical Narrative," Journal of Religious Ethics 47, no. 3 (2019): 443–69.

3. Genesis 32:31. Translation is my own. JPS translates this verse as "I have seen a divine being face to face." The Hebrew speaks of elohim, a common way of naming God.

4. Rashi on Genesis 33:18. Translations from Rashi are my own.

5. Dale Evans Rogers, Angel Unaware: A Touching Story of Love and Loss (Grand Rapids, MI: Fleming Revell, 1953).

6. Andrew Walker-Cornetta, "Unsingular Subjects," American Religion, https://www.american-religion.org/provocations/unsingular, accessed January 28, 2022.

7. The case of Ashley X has been widely discussed by disability studies scholars and activists. For a powerful and accessible account, see Eli Clare, Brilliant Imperfection: Grappling with Cure (Durham, NC: Duke University Press, 2017), 152–56. For a discussion of the medical controversy and an account of her parents' motivations, see Amy Burkholder, "Disabled Girl's Parents Defend Growth-Stunting Treatment," CNN Health, March 12, 2008, http://www.cnn.com/2008/HEALTH/conditions/03/12/pillow.angel/index.html.

8. Rabbi Ruti Regan, "Disability, Idolatry, and the Divine Image," workshop, Summer Institute on Disability and Theology, 2017.

9. James Kugel, *How to Read the Bible: A Guide to Scripture, Then and Now* (New York: Free Press, 2007), 111.

10. Judges 13:6.

11. Genesis 32:25. JPS translates *elohim* as "divine being," but in biblical Hebrew, this term is most commonly used as a way of naming God.

12. Rosemarie Garland-Thomson, "Becoming Disabled," *New York Times*, August 19, 2016.

13. Harriet McBryde Johnson, *Too Late to Die Young: Nearly True Tales from a Life* (New York: Picador, 2005), 11.

14. On Freud's use of the uncanny in connection with disability, see Lennard Davis, *Enforcing Normalcy: Disability, Deafness, and the Body* (London: Verso, 1995), 141.

15. For a discussion of Duffy's work, see Rosemarie Garland-Thomson, "Staring Back: Self-Representations of Disabled Performance Artists," *American Quarterly* 52, no. 2 (2000): 334–33.

16. Edward Carpenter, *Angels' Wings: A Series of Essays on Art and Its Relation to Life* (London: Swan Sonnenschein, 1898), 26.

17. Carpenter, *Angels' Wings*, 27.

18. For many contemporary readers, the tale of Jacob wrestling the angel has become a touchstone for recognizing the spiritual insight gained through gay men's experience. In 1993, Steve Greenberg penned a powerful account of his experience as a gay Orthodox rabbi under the pseudonym Rabbi Yaakov Levado—Jacob Alone—a name that gave voice to Greenberg's own sense of loneliness and struggle. A decade later, Greenberg turned again to Jacob's story for the title of his book, *Wrestling with God and Men*, reconciling same-sex love with Jewish tradition. The title recalls that nighttime struggle at the river when Jacob is renamed Israel; the Bible recognizes him as one who has "wrestled with God and with men, and prevailed." Steven Greenberg, *Wrestling with God and Men: Homosexuality in the Jewish Tradition* (Madison: University of Wisconsin Press, 2004).

19. Joe Perez, *Soulfully Gay: How Harvard, Sex, Drugs, and Integral Philosophy Drove Me Crazy and Brought Me Back to God* (Boston: Shambhala Publications, 2007), 247; Andrew Ramer, *Queering the Text: Biblical, Medieval, and Modern Jewish Stories* (Maple Shade, NJ: Lethe Press, 2010), 11–13.

20. Rashi on Genesis 32:35. The Aramaic expression is drawn from the Babylonian Talmud, Sanhedrin 63b. Targum Neofiti offers a similar translation, that Jacob and the angel "embraced."

21. Geoffrey Hartman, *The Third Pillar: Essays in Judaic Studies* (Philadelphia: University of Pennsylvania Press, 2011), 26.

22. Ruth 2:9.

23. Genesis 3:3.

24. Leviticus 5:2.

25. Rosemarie Garland-Thomson, "The Case for Conserving Disability," *Bioethical Inquiry* 9 (2012): 339–55, 342.

CHAPTER ELEVEN: THE POLITICS OF BEAUTY

1. Babylonian Talmud, Ketubot 16b–17a.

2. Daniel S. Hamermersh and Jeff E. Biddle, "Beauty and the Labor Market," *American Economic Review* 84, no. 5 (1994): 1175.

3. Hamermersh and Biddle, "Beauty and the Labor Market."

4. Dana Dunn, *The Social Psychology of Disability* (Oxford: Oxford University Press, 2015), 49.

5. Tobin Siebers, *Disability Aesthetics* (Ann Arbor: University of Michigan Press, 2010), 23.

6. Siebers, *Disability Aesthetics*, 25.

7. While Siebers has discussed this claim at length in his book *Disability Aesthetics*, an excellent short introduction to his argument can be found in Tobin Siebers, "Disability Aesthetics," *Journal for Cultural and Religious Theory* 7, no. 2 (Spring/Summer 2006): 63–73.

8. Mia Mingus, "Moving Toward the Ugly: A Politic Beyond Desirability," Femmes of Color Symposium Keynote Speech, Oakland, CA, August 21, 2011, https://leavingevidence.wordpress.com/2011/08/22/moving-toward-the-ugly-a-politic-beyond-desirability.

9. Mingus, "Moving Toward the Ugly."

10. Mingus, "Moving Toward the Ugly."

11. For a powerful analysis of Bilhah and Zilphah in the Hebrew Bible and a reconsideration of their significance, see Wilda C. Gafney, *Womanist Midrash: A Reintroduction to the Women of the Torah and the Throne* (Louisville, KY: Westminster John Knox Press, 2017), 57–71. See also Wil Gafney, "Torat Bilhah: The Torah of a Disposable Woman," December 3, 2011, https://www.wilgafney.com/2011/12/03/torat-bilhah-the-torah-of-a-disposable-woman.

12. Babylonian Talmud, Baba Batra 123a.

13. For an overview of some traditional commentary on Leah's eyes and eyesight, see Morton Seelenfreund and Stanley Schneider, "Leah's Eyes," *Jewish Bible Quarterly* 25, no. 1 (1997): 18–22.

14. R. Gradwohl, "Waren Leas Augen hässlich?" *Vetus Testamentum* 49, no. 1 (1999): 119–24.

15. Claire Cunningham gives a powerful account of Orthodox disabled people's experiences in this regard in her 2014 performance "Guide Gods." On the stigma faced by women with disabilities in Orthodox Jewish contexts, see Ariella Barker, "Dating with a Disability in the Jewish World," RespectAbility, April 30, 2021, https://www.respectability.org/2021/04/dating-with-a-disability-in-the-jewish-world.

16. Mingus, "Moving Toward the Ugly."

17. Exodus 15:20; Babylonian Talmud, Megilah 14a.

18. Alicia Suskin Ostriker, "Songs of Miriam," in *The Nakedness of the Fathers: Biblical Visions and Revisions* (New Brunswick, NJ: Rutgers University Press, 1997), 146.

19. Exodus 15:1. The translation I have quoted is the translation that appears in Ostriker's poem.

20. Midrash Tanhuma, Tzav 13.

21. 2 Kings 19:9.

22. Elad Filler, "Moses and the Kushite Woman: Classic Interpretations and Philo's Allegory," TheTorah.com, https://www.thetorah.com/article/moses-and-the-kushite-woman-classic-interpretations-and-philos-allegory, accessed October 19, 2022.

23. For a discussion of Miriam's experience with tsaraat in biblical and other ancient Jewish sources, see Hanna K. Tervanotko, *Denying Her Voice: The Figure of Miriam in Ancient Jewish Literature* (Gottingen: Vandenhoeck & Ruprecht, 2016).

24. Numbers 12:13. Translation is my own. JPS has "O God, pray heal her." I prefer simpler language, to better capture the urgency and the spareness of Moses's words.

25. Numbers 12:14.

26. Babylonian Talmud, Arakhin 16a.

27. Alexander Rysman, "How the Gossip Became a Woman," *Journal of Communication* 27, no. 1 (1977).

28. Reina Gattuso, "Gossip as an Act of Resistance," Feministing, August 23, 2006, http://feministing.com/2016/08/23/gossip-as-an-act-of-resistance.

29. Yocheved Bat-Miriam, *Shirim* (Tel Aviv: Sifriyat Po'alim, 1973), 179–80. Translated by Ilana Pardes in "The Poetic Strength of a Matronym," in *Gender and Text in Modern Hebrew and Yiddish Literatures*, ed. Kathryn Hellerstein, Anne Lapidus Lerner, and Anita Norich (New York: JTS Press, 1992), 41.

30. Wendy Zierler, "Re-Encountering Miriam," TheTorah.com, https://www.thetorah.com/article/re-encountering-miriam, accessed October 19, 2022. This modern midrash was included as a commentary on Parshat Beha'lotkha in *The Torah: A Woman's Commentary* (New York: URJ Press, 2008), 868.

31. Yiskah Rosenfeld, "The Murmurings of Miriam," *Bridges: A Jewish Feminist Journal* 12, no. 1 (2007).

32. Ostriker, "Songs of Miriam," 146–47.

CHAPTER TWELVE: THE RADICAL PRACTICE OF REST

1. Genesis 2:2. The phrasing is mine, an evocative translation that deliberately avoids the gendering that is present in the original Hebrew. JPS reads "On the seventh day God finished the work that He had been doing, and He ceased on the seventh day from all the work that He had done."

2. The quote is from Ahad Ha'am, "Sabbath and Zionism," *Hashiloach* 3 (1989); it is sometimes rendered, "More than Israel has kept Shabbat, Shabbat has kept Israel." Ha'am's quote predates the founding of the modern state of Israel; he uses Israel as a way to refer collectively to the Jewish people.

3. Abraham Joshua Heschel, *The Sabbath: Its Meaning for Modern Man* (1951; New York: Farrar, Straus, and Giroux, 1995), 13.

4. Patty Berne, "Disability Justice: A Working Draft," Sins Invalid, June 10, 2015, https://www.sinsinvalid.org/blog/disability-justice-a-working-draft-by-patty-berne.

5. Ellen Samuels, "Six Ways of Looking at Crip Time," *Disability Studies Quarterly* 37, no. 3 (2017), http://dx.doi.org/10.18061/dsq.v37i3.5824.

6. Susan Wendell, "Unhealthy Disabled: Treating Chronic Illnesses as Disabilities," *Hypatia* 16, no. 4 (2001): 21.

7. US Bureau of Labor Statistics, March 2020, https://www.bls.gov/ncs/ebs
/factsheet/paid-sick-leave.htm.

CHAPTER THIRTEEN: GOD ON WHEELS

1. I've written about this experience in Julia Watts Belser, "God on Wheels:
Disability and Jewish Feminist Theology," *Tikkun Magazine* (Fall 2014).

2. While the medieval Jewish philosophical tradition strongly rejected anthro-
pomorphism, earlier Jewish conceptions of God are thoroughly embodied and
relational. Moshe Halbertal shows how rabbinic parables and teachings about
God commonly describe God in bodily terms. See Moshe Halbertal, "The God
of the Rabbis," in *The Cambridge Companion to Jewish Theology*, ed. Steven Kepnes
(Cambridge: Cambridge University Press, 2020). On the frequent use of anthro-
pomorphic imagery for God in rabbinic literature, see Yair Lorberbaum, *In God's
Image: Myth, Theology, and Law in Classical Judaism* (New York: Cambridge University Press, 2015).

3. Ezekiel 1:4.

4. Ezekiel 1:5-7. Translation is my own.

5. Ezekiel 1:8-12. Translation is my own.

6. Sunaura Taylor offers a powerful account of the intersections between
disability liberation and animal liberation, as well as the way that common assumptions about animal inferiority are rooted in ableist claims: that animals are
less worthy of care because they do not speak, reason, or feel the way that most
humans do. Sunaura Taylor, *Beasts of Burden: Animal and Disability Liberation* (New
York: New Press, 2017).

7. Eli Clare, *Brilliant Imperfection: Grappling with Cure* (Durham, NC: Duke University Press, 2017), 6.

8. I first encountered this powerful image through the work of disabled theologian Nancy Eiesland, whose work I will discuss in more detail later in the chapter. She tells the story of being asked to lead a Bible study for a group of people
with disabilities in a rehabilitation hospital. Asking the residents there "how
they would know if God was with them and understood their experience," she
recounts that, after a long silence, "a young African-American man said, 'if God
was in a sip-puff, maybe He would understand.'" Nancy Eiesland, "Encountering
the Disabled God," *The Other Side* (September–October 2002): 13.

9. Ezekiel 1:16. Translation is my own.

10. Accounts of ancient chariot warfare are filled with tantalizing details about
the exhilaration and challenge of driving a chariot in practice. Deborah Cantrell
observes that "speed for ancient chariots was easy; the problem was in stopping
them," a detail that resonates all too well with my own experience as a manual
wheelchair user, where the only brakes I have are my own hands. Sawyer recounts
the difficulty chariot drivers faced in ancient China, where the complexity of the
terrain and the treacherous ruts of a battlefield often turned chariots into stationary
platforms for archery. Deborah O'Daniel Cantrell, *The Horsemen of Israel: Horses and
Chariotry in Monarchic Israel* (University Park, PA: Penn State University Press, 2011),
64; Ralph D. Sawyer, *Ancient Chinese Warfare* (New York: Basic Books, 2011), 371.

11. Ezekiel 1:19-20. Translation is my own.

12. See Mel Chen, *Animacies: Biopolitics, Racial Mattering, and Queer Affect* (Durham, NC: Duke University Press, 2012).

13. See Robin Wall Kimmerer, *Braiding Sweetgrass: Indigenous Wisdom, Scientific Knowledge, and the Teachings of Plants* (Minneapolis: Milkweed Editions, 2013). This quote is drawn from Robin Kimmerer, "Speaking of Nature," *Orion Magazine*, June 12, 2017, https://orionmagazine.org/article/speaking-of-nature.

14. I've written in more detail about these ideas in Julia Watts Belser, "Vital Wheels: Disability, Relationality, and the Queer Animacy of Vibrant Things," *Hypatia* 31, no. 1 (October 2015): 5–21.

15. JPS translates this verse as "Let us make *man*," but I prefer "human" instead. The Hebrew word *adam* is at this point used to describe a human who is not yet gendered. In the next verse, Genesis will describe the *adam* as both male and female.

16. David Seidenberg offers a comprehensive assessment of the complex ways that rabbinic and later Jewish sources understood the idea of God's image, with a particular focus on the ecological implications of this theological claim. He shows that while traditional sources often use the idea of divine image to craft a sharp distinction between humans and other animals and to argue for the superiority of the human being, some passages within rabbinic sources affirm a much more egalitarian understanding of the divine image and extend that idea to all of creation—a motif that becomes much more prominent in medieval Jewish mysticism. David Mevorach Seidenberg, *Kabbalah and Ecology: God's Image in the More-Than-Human World* (New York: Cambridge University Press, 2015).

17. Moses Maimonides, *Guide for the Perplexed* 1:1. Translation follows Seidenberg, *Kabbalah and Ecology*, 67.

18. Eli Clare offers a powerful account of Carrie Buck's life and her involuntary sterilization. See Clare, *Brilliant Imperfection*, 103–12.

19. Susan Burch and Hannah Joyner, *Unspeakable: The Story of Junius Wilson* (Chapel Hill: University of North Carolina Press, 2007).

20. Disability activists have taken aim against legal rules that allow employers to circumvent minimum wage and fair labor standards in the case of people with disabilities. In a 2018 report, the National Council of Disability notes that more than three hundred thousand Americans with disabilities are employed in subminimum wage positions in segregated sheltered workshops, where they are often paid mere pennies per hour. National Council on Disability, *National Disability Employment Policy: From the New Deal to the Real Deal; Joining the Industries of the Future* (Washington, DC: NCD, October 11, 2018). For analysis of Vermont's ban on sheltered workshops, see Theresa Gold, "Pennies an Hour: Was This Really the Intent Behind § 14(C) of the Fair Labor Standards Act? A Note Calling for a System Change to an Otherwise Broken System," *Texas Tech Law Review* 48 (2016): 459–503.

21. On the powerful Autistic-led campaign to document brutality against Autistic people and to shut down institutions practicing electric shock treatments as a means of behavior modification, see Shain M. Neumeier and Lydia XZ Brown, "Torture in the Name of Treatment: The Mission to Stop the Shocks in the Age of Deinstitutionalization," in *Autistic Community and the Neurodiversity Movement: Stories from the Frontline*, ed. Steven K. Kapp (Singapore: Springer, 2020), 195–210.

22. On the brutal conditions at many institutions and group homes, as reflected in the life experiences of residents who attend a church in Atlanta, see Rebecca Spurrier, *The Disabled Church: Human Difference and the Art of Communal Worship* (New York: Fordham University Press, 2019), chapter 5.

23. For a powerful response to the use of the R-word as an insult by a man with an intellectual disability, see John Franklin Stephens, "An Open Letter to Ann Coulter," *Special Olympics Blog*, October 23, 2012.

24. On sexuality and intellectual disability, see Michael Gil, *Already Doing It: Intellectual Disability and Sexual Agency* (Minneapolis: University of Minnesota Press, 2015).

25. Genesis Rabbah 8:11.

26. Seidenberg, *Kabbalah and Ecology*, 90–91.

27. Grace Ji-Sun Kim, *Invisible: Theology and the Experience of Asian American Women* (Minneapolis: Fortress Press, 2021), 127.

28. Judith Plaskow, "God: Some Feminist Questions," *The Coming of Lilith: Essays on Feminism, Judaism, and Sexual Ethics, 1972–2003* (Boston: Beacon Press, 2005).

29. Nancy Eiesland, *The Disabled God: Toward a Liberatory Theology of Disability* (Nashville: Abingdon Press, 1994), 89.

30. Eiesland, *The Disabled God*, 99.

31. Eiesland, *The Disabled God*, 100.

32. Sins Invalid, *Sins Invalid: An Unshamed Claim to Beauty*, film, 32 mins. (2013). A portion of Bell's performance can be viewed at https://www.youtube.com/watch?v=VUkKCpBEa0Q.

INDEX

Bolded page numbers refer to terms in the glossary

Aaron (biblical figure), 76–78, 80, 82, 88, 94, 109, 191–92

ableism: accomplishment as value of, 200–201; anti-Judaism, 47, 128–29, 132–36, 208; in the bible, 10–11, 18, 43–44, 250n7; caricatures of disability, 219; cognitive ableism, 49–50, 251n17, 251n19; covering, 30–32, 40, 71–72, 249n10, 249n11, 249n15; defective (use of term), 57–58; defined, **39**, 47–48; disability as consequence of sin, 94–95, 125–27, 136; disability justice, 47, 200, 201, 231, 264n32; emotions, display of, 100, 101–3; excellence, 47–48, 49, 50–51, 141–44, 212; intelligence, 39, 47–50, 60, 224–26, 235, 263n20, 264n23; language of, 38–39, 42, 225, 264n23; parenthood, 39; privilege, 16–17, 22, 29–32, 40, 47–48, 120–21, 191, 201, 228, 251n17; productivity, 52–53, 200, 202, 212–13; racism, 16–17, 22–23, 46–48, 52, 122, 168, 191, 228, 249n15, 251n16, 251n17, 256n8; Sodom (biblical city) as account of, 43–44, 250n7; as structural violence,

39, 44–46, 250n4; trope of disability as tragic suffering, 100–101, 214; value of life, 46, 144–48, 211, 225, 257n5. *See also* barriers; beauty; cure; healing; mum (blemish); nondisabled people

Abraham (biblical figure), 148–49, 150–53, 257n7

access: barriers to, 2, 39, 105–6, 113–14, 122, 202, 210–11, 233; biblical sources on, 12, 117–18, 247n5; as communal responsibility, 45; employment, 27–28, 30, 39, 46, 52, 213, 225–26, 263n20; to health care, 29–30, 39, 46, 119–20, 146–48, 151, 248n7; Moses's access to the land, 95–99, 97, 102–4, 107, 255n5; to nature, 95–99, 102–4, 106–8, 111–12; privilege, 16–17, 22, 29–32, 40, 47–48, 120–21, 191, 228, 251n17; restrooms, 28, 142, 237; sensory access, 72, 81–82, 235, 253n21; Shabbat observance, 199–200, 201–7, 209–10, 212–13; signs as alternatives to speech, 81–82; in synagogues, 5, 202–3, 210–11; transportation, 29, 144, 203, 205–6, 222, 233, 237

accommodation: Aaron as accommodation to Moses, 76–78, 80, 82,

88; burden of disclosure, 26–30, 248n4; discrimination, 24–26, 27, 37–39; qualifications for, 27, 28–29, 44–45

activism, 26, 37–39, 248n7, 250n4, 253n21

Acts, book of, 87

ADA (Americans with Disabilities Act), 26, 37–39

African Americans, 23, 46–47, 122, 249n15, 256n8

aging, 146–48, 211, 257n5

Ahad Ha'am, 199, 261n2

Akedah (binding of Isaac), 148–49, 150–53, 257n7

Amalek, battle with, 109

Americans with Disabilities Act (ADA), 26, 37–39

angels: in art, 170; bodies, description of, 170–71, 217–19; in book of Ezekiel, 217, 218; encounters with, 167, 169–70, 178–79; faces of, 217–18; Jacob wrestles with angel, 162–68, 169–70, 175–76, 259n18, 259n20; in popular culture, 165–66; recognition of, 167–70, 226; weeping of, 149–50, 152, 257n11; with wings, 170–71, 218

animacy, 221–22

animal intelligence, 224

animal liberation, 262n6

animals: caricatures of disability, 219; human exceptionalism, 223–24, 263n16

anti-Judaism, 47, 128–29, 132–36, 208, 255n6

art, 109–10, 170, 172, 183, 249n8. See also dance

Ashley X, 166, 258n7

Autism: ableism, 50, 127, 155, 225; advocacy, 248n7, 253n21; Autistic God, 237; behavioral therapy, 155, 263n21; identification of, 25, 42, 50, 71–72; stimming, 72, 235, 253n21

Babylonian Talmud (Bavli). See Talmud

barriers: ADA (Americans with Disabilities Act), 26, 37–39; biblical texts on, 6, 12; in commercial spaces, 26, 33, 113–14; housing, 29, 39, 122, 202; restrooms, 28, 142, 237; sidewalks, 105–6, 210, 216, 236, 237; in synagogues, 5, 202–3, 210–11. See also transportation

Batya (Pharaoh's daughter), 86, 87

beauty: aesthetic judgments, 19–21, 60, 63, 180, 181–83, 189; as desirable, 123, 124, 181, 185–88; of disability, 11, 20–21, 170, 180–81, 183–84; ethnic identity, 191; self-image, 170, 181, 188–89; ugliness, 181–83, 184–85, 189; and women, 20–21, 170, 180–81, 185–87

Bell, Alexander Graham, 46

Bell, Rodney, 230–31, 264n32

Ben Bag-Bag (Talmud figure), 21–22

Berne, Patty, 47, 200

Biddle, Jeff, 181

Bilhah (biblical figure), 186

bimah, 72, 202, **238**

binding of Isaac (Akedah), 148–49, 150–53, 257n7

Black disability activism, 48, 168, 251n15

blemish (mum): defective (use of term), 57–58; as disqualification, 56–57, 67–68, 70–71; Mishnah on, 65–68; of priests, 54–63, 64, 69–70; sacrifices without, 56, 57; tsaraat, 81–82, 192–95, **240**, 254n10, 254n11; visibility of, 59–61

blessings, 5, 66, 67, 69–70, 158–59, 163, 176, 252n14, 258n23

blindness: blind Jews, trope of, 132, 134; as choice, 137–38; depictions of, 139–41, 257n3; as end of life, 144–46; exploitation of,

126–27, 160; of Isaac, 139–41, 144–45, 146, 150, 152; markers of, 26; as metaphor for sin, 155; navigation without sight, 154–56; sensory knowledge, 140–41, 155–57; the spiritual, 126–27, 131–34; weeping, 150, 152–53, 257n11

"the blue of distance" (Solnit), 109–10

bodies: aesthetic judgments, 17, 54, 55, 181–83, 189; aging, 146–48, 211, 257n5; athleticism, 171, 174, 177; *b'tselem Elohim*, 6, 200, 223, 224–25, 226, 227, **238**; exploitation of, 126–28, 150–51; eyes, imagery of, 186–87; familiarity (concept), 71–72; gaze, 35, 67, 68–69, 71, 94–95, 111, 169, 214; hand imagery, 67–68, 70, 156; in healing stories, 114–16, 118, 123, 127, 255n1; limits of, 109, 145, 177–78; limp, 3, 26, 162–65, 168, 175; mind, 49–50; normate, 40–41, 43–44, 52, 168; race, 16–17, 22, 47–48, 52, 191, 219, 228, 251n17; resurrection of, 230; self-image, 170, 188–89; violence, 43–44, 46, 57, 62, 83, 86–87, 148–50, 225, 250n7; in wheel chair life, 221; wrestling, 162–68, 169–70, 175–76, 259n18, 259n20. *See also* blemish *(mum);* dance

brides, 19–21, 180

Britain, 29, 38–39

b'tselem Elohim, 6, 200, 223, 224–25, 226, 227, **238**

Buck, Carrie, 225

burning bush, 90

canes, 26, 131

Cantrell, Deborah, 262n10

care givers, 29, 147–48, 213

Carpenter, Edward, 170–71

cerebral palsy, 3, 168

challah baking, 204

chariots, 8–9, 215, 218, 220–21, 228, 234, 262n10

children: abuse of, 39, 58, 83, 86, 87, 154–55, 166, 219, 258n7; achievement, 39; assistive communication devices, 166; deafness, 11, 75, 175–76; disability services for, 29, 46; disabled parents of, 39; interest in angels, 170–71; Jacob's deception of Isaac, 139–40, 141, 156–61; spirituality of, 3, 14; stuttering, 88, 89, 254n19

choices, responsibility for, 191–92

choreography, 172–74, 177–78

Christian Bible: healing stories in, 114–16, 118, 123, 125–26, 128, 130, 135, 255n1; on Moses, 87

Christianity: blindness, 134; the Disabled God in, 228–30; Judaism, 129–33, 134, 136–37, 208. *See also* Gospels; Jesus

chronic illness, 59, 122, 211–12, 250n3

Clare, Eli, 43, 57, 121, 219

cognitive effects: of physical disability, 49–50

Coleman, Monica, 46, 122, 249n15, 256n8

communication technologies, 46, 81, 166, 207, 235

community, 2, 23, 46, 129, 187, 260n15

covering, 30–32, 40, 71–72, 249n10, 249n11, 249n15

creation narratives, 6, 74–75, 78, 81, 198–200, 223–26, 261n1

crossing into the land, 95–99, 97, 102–4, 107–9, 255n5

crutches, 81, 172, 174

Cunningham, Claire, 123, 172–74, 177, 260n15

cure: as choice, 115, 121, 122–25; ethics of, 166, 258n7; healing compared with, 135; health care, 38, 121–22, 146–47; medical culture, 37–38, 46, 119–20, 123–24, 188–89, 250n3; politics of, 120, 121. *See also* healing

Curtis, Jess, 173–74, 177, 178

Cushite nation, 191, 260n21

dance: athleticism, 231; body changes limiting, 177–78; choreography, 172–74, 177–78; with crutches, 81, 172, 174; Cunningham, Claire, 123, 172–74, 177, 260n15; physical contact, 173–74; Sins Invalid, 47, 231, 264n32; spin, 9, 230–33; in wheelchairs, 2, 230, 231, 232–33

Daniel, book of, 61

deafness, 10–12, 42, 46, 59, 74, 169, 224, 246n1

death, 46, 96, 144–47, 169, 257n5, 275n5

defective (use of term), 57–58

Della Francesca, Piero, 171

desire, 95–96, 99, 109–10, 123–25

Deuteronomy, book of, 6, 96–97, 102–3, 107, 146, 155, 255n5, 255n8

disability: ADA (Americans with Disabilities Act), 26, 37–39; agency, 137–38; aging, 146–48, 211, 257n5; anonymity in, 84, 114, 115, 118; caricatures of, 219; as consequence of sin, 94–95, 125–27, 131, 136; covering, 30–32, 71–72, 249n10, 249n11, 249n15; cultural determination of, 57–59; definitions of, 3, 24, 28–29, 40–42, 41, 46–47, 85–86; denial of, 23, 31–32, 35–36, 165, 168; disclosure of, 23, 29, 30–32, 165, 168, 248n8, 249n10; as divine intervention, 84–85; as end-of-life (euphemism), 144–46, 147; familiarity (legal concept), 71; identity, 25, 27–29, 41–43,

50, 71–72, 99–101, 108–9, 122–23, 131–32, 137, 168; intellectual disabilities, 39, 47–50, 60, 224–26, 235, 263n20, 264n23; pain, 25, 32, 50, 100–102, 104, 123, 150–51; race and racism, 16–17, 22–23, 46–48, 52, 122, 168, 191, 219, 228, 249n15, 251n16, 251n17, 256n8; Shabbat observance, 206–12; social model of, 26, 37–39, 250n3; sympathy, 2, 100–101, 113–14; trauma, 100–101, 148–52; tropes of, 50, 90, 100–101, 115–16, 214; visibility of, 11, 24–26, 27, 33–35, 59–61, 214; vulnerability, 159–60, 169. *See also* barriers; beauty; healing

disability con, 25–26, 27

the Disabled God, 228–30

Dorff, Elliot, 59

Down Syndrome, 237

Duffy, Mary, 170

education, 29–30, 39, 154–55, 235, 251n17

Eiesland, Nancy, 229–30, 262n8

electric shock treatments, 225, 263n21

Elisha ben Abuya (rabbinic figure), 254n19

employment, 27–28, 30, 39, 46, 52, 147–48, 212–13, 225–26, 250n4, 263n20

end-of-life, 144, 146, 147

Esau (biblical figure), 139–40, 156–57, 159, 186, 258n23

eugenics, 45, 46, 47, 48, 225

euthanasia, 46

Evans, Heather Dawn, 249n10

excellence, 47–48, 49, 50–51, 141–44, 212

Exodus, book of, 73–82, 87, 109, 254n10, 255n21

eyes, imagery of, 186–87

Ezekiel: disability envisioned in, 217–18; in exile, 214–15;

muteness of, 88, 254n18; visions of, 8–9, 215, 217–18; wheel imagery in, 8–9, 220, 246n3; wing imagery in, 170

familiarity (concept), 71–72
Findlay, Carly, 38
food resources, 29, 150
fraud, 25–26, 27
Freud, Sigmund, 169–70

Gallagher, Hugh, 31–32
Garden of Eden, 176–77, 216
Garland-Thomson, Rosemarie, 35–36, 40, 68, 168
Gattuso, Reina, 194
gaze, 35, 67, 68–69, 71, 94–95, 111, 169, 214
gender, 16, 32–35, 113–15, 223, 228
Genesis, book of, 139–41, 140, 153, 156–57, 162–64, 186, 257n1, 257n2, 257n5, 258n18, 258n19, 258n21, 258n22
God: aesthetic desires of, 11, 63–65, 89; Akedah, 148, 150; anger of, 80, 96, 102–3, 108, 255n6; b'tselem Elohim, 6, 200, 223, 224–25, 226, 227; creation narratives, 6, 74–75, 78, 81, 198–200, 223–26, 261n1; and disability, 11–12, 84–85, 215–16, 228–30, 262n8; discovery of, 14–15; Ehiyeh Asher Ehiyeh, 16–17, 247n9; in Ezekiel's visions, 215; frustration of, 76–77, 78, 79–80; gender of, 15, 16, 17, 62, 228, 232, 236; his act of rest, 199, 261n1; human intervention, 78–80; Jacob's encounter with, 163; Miriam and Aaron rebuked by, 192–93; Miriam rebuked by, 192, 195; Moses's encounters with, 74–75, 76–80, 97–99, 103, 192–93, 255n7; physicality of, 15–17, 60, 216–18, 228, 247n8, 262n2, 263n16; ruach (breath) of,

219–20, 262n8; visual representations of, 60; on wheels, 9, 16, 215, 230–36; wonder, sense of, 14
Goffman, Erving, 40
Gospels: anti-Judaism in, 128–29, 132–35; blindness, 126–27, 131, 132–33, 138; healing stories in, 114–16, 118, 123, 125–26, 128–29, 130, 135, 255n1; Jewish background of, 129–33, 135–36; transformation of the disabled, 128
gossip, 115, 193, 194
government: ADA (Americans with Disabilities Act), 26, 37–39; cuts to public services, 29; disability determinations, 29–30; institutional care, 29, 225, 248n7
Gracer, Bonnie, 77
Graybill, Rhiannon, 109
Green, Tamara, 59
Greenberg, Steve, 259n18
grief, displays of, 101–2
group homes, 225, 264n22

halakhah (Jewish law), 5, 71, 203, 207–8, **238**, 247n14
Halbertal, Moshe, 262n2
halo effect, 181
Hamermesh, Daniel, 181
hand imagery, 67–68, 70, 156
Hartman, Geoffrey, 176
healing: anonymity in, 84, 114, 115, 118; as choice, 137–38; cure compared with, 135; expectations of healing, 91–92, 117–19; in Gospels, 114–16, 118, 123, 125–26, 128–29, 130, 135, 255n1; Moses's request to God to heal Miriam, 193; prayers for, 104–5, 113–14, 123, 125, 193, **239**, 261n25; Sabbath observance, 130; as spectacle, 114–17; of women, 113–17
health care access, 29, 39, 46, 119–20, 146–48, 151, 248n7

Hebrew Bible, **239**; blindness, 139–41, 144–45, 146, 150, 152; dignity, 6; disability reversal, 10–12, 117–18, 247n5; emotion in, 102; investment in sight, 155; sacrifices in, 21, 55–56, 57; speech disability, 73–74, 83–84, 87–88, 253n2; wheel imagery, 246n3. *See also* God; kohanim (priests); *mum* (blemish); Shabbat (Sabbath, Shabbos); individual biblical figures (e.g. Moses); individual books of the bible (e.g. Leviticus)
Hershey, Laura, 36
Heschel, Abraham Joshua, 199–200
Hillel (rabbinic figure), 20, 21, 180
hip, Jacob's, 162, 163, 175, 177
Hiyya, Rabbi (rabbinic figure), 33–35
Holmes, Oliver Wendell, 225
homosexuality, 18, 247n11, 259n18
housing, 29, 39, 45, 122
Hull, John, 138

"I" (Jacob's answer to Isaac), 158, 258n20
Ibn Ezra, Abraham (rabbinic figure), 191
identity-first language, 42
immigration, 57, 98
infanticide, 83, 86, 87
inspiration porn, 128
institutional care, 29, 225, 248n7, 263n21, 264n22
intelligence, 39, 47–50, 60, 224–26, 235, 263n20, 264n23
Isaac (biblical figure): Akedah, 148–49, 150–53, 257n7; blessings given by, 158–59, 258n23; blindness of, 139–41, 144–45, 146, 150, 152; death of, 257n5; Esau, relations with, 139–40, 156–57, 159, 186, 258n23; "I" (Jacob's answer to Isaac), 158, 258n20; Jacob's deception of, 139–40, 141, 156–61; longevity of, 144–45, 146, 257n5; Rebecca,

139–40, 153–54, 156, 160, 257n15; sensory perception of, 153–54, 157; as survivor of violence, 149, 257n10. *See also* Jacob
Isaiah, book of, 10–11, 88, 155, 170, 246n3, 257n11
Islam, 127, 253n3
Israelites, 73–74, 79, 93–94, 98, 103–4, 109, 255n7

Jacob (biblical figure): arrival in Shechem, 162–65; deception of Isaac, 139–40, 141, 156–61; engagement with disability, 165; "I" (Jacob's answer to Isaac), 158, 258n20; Isaac's blessing, 156–58, 258n23; as Israel, 163, 259n18; limp of, 162–65, 168; Rebecca, 139–40, 153–54, 156, 160, 257n15; wives of, 185–86; wrestles with angel, 162–68, 169–70, 175–76, 259n18, 259n20
Jeremiah, book of, 12, 247n5
Jerusalem Temple: destruction of, 215
Jesus: belief in, 113; and the blind man, 126–27, 131, 132–33, 137–38; on disability, 125–26; healing by, 114–16, 118, 123, 125–26, 128–29, 130, 135, 255n1; incarnation of, 16; as Jew, 128–29; resurrection of, 230; the Sabbath and, 114, 129–30
Jewish community, 5, 71, 72, 187, 202–3, 207–8, 210–11, 237, 238, 260n15
John (Gospel), 118, 125, 126–27, 129–33
Johnson, Harriet McBryde, 169
Jones, Kirsty, 253n7
Joshua, 147
Judaism: anti-Judaism, 47, 128–29, 132–36, 208, 255n6; blindness as stereotype of, 132, 134; in Christianity, 129–33, 134, 136–37, 208; halakhah (Jewish law), 5, 71, 203, 207–8, **238**; Shavuot, 8–9;

synagogues, 5, 72, 104–5, 202, 210–11, 237. *See also* Shabbat (Sabbath, Shabbos)
justice, 6, 18, 46–47, 94, 247n10

keeping Shabbat, 199–200, 201–6, 209–10, 212–13, 261n2
Kenny, Amy, 127
Kierkegaard, Søren, 148
Kim, Eunjung, 121
Kim, Grace Ji-Sun, 228
Kimmerer, Robin Wall, 222
Kleege, Georgina, 155–56, 257n3
kohanim (priests), **239**; access to the sacred, 58; blemishes, 54–63, 69–70; blessings, 66, 67, 69–70, 252n14; destruction of the Temple in Jerusalem, 66, 214–15, 252n14; disqualification of, 58–60, 59, 67–68, 70; hands of, 67–68; holiness of, 60; relations with community, 60, 67–69; sacrifices, 21, 54–57, 215; visual perfection, 58–60
Kugel, James, 167
Kushner, Harold, 247n8

Land of Israel, 95–99, 96, 97, 102–4, 107–9, 255n5
Leah (biblical figure), 185–87
Lehrer, Riva, 124
Leigh, Darby, 75
leprosy, 81–82, 195, 254n10
Levine, Amy-Jill, 132, 135–36, 256n18
Leviticus, book of, 6, 18, 54, 55, 56, 58, 59, 60–64, 66
Lewis, Talila "TL," 47, 51–52, 251n15
limp, 3, 26, 71, 162–65, 168, 175
longevity, 146–47
Longmore, Paul, 250n4
Lot (biblical figure), 43–44, 250n7
Luke (Gospel), 114–16, 130, 255n1, 256n16

Maharal of Prague (rabbinic figure), 226, 227
Maimonides, Moses (rabbinic figure), 16, 64, 94, 216, 224–25, **239**, 252n13
Malachi, book of, 61–62, 252n12
Manoah (biblical figure), 167, 169–70
marriage, 33–35
Mbuvi, Amanda, 86, 88
Medicaid, 29, 248n7
medical culture, 37–38, 46, 57, 119–20, 123–24, 188–89, 250n3
mental health, 46, 49, 122, 170, 249n15, 256n8
Michaelson, Jay, 43
Midrash, **239**; ableism (example) in, 43–44, 250n7; angels weeping, 149–50, 257n11; on the binding of Isaac (Akedah), 149–50, 152–53; God's face, 15, 247n8; on Isaac's blindness, 149–51; Jacob's limp, 164–65; Jacob's reconciliation with Esau, 164; on Leah, 186; Miriam's rebuke of Moses, 191, 260n20; Moses asking for people's prayers, 103–4, 255n7; Moses pleads with God, 99, 255n7; Moses's inability to enter the land, 103–4; on Moses's speech, 82–83, 89, 91; on Moses's staff, 81; priestly blessing, 67, 252n15; Sodom in, 43–44, 250n7; on speech disability, 83–84, 91; story of the angel and the coal, 83–84
Midrash Tanhuma, 91, 144, 257n4
mikveh, 5, **239**
Mingus, Mia, 184, 185, 188, 196
Miriam (biblical figure): merit of, 93, 189, 191–92, 195–96; Moses and, 86, 191, 192, 193, 260n20, 261n25; as prophetess, 195; skin affliction (*tsaraat*), 192–93, 194–95; song of Miriam, 189–90, 260n19; Zipporah supported by, 191, 192

Mishnah, 65–68, 71, 81
Montgomery, Cal, 251n19
Moore, Leroy, 48, 168
Morrison, Toni, 23
Moses (biblical figure): Aaron, 76–78, 80, 82, 88, 94, 109, 191–92; aging of, 146–48; battle with Amalek, 109; crossing into the land, 95–99, 102–4, 107–10, 255n5; death of, 96; early life, 86–89, 195; in Islam, 127, 253n3; Israelites' relations with, 73–74, 79, 93–94, 98, 103–4, 109, 255n7; Midrash on, 83–84; Miriam, 86, 191, 192, 193, 260n20, 261n25; on the mountain, 107, 109, 146; in New Testament, 87; orations of, 91–92, 255n21; in Pharaoh's court, 83–84, 86–87; rebuke of, 191–93, 195; relations with God, 74–75, 76–80, 97–99, 103, 192–93, 255n7; requests for healing, 193, 261n25; speech disability, 73, 83–84, 87–88, 253n2; spiritual leadership of, 88–89; staff of Moses, 81; story of the angel and the coal, 83–84; striking the rock, 80, 94, 96; water turns into blood, 82; wives of, 191–92, 193
mountain imagery, 107, 109, 146, 148, 149, 150, 153
Mount Moriah, 148, 149, 153
mouth imagery, 74, 75, 78, 83, 84, 253n4
mum (blemish), 239; defective (use of term), 57–58; as disqualification, 56–57, 67–68, 70–71; Mishnah on, 65–68; of priests, 54–63, 64, 69–70; sacrifices without, 56, 57; tsaraat, 81–82, 192–95, 240, 254n10, 254n11; visibility of, 59–61

Nachmanides (rabbinic figure), 94
National Center for Learning Disabilities, 251n17

nature, 13–14, 95–99, 102–4, 106–8, 111–12, 151, 221, 222
Nazi Germany, 46
nondisabled people: as insulting , 38–39, 225, 264n23; as normate, 40–41, 168; reaction to disability, 1, 94–95, 100, 113–14, 117–20, 168–69, 173–74, 177, 214; as temporarily able-bodied, 146; trope of disability as tragic suffering, 100–101, 214; visibility of disability, 11, 24–26, 27, 33–35, 59–61, 214
Numbers, book of, 79–80, 94, 96–97, 191, 252n14, 255n2, 255n3

Olyan, Saul, 60, 63
Orthodox Jewish community, 187, 203, 207, 259n18, 260n15
Ostriker, Alicia, 189–90, 196, 260n19

pain, 25, 32, 50, 100–102, 104, 123, 150–51
passing, 30–32, 40
paternalism, 17, 48
Perez, Joe, 175
perfection, 58–60, 89, 183
person-first language, 42
Pervez, Noor, 127
Pharaoh, 73, 79, 83–84, 86–87, 88
Pharisees, 132
physical appearance, 182
physician-assisted suicide, 146
Piepzna-Samarasinha, Leah Lakshmi, 151
Pirke de-Rabbi Eliezer, 81, 254n9
Plaskow, Judith, 228
police violence, 48, 251n16
political activism, 2, 26, 29, 37–39, 46, 248n7, 253n21
power, tsaraat as sign of, 195–96
prayers, 2, 5, 103–6, 113–14, 123, 239, 255n7
Price, Margaret, 50
priests (kohanim), 239; access to the sacred, 58; blemishes, 54–63,

69–70; blessings, 66, 67, 69–70, 252n14; destruction of the Temple in Jerusalem, 66, 214–15, 252n14; disqualification of, 58–60, 59, 67–68, 70; hands of, 67–68; holiness of, 60; relations with community, 60, 67–69; sacrifices, 21, 54–57, 215; visual perfection, 58–60

privilege, 16–17, 22, 29–32, 40, 47–48, 120–21, 191, 201, 228, 251n17

productivity, 52–53, 200, 202, 212–13

prophecy, 88–89, 195–96, 253n7, 254n19

queerness, 2, 4, 9, 17, 18, 21–23, 32, 43, 52, 175, 201

rabbinic Judaism: on blemished priests, 64, 67–71; on disability, 19–20, 32–35, 247n12, 247n13, 249n16, 249n17; human qualities defined, 225, 226, 227; on Jacob, 164, 175, 187, 259n20; on Moses, 88, 94, 191–92; Pharisees in, 132; on praising beauty, 20, 21, 180; priests in, 7, 65–68; self-images in, 32–35; stuttering in, 83–84, 88–89, 91–92, 94; on women, 69

race and racism, 16–17, 22–23, 46–48, 52, 122, 168, 191, 219, 228, 249n15, 251n16, 251n17, 256n8

Rachel (biblical figure), 185–87

Ramer, Andrew, 175

rape, 43–44, 250n7

Raphael, Rebecca, 60, 153

Rashbam (rabbinic figure), 88, **239**

Rashi (rabbinic figure), 61–62, 67, 78, 94, 164, 175, **239**, 259n20

Rav (rabbinic figure), 33

Rebecca (biblical figure), 139–40, 153–54, 156, 160, 257n15

Regan, Ruti, 23, 166

religious communities, 2, 5, 54, 71–72, 187, 202–3, 207–8, 210–11, 228, 237, 238, 260n15

restrooms, 28, 142, 237

Rich, Adrienne, 7

right to life, 46

ritual conduct within the tabernacle, 54, 55, 56, 59, 60–64, 66

rock, striking of, 94, 96

Rogers, Dale Evan, 165–66

Roosevelt, Franklin D., 31–32

Rosenfeld, Yiskah, 195

ruach (breath) of God, 219–20, **240**, 262n8

Ryan, Francis, 29

Rysman, Alexander, 194

Saadiya Gaon, 216

sacrifices, 21, 55–57, 215

Samuels, Ellen, 211

Sawyer, Ralph D., 262n10

Schipper, Jeremy, 61, 63

Schumm, Darla, 134

scooters, electric, 2, 32, 33, 119–20, 131, 142, 203, 208, 221

Seidenberg, David, 263n16

sexuality: denial of, 225; of gay men, 175, 259n18; homosexuality, 18, 43, 247n11, 250n7; queerness, 2, 4, 9, 17, 18, 21–23, 32, 43, 52, 175, 201; of women, 69

sexual violence, 43–44

Shabbat (Sabbath, Shabbos), **240**; challah baking, 204; challenges of keeping, 199–200, 201–6, 209–10, 212–13; in Genesis, 198–99, 261n1; God's act of rest, 199; Jesus and, 114, 129–30; preparations for, 197, 198, 204–5, 210; solitary observance of, 198, 202, 208, 210; technology use on, 202–3, 207–8; transportation on, 27–29, 144, 203, 205–7, 222, 233, 237

shame, 36, 41–42, 90, 92, 119, 184

Shammai (rabbinic figure), 20, 180
Shavuot, 8–9, 214
Shell, Marc, 90, 253n2, 253n3, 254n9
sheltered workshops, 225–26, 263n20
shoes, 123, 124
Shulḥan Arukh, 71
sidewalk surfaces, 105–6, 210, 216, 236, 237
Siebers, Tobin, 182, 183
signs as alternatives to speech, 81–82, 253n7
sin: blindness as metaphor for, 155; disability as consequence of, 94–95, 125–27, 136; sexuality, 43, 250n7; *tsaraat* associated with, 193–94, 195; ugliness, 182
Sins Invalid, 47, 200, 231, 264n32
sip-puff wheelchairs, 219, 229, 262n8
"Six Ways of Looking at Crip Time" (Samuels), 211
skin disease, 38, 81–82, 192–96, 254n10
social hierarchy, 38–39, 158–60, 181–82, 250n3
Sodom (biblical city), 43–44, 250n7
Solnit, Rebecca, 109–10
"Songs of Miriam" (Ostriker), 189–90, 196, 260n19
Soulfully Gay (Perez), 175
speech: Aaron as accommodation to Moses, 76–78, 80, 82, 88; divine intent, 74–76; justifying specialness, 226; linguistic history, 87–88; Midrash on, 83–84; mouth imagery, 74, 75, 78, 83, 84, 253n4; in Muslim tradition, 253n3; muteness of Ezekiel, 88, 254n18; prophecy, 88–89, 195–96, 253n7, 254n19; signs as alternatives to, 81–82, 253n7; stuttering, 25, 88–89, 90, 91, 94, 253n2, 254n19
spin, 9, 232–33
the spiritual: blindness, 126–27, 131–34; children and, 14–15; mis-use of, 84–86, 113–14,

126–28, 166; nature, 13–14, 95–99, 106, 108, 111–12, 151, 221, 222; Shabbat observance, 199–200, 201–6, 209–10, 212–13; spiritual leadership of Moses, 88–89
Stackert, Jeffrey, 61, 63
staff of Moses, 81
standing, 25, 228
staring, 35, 67, 68–69, 71
sterilization, 46, 225
stigma, 27, 30, 32, 39, 57–58, 81–82, 168, 170, 214, 254n10, 254n11
striking the rock, 94, 96
stuttering, 88–89, 90, 91–92, 94, 253n2, 254n19
suspicions of disability, 26, 27
sympathy, 2, 100–101, 113–14
synagogues, 5, 72, 104–5, 202, 210–11, 237

Talmud, **238**; ableism in, 19–21, 32–35, 180; on blemished priests, 69–71; on disability, 33–34, 249n16, 249n17; on praising beauty, 20, 21, 180; on priestly blessing, 69–70; priests in, 65–66; sources related to body image, 19–20, 32–35, 180; study of, 18–21; on the stuttering child, 254n19; *tsaraat* in, 193–94; women in, 20, 32–35, 69, 186, 260n12
taxis, 144, 203
Taylor, Charles, 14
Taylor, Sunaura, 262n6
Temple in Jerusalem, 55, 66, **240**
Thank You Very Much (Cunningham), 123
"the uncanny" (Freud), 169–70
The Way you look (at me) Tonight (Cunningham), 173–74
Torah, **240**. *See* God; Hebrew Bible; *kohanim* (priests); individual biblical figures (e.g. Moses)
Torah study, sources on, 21–22, 247n15

touch: in dance, 173–74; as deceptive, 139, 156–57; Hebrew words for, 174, 176–77; as transformative, 114, 162, 165, 168, 172–75, 178; value of, 104, 155; vision related to, 111; wrestling, 162–68, 169–70, 175–76, 259n18, 259n20
transportation: public transport, 202–3, 205; scooters, electric, 2, 32, 33, 119–20, 131, 142, 203, 208, 221; on Shabbat, 27–29, 144, 203, 205–7, 222, 233, 237; sidewalk surfaces, 105–6, 210, 216, 236, 237; taxis, 144, 203. *See also* wheelchairs
trauma, 148–52
trope of disability as tragic suffering, 100–101, 214
tsaraat, 81–82, 192–95, **240**, 254n10, 254n11
tsedek, tsedek tirdof, 6, 18
Tuchman, Lauren, 160
the twelve scouts, 96, 255n4
Tzippora (biblical figure), 87, 88

ugliness, 181–83, 184–85, 189
Umansky, Laurie, 251n18
United States: ADA (Americans with Disabilities Act), 26, 37–39; Ashley X, 166; disability activism in, 38–39; disability determinations, 29–30; institutional care, 29, 225, 248n7; Junius Wilson, 225

violence: Ashley X, 166, 258n7; in battle, 109; and border crossings, 98; defectiveness, 57–58; electric shock treatments, 225, 263n21; environmental pollution, 151; eugenics, 45, 46, 47, 48, 225; forced sterilization, 46, 225; impairment produced by, 150–51; infanticide, 83, 86, 87; of patriarchy, 62; police violence, 48, 251n16; racism, 16–17, 22–23, 46–48, 52, 122, 168, 191, 219, 228, 249n15,

251n16, 251n17, 256n8; sexual violence, 43–44, 250n7; state violence, 86–88; trauma, 148–50
visual signs, 81–82, 253n7, 254n11

Walker-Cornetta, Andrew, 166
walking, 3, 118–19, 226
war chariots, 220, 262n10
Waters of Meribah, 93–94
The Way You Look (at me) Tonight, 173–74, 177
weeping, 150, 152–53, 159, 257n11
Wendell, Susan, 212
Wening, Margaret Moers, 11
wheelchairs: animacy of, 221–22; athleticism needed for, 171; covering use of, 31–32; in dance, 231–33, 264n32; electric scooters, 2, 32, 33, 119–20, 131, 142, 203, 208, 221; God on wheels, 9, 16, 215, 230–35; in popular culture, 24–25, 29, 114, 145–46, 169; reactions to, 94–95, 100–101, 117–18, 131, 142–43, 169, 214; sidewalk surfaces, 105–6, 210, 216, 236, 237; sip-puff wheelchairs, 219, 229, 262n8; spin, 232–33
wheels, 8, 9, 16, 215, 220, 230–35, 246n3, 262n10
whiteness, 16, 22, 40, 47, 221, 228
wilderness, 13–14, 95–99, 102–4, 106–8, 111–12, 151, 221, 222, 255n5
Wilson, Junius, 225
wings, 170–71, 172, 218
women: anonymity of, 86, 114, 115; assessment of women's disabilities, 32–35, 113–15; and beauty, 20–21, 170, 180–81, 185–87; as disruptive, 69; gossip, 194; in healing narratives, 113–17; healthcare, 119, 123–25, 151; as inferior, 49; in rabbinic Judaism, 20, 32–35, 69, 260n12
word, revelatory power of, 253n7

working conditions, 27–28, 30, 39, 46, 147–48, 211–13, 225–26, 250n4, 263n20
wrestling, 162–68, 169–70, 175–76, 259n18, 259n20

Yehudah, Rabbi (rabbinic figure), 68
Yitzhak, Rabbi (rabbinic figure), 91–92

Yoshino, Kenji, 30, 249n11
Young, Thelathia Nikki, 23

Zhelezhniak, Yocheved, 195, 261n29
Zierler, Wendy, 195
Zilpah (biblical figure), 186
Zipporah (biblical figure), 191, 192
Zornberg, Aviva Gottlieb, 104